D1301416

Messages from Home

MESSAGES FROM HOME

The
Mother-Child
Home Program
and
the Prevention
of
School Disadvantage

PHYLLIS LEVENSTEIN

OHIO STATE UNIVERSITY PRESS · COLUMBUS

385623 Tennessee Tech. Library
Cookeville, Tenn.

Copyright©1988
by the Ohio State University Press.
All rights reserved.

Library of Congress Cataloging-in-Publication Data

Levenstein, Phyllis, 1916–
Messages from home : the Mother-Child Home Program and the
prevention of school disadvantage / Phyllis Levenstein.
p.   cm.
Bibliography: p.
Includes index.
ISBN 0–8142–0447–3
1. Child development—United States.   2. Learning ability.
3. Education, Preschool—United States—Parent participation.
4. Mother and child—United States.   5. Academic achievement.
I. Title.   II. Title: Mother-Child Home Program.
LB1134.L48 1987
372'.21—dc19   87–17315
CIP

To
Sidney Levenstein
1916–1974

Contents

List of Tables • ix

List of Abbreviations • xi

Introduction:
A Way Up? • 1

1
Climbers: Two Mothers, Two Children • 5

2
Mother-Love and the Underclass • 29

3
Getting Up from Under • 49

4
On the Shoulders of Giants • 99

5
How High Was Up? • 113

6
From Laboratory to Real World • 163

7
Messages from Home • 203

Afterword
In Appreciation • 219

Appendix 1
Index to Technical Materials for Operating
a Mother-Child Home Program • 223

Appendix 2
Replicators of the Mother-Child
Home Program, 1986–87 • 225

Appendix 3
Criteria for VISM Books and Toys,
with Examples • 229

References • 231

Index • 243

Tables

Table 5.1   Design I: Children's mean IQ and Academic
                 Scores at Entry (Age 2), Program's End (Age 4
                 & 6), and in 3rd Grade (Age 8) • 121

Table 5.2   Mean IQ Score for Early Education and
                 Control by Project, By Age • 122

Table 5.3   Effect of Mother-Child Home Program
                 (MCHP) on Reading Scores • 124

Table 5.4   Correlations of Mothers' Home Verbal
                 Interaction at Child's Age 4 with Child
                 Competencies in First Grade at Age 6
                 (Pearson's r, N = 39) • 135

Table 5.5   Design II: Children's Mean IQ Scores, and
                 Rates of Mothers' "Lottery" Acceptance • 138

Table 5.6   Striver and Hesitater Program Mothers in
                 Design I (1969 Program) and Design II (1976
                 Program) • 143

Table 5.7   Design II: High School Graduation of Strivers
                 and Hesitaters Among 1976 Program
                 Mothers • 144

Table 5.8   Design I: High School Graduation of Strivers
                 and Hesitaters Among 1969 Program
                 Mothers • 145

Table 5.9   Design II: 1976 Children's Mean IQ and
                 Academic Scores at Entry (Age 2), At
                 Program's End (Age 4), and at End of Second
                 Grade (age 8) • 147

Table 5.10   MIB (Maternal Interactive Behavior) Scores of
                 1976 Program and Non-Program Mothers in
                 1980 Follow-up Study • 154

Abbreviations

AFDC	Aid to Families with Dependent Children
CAT	California Achievement Test
CBT	Child's Behavior Traits
DHEW	Department of Health, Education, and Welfare
ECIA	Educational Consolidation and Improvement Act
HOME	Home Observation for Measurement of the Environment
IQ	Intelligence Quotient
KEEP	Key Elements for Establishing [Mother-Child Home] Program Instrument
MCHP	Mother-Child Home Program
MDRC	Manpower Demonstration Research Corporation
MIB	Maternal Interactive Behavior
NCE	Normal Curve Equivalents
PACT	Parent and Child Together
PCHP	Parent-Child Home Program (Pittsfield, Massachusetts)
PPVT	Peabody Picture Vocabulary Test
PROP	People's Regional Opportunity Program (Portland, Maine)
TD	Toy Demonstrator
VIP	Verbal Interaction Project
VISIT	Verbal Interaction Stimulation Intervention Techniques
VISM	Verbal Interaction Stimulus Materials
WIN	[Federal] Work Incentive Program
WISC	Wechsler Intelligence Scale for Children
WRAT	Wide-Range Achievement Test

Introduction:
A Way Up?

Humanity's most ancient dialogue—the verbal exchange between mother and child—was at the core of the model Mother-Child Home Program that reached into the homes of families in a poverty pocket of Long Island, New York, and was replicated widely elsewhere.

The Program is a low-cost, pre-preschool method, which was developed from 1967 to 1982 by the nonprofit Verbal Interaction Project, Inc., with $3,000,000 of federal and private funding. It was intended to help low-income mothers to prevent their toddlers' future school problems. Sixteen years of experimental research measured the results of the original Program and tested its assumption that children's best preparation for school is their early participation in cheerful, casual exchanges of concept-building conversation with their parents at home.

Talking to infants comes naturally to all mothers (or mother substitutes). For most mothers, especially those who are at least high school graduates, talking to baby becomes conversation. The dialogue is often focused around the toys and books which middle-income parents can afford. The Program's hypothesis was that this verbal interaction gradually fosters a parent-child network that is both intellectually and emotionally supportive for the child, whatever the family's ethnolinguistic style.

The social and emotional bonding between mother and child is the matrix for the network. Important as it is for the child's emotional development, the mother-child bond can evolve with scarcely a word ever being said. However, the exchange of language within the context of that emotional relationship creates cognitive skills that enable children to meet increasingly complex intellectual challenges. The child's growing intellectual abilities send positive messages to the mother about her own constructive role in the child's competence. They encourage her to continue the good work by sending more of her own pleasant cognitive "strands" to the child. Child and mother together thus weave a network that has both emotional and cognitive links. The Program conjectured that the network's supports last into children's school years to reinforce their skills with school tasks—that they are, in fact, crucial to children's school success.

The Program's view was that family factors linked to poverty often hamper the full development of the parent-child network. For children thus at risk for educational disadvantage, an intervention program should begin at home when they are about two years old. The program should center around toys and picture books of high quality, permanently assigned to the family and used as the focus of the child's verbally oriented play with his or her mother. The mother herself might make gains in parenting skills and self-esteem through her participation in the Program.

School as a Gateway

The opportunities offered by the American public education system, however imperfect it is, afford all citizens the promise of a fair chance at the pursuit of happiness. Education is the gateway to success in a career and to the fulfillment that this can bring. It is literally true that for almost all occupations past the semi-skilled level, only education admits people to the careers they want, in mainstream culture and in most subcultures. Plumbers, doctors, electricians, computer programmers, teachers, mechanics, lawyers all require education in larger or smaller amounts.

For the past few decades, a very large number of students, especially in the inner cities, have failed to take full advantage of the public schools to escape from poverty into a better life. Not only is the high school dropout rate alarming, but the academic lacks of children still in school are startling. These problems have continued even after remedial programs aimed at low-income children began to be infused on a large scale into the schools 20 years ago, with massive federal support (Title One). No doubt, without these programs the situation would be even worse today; certainly many individual students were helped.

Nevertheless, countless young people who are ill prepared *for* school to begin with, and inevitably *by* school for any skilled occupation, fill the ranks of the jobless and the aimless, having left high school before graduating. From their ranks come recruits for street crime, for welfare dependency, and for other social problems. Ironically, as those ranks are swelled in ever-increasing numbers by high school dropouts without job skills, the work base of our society is becoming so transformed by technology toward a services/skills orientation, that a high school diploma is the minimum requirement for almost any satisfying and well-paying job.

A Way Up?

The Verbal Interaction Project explored, through its research of the Mother-Child Home Program, whether the way up for many disadvantaged children should start at home and long before a child might enter a classroom preschool program. Its task was to find out if the shared joy of young children and their mothers—playing, laughing, and talking together in their livingrooms—could lead to the serious business of school success.

Was it really possible that a modest, low-key pre-preschool program to aid mother-child play interaction, at home in the family livingroom, could appeal to most families, regardless of their differences from mainstream culture, and could prevent the educational disadvantage of low-income children? Could economically disadvantaged children thus enter first grade with a reasonable prospect of graduating from high school?

This book will describe in some detail the nonobtrusive, relatively simple—and inexpensive—Mother-Child Home Program, as well as the systematic research intended to answer questions about Program effectiveness. A more basic question to be answered was whether children's school competence was indeed related to early verbal interaction between mother and child: does the parent-child network conjectured at the outset of the Mother-Child Home Program really exist?

However, the most socially pressing research question was whether the pre-preschool Mother-Child Home Program, predicated on that network's existence, would achieve its goal of preventing the educational disadvantage of low-income children while fostering mothers' parenting skills and self-esteem. Would the Program in truth prove to be a way up for children at risk for school failure, and for their mothers too?

1

Climbers:
Two Mothers,
Two Children

The Invitation: July

Mrs. Willard and Carol

The July morning was hot. Mrs. Willard[1] was awake, had to be. Two-year-old Carol had dragged the sheet until she had almost tumbled her mother out of bed. Demanded breakfast. Paid no attention to the heat in the small room, which was crowded by a loaded dresser, a chair without a back, and several overflowing boxes. Mrs. Willard's welfare checks didn't provide much furniture. When the sun came around to that side of the housing project, it would beat into the curtainless window. Yet better to lie still now than get up.

But Carol wanted breakfast. She was crying and pulling. The three older ones could get their own cereal off the shelf, their own milk out of the refrigerator—and leave it on the table to sour. Tug their own clothes out to dress and run barefoot into the street. At twenty-five months, Carol couldn't do those things for herself. She could run to her mother and scream and even talk. Ask questions. Sometimes Mrs. Willard thought she was a nuisance, wanted too much. The older ones seemed to have gotten used to doing things for themselves, not bothering

---

1. *The names of participants in the Mother-Child Home Program, and information about them, are disguised. Their inner thoughts and feelings are extrapolated from their Program records; however, the records, when reproduced here, are otherwise exactly as originally written. Program staff members who appear in this book are identified by their real names.*

her with their inquisitiveness.

Then Mrs. Willard heard the sound of mail being pushed into the empty, oblong spaces in the entry hall, into what had been a set of mailboxes. One space had "Willard" crudely penciled across the top. She heard the mailman say good morning to someone in the hall, not too far from her own apartment door. "Must be around ten," she thought. Carol had a right to want her breakfast.

Mrs. Willard, a statuesque, calm-featured, brown-skinned woman, walked heavily to the bathroom, threw cool water on her face. Felt better. By the time Carol was sitting in the tiny kitchen, with cold cereal in a bowl hastily rinsed from the pile in the sink, Mrs. Willard was ready to see if anything had been pushed into her own mailbox.

She slipped through the door, leaving Carol at the table and the coffee for her own breakfast—still enough from yesterday—heating on the stove. Quickly came back, with an advertisement (SHOP YOUR MINIMALL!) and a long white envelope addressed to "Mrs. Helen Willard." She crumpled the ad, put the envelope face up on the table, searched out a sweet roll from a bag and started to eat it with her coffee. "Hush, Carol," she said gently as the little girl jabbered away about a cartoon she had been watching on TV.

Presently she opened the envelope. It appeared to be only a typed letter with an unfamiliar name at the top: "Mother-Child Home Program."

"Dear Mrs. Willard," it began. Before she could read further, Carol began clamoring to get down. At the same time, the six year old twins—girls—burst into the door, shouting and hitting each other. The letter and envelope slipped into the puddle of milk that surrounded Carol's cereal bowl. They were thrown out that evening when a space was cleared on the table for someone's supper.

A FEW DAYS LATER

When Mrs. Willard answered a knock at her door a few days later (the bell had long since given out), she saw an unknown woman standing there, brown-skinned like herself.

A briefcase was in her hand. Welfare worker? Saleswoman? Mrs. Willard braced herself.

The woman smiled. "Mrs. Willard? I'm Myrtle Crawford. I wrote to you about our free Mother-Child Home Program a little while ago. Miss Bailey told me you might be interested in being in it."

"Yeah." Mrs. Willard's face relaxed fractionally. She liked Miss Bailey, a social worker at the twins' school who had helped her get an extra welfare allowance for Carol's crib.

"In the Program, we visit you and your two-year-old together twice a week, starting in October and going on till the end of the school year. Every week we bring a toy or a book for . . . what's your little one's name?"

"Name? Her name? Oh . . . Carol . . . her name's Carol."

"Well, if you join the Program, Carol will get a new book or toy every week. A Toy Demonstrator will bring it and will show you both how to use it, especially you, so you can use it with Carol on your own. The books and toys will be yours to keep. We think if mothers use them with their children every day, it will help get them ready for school when they start later on."

Mrs. Willard thought of her son, Vincent. At age eight, he had just entered a special class for slow learners.

"Yeah. Well . . . what will it cost?"

"Not a thing. If she's between eighteen and thirty months old, we are able to offer you the Mother-Child Home Program without your spending a penny. Can you tell me her birthday?"

Incredulous, skeptical, Mrs. Willard looked at the stranger. But what harm could it do? Maybe it might help Carol keep on being as smart as she was now, not end up in a Special Class, like Vincent. "I guess it's OK. She was two years old last month . . . June. But what would I have to do?"

"Just be there, together with Carol, every time the Toy Demonstrator comes, twice a week—and watch what she does—and try to do the same things with Carol, a little every day. Most mothers think it's fun—and the kids sure do. Even the olders ones sometimes play with the toys and books."

Mrs. Willard made up her mind, faster than she usually did.

"All right . . . I'll do it!"

"Great! You can always just stop, if you change your mind any time after the Program begins. Now, I need to ask you a few questions, so we can help you better—but you just answer the ones you want to. May I sit down?"

Still hesitant, Mrs. Willard showed Myrtle Crawford to the sofa in the livingroom and sat down herself on the chair crowded against it. As it turned out, she tried to answer all the questions: the names and school grades of Carol's three older brothers and sisters; her own age (thirty-one years) and last school grade (eleventh); a little about her health; whether Carol's father lived at home at all (he didn't, and in fact Mrs. Willard didn't know exactly where he was living); also, a couple of questions about the grandparents on both sides (she couldn't tell anything about Carol's grandparents on her father's side). There were no questions about things Mrs. Willard preferred to keep to herself, such as why she had come up from South Carolina four years ago, whether she had been legally married to Carol's father, and where he was now.

Myrtle (she said to call her that although she called Mrs. Willard Mrs. Willard) told her when she would be back with Mrs. Willard's Toy Demonstrator, to introduce them. The Toy Demonstrator and Mrs. Willard would set up a toy chest first thing. Then the Program would begin.

When Myrtle asked if *she* had any questions, Mrs. Willard couldn't put anything into words, but she had plenty. Mainly, would Myrtle and the Program really do what they said? Would there really be toys and books for Carol? Would they really leave it to her how much she did in the visits, as Myrtle had implied? Or would they nag or talk down to her like teachers in school? What was the catch?

Mrs. Carter and Jo-Jo

It was a hot July morning.

Mrs. Carter let cool water run over her hands as she washed dishes at the kitchen sink. She was a small, trim-figured, brown-skinned woman with a mobile face. She looked as if she could be Jo-Jo's sister rather than his mother. Jo-Jo had had his break-fast and was experimentally opening a low cupboard in the kitchen. "Jo-Jo, stop!" she ordered, automatically stern. "Go watch TV!" She plunked him in front of the television set, which was already on, and loud. A children's cartoon animated the Saturday morning. Her six-year-old daughter, Dee-Dee, had for once deserted TV. Mrs. Carter had given Dee-Dee ready permission to go out. That left her with two year old Jo-Jo, but she didn't object too much. He minded pretty well. He learned fast from briskly slapped hands and reprimands. He was smart. He was beginning to talk a lot—too much, even had started asking questions as the older one had done. But he was already beginning to learn, as the six year old had, to mind his own business. She wanted him to grow up polite, like Dee-Dee. Maybe do well in school, get a good job. Someday she hoped to get a good job herself and get off of welfare. But sometimes Mrs. Carter felt so discouraged, she couldn't get herself to figure out how to do it.

She glanced out of the neatly curtained window of the bare little kitchen to see the mailman coming up the walk. That was one advantage of living in a ground floor apartment of the housing project. That way she could get to her doorless mailbox in the entry ahead of anyone else who might take a notion to investigate its contents. She scooped Jo-Jo up and quickly went out to the mailbox. Two advertising flyers (she noticed a couple of the orange ones on the floor where they had fallen—or been thrown—from other mailboxes) and an envelope.

Back to her own door, fast, to shut it behind her before she put Jo-Jo down to look at her mail. The orange ad was about a prewinter sale of school clothes. This she laid open on the table, bare now except for a pencil. The other flyer was a general admonition to "SHOP YOUR MINIMALL!" This she crum-pled and threw into a paper bag standing ready near the sink.

The third item was a long white envelope addressed to "Mrs. Nancy Carter." She studied this for a moment and then opened the envelope. It appeared to be a typed letter with a name new to her at the top: "Mother-Child Home Program."

"Dear Mrs. Carter," it began. Before she could read further, Dee-Dee came running into the apartment from outdoors, loudly complaining about a neighbor's child.

"Sit down!" she ordered Dee-Dee, glaring the six-year-old into instant obedience. In the mutinous silence that followed, broken only by Jo-Jo's noisily sucking his thumb, and the television's loud voices, she read on:

> We are happy to tell you that a new program for two-year-olds and their mothers is starting in your neighborhood. It will be free and will be conducted in your own home. Miss Bailey, Dorothy's school social worker, thought you might like to join. We will visit you in a few days to find out if you do. Or, if you wish, you are welcome to call me at 611–5017. Then we can make an appointment at your convenience.
>
> Sincerely yours,
>
> Myrtle Crawford
> Program Coordinator

Mrs. Carter looked reflectively at Jo-Jo, ignoring Dee-Dee's squirming and her rebellious face. Then she said sternly, "You— watch Jo-Jo. I'll settle you later. And don't either of you move while I go across the hall to Mrs. Smith's."

The two subdued children heard her knocking at the Smith door and a moment later asking, "Can I use your phone? It's a local call."

A FEW DAYS LATER

The woman knocked on her door precisely at two o'clock, at exactly the time and on the day Mrs. Carter had arranged by telephone with the Mother-Child Home Program.

"Hello! Mrs. Carter? I'm Myrtle Crawford, the Coordinator of the Mother-Child Home Program. We talked together on the phone about your joining our Program. I'd like to tell you more about it, so you can decide."

Mrs. Carter's face was solemn as she gestured Myrtle Crawford into the livingroom to sit down. She sat herself on the edge of a worn chair. Jo-Jo wandered in and she lifted him onto her lap without looking at him or at the curious face of the older sister hanging back in the bedroom doorway.

The Program Coordinator launched into her Program description as she had with Mrs. Willard.

"You mean I get to keep the toys and books? And none of it costs anything? How come?"

"I know it sounds sort of unusual, but we're lucky enough to be funded by the government and some private foundations especially to give you and other mothers in the neighborhood this Program, along with their two-year-olds. That's why Miss Bailey was glad to give us your name—to give you a chance at the Program if your little one is the right age. When is Jo-Jo's birthday?"

"His name is really Harry; we just call him Jo-Jo. He was born June 9th . . . two years old last month. Would that make him OK, Mrs. Crawford?"

"Just right. By the way, most people call me Myrtle. Would you like to participate in the Mother-Child Home Program?"

"Sure would. When do we begin . . . Myrtle?"

It wasn't so hard to say the first name as she had feared, nor to answer Myrtle's questions. She told Myrtle that Jo-Jo had only one sister, Dorothy, who at age six was going into first grade and was nicknamed "Dee-Dee." She herself was 24-years-old and had graduated from high school. Like Mrs. Willard, her own health was good, she was a full-time housewife, and she and the children were supported by welfare. Mrs. Carter could tell a bit about Jo-Jo's father, who lived away from them: he was her age, had been born in Georgia (she had been born in New York City), was a high school graduate, and was a park attendant. She said that both of her parents had had "some college" and that her mother was a nurse, but that her father's occupation was "unknown." The father's parents were high school graduates, she thought. His mother was a domestic worker, but his father's occupation was "unknown." Mrs. Carter noted with relief that the questions were few and innocuous. She could see for herself that the answers would probably help them to understand Jo-Jo better.

Mrs. Carter drew a deep breath after the door closed behind Myrtle Crawford.

"OK, Dee-Dee, you can come in now. Jo-Jo and I are going to school at home—right, Jo-Jo? I don't want you bothering the teacher when she comes—hear?"

Children's Evaluations before the Program: September

Mrs. Willard and Mrs. Carter had been enrolled in the Mother-Child Home Program in July, although it was not to start until October, to allow time for careful pre-Program evaluations of their children.

One of the Program's aims for the children was to give them a good chance for future school success with such fundamentals as reading and arithmetic, through encouraging their early verbal and other positive interactions with their mothers. Because their learning these subjects was far in the future, Carol Willard and Jo-Jo Carter were given IQ ("intelligence quotient") tests, whose scores usually predict school success. In effect, these tests were measurements of their future ability to learn school subjects when they eventually would be exposed to them in elementary school. They played "test games" at the Program's office, sitting on their mothers' laps—with blocks, with small pegs that fit into round holes, with a tiny painted cat that could be hidden under a little cup.

Their IQ scores (mental age divided by chronological age) should not only improve by the end of their two years in the Mother-Child Home Program, but they should be high enough to assure the likelihood that Carol and Jo-Jo would do well in school when that remote time came. Two aims of the Mother-Child Home Program were to help them make normal school progress from grade to grade (be promoted regularly) and to avoid placement in special classes.

Another important Program aim was to enhance the mothers' self-respect, and thus their mental health, by making them the principal agents of their children's good progress. They and their children, together, would be social climbers of a special kind.

Carol and Jo-Jo seemed to enjoy the test games. Their pre-Program scores on the Cattell Infant Intelligence Scale were similar, both on a low-average level. Carol's Cattell IQ was 93, and Jo-Jo's was 91.

These scores predicted moderate school difficulties in later years. Most classroom activities in their Long Island town were geared to the abilities of children with somewhat higher IQs, around 100, or mid-average. Moreover, they risked the gradual downward slope in their IQs which often occurs in low-income children.

The psychologist who evaluated the children wrote comments on each of them:

Carol

> *"Extremely shy but involved in a placid, passive way. Sweet smile when pleased. Carol was very reluctant to speak—very shy."*

Jo-Jo

> *"Sweet, cooperative child. Jo-Jo is shy at times, refuses to try if fears failure. Basically cooperative, involved. Very affectionate with mother and vice-versa."*

First Year of Mother-Child Home Program: October to June

Mrs. Willard and Carol: Year One

FIRST HALF OF YEAR ONE

When Myrtle Crawford first brought Mrs. Willard's "Toy Demonstrator" to meet her early in October, Mrs. Willard couldn't make up her mind about whether she liked the Toy Demonstrator or not. She seemed a little young and didn't use much better grammar than Mrs. Willard did herself. Mrs. Willard had found it awkward, but sort of fun, to help the Toy Demonstrator build a toy chest from a big flat package that Myrtle had brought along. The toy chest stayed right there in the livingroom when it was finished.

The Toy Demonstrator got Carol interested from the start during the Home Sessions, which they arranged for a time when the five older children were in school. While Mrs. Willard watched silently from the backless chair she had carried into the livingroom from her bedroom, the woman showed Carol in the first Home Session the colored blocks in a little cart she had brought. She told Carol the colors and then said, "Show mommy the blue block."

And Carol did!

Mrs. Willard's face came alive when Carol showed her the blue block—then a red one, a yellow one. Then she retreated into voicelessly watching the Toy Demonstrator play with Carol. In almost no time the Toy Demonstrator said to Carol, "I have to go now, Carol. Please—help me put the blocks back into the cart."

Mrs. Willard waited for the Toy Demonstrator to put the cart and all the blocks back into her own big white shopping bag that said "Mother-Child Home Program" on it. But she didn't. She helped Carol put them into the empty toy chest that she had put together with Mrs. Willard. They were keeping their promise! Good thing. The mother could tell that Carol really loved that toy. She would cry a lot if she ever had to give it up.

The following week the Toy Demonstrator brought a book for Carol. This time she sat right down near one end of the sofa and patted the place beside her, in the middle of the sofa, for Carol to sit. Then she said, "Mommy, you come too—you sit on the other side of Carol—we'll read to her together."

Mrs. Willard hesitated. She hadn't counted on that. She didn't read out loud so well. But she came and sat down on the other side of Carol, who snuggled against her. A sort of jealous feeling she had begun to have about the Toy Demonstrator relaxed. She herself listened as the Toy Demonstrator read a book called *Pat the Bunny,* pausing at each page to tell Carol to do something like, "Now show Mommy how you pat the bunny!"

Afterward the Toy Demonstrator, a former mother-partici-pant herself, wrote some comments on that early Home Session, for Myrtle Crawford to read:

> Mother, child and I sat on the sofa together. Carol
> sat in the middle. Mother and I held the book, Carol

turned pages. Carol smiled very friendly during the session. She also patted the bunny, played peek-a-boo, smelled flowers, pointed to parts of her face while Mrs. Willard named each part for her. Mrs. Willard also re-read the book to Carol. After the session was over, mother commented that the session was very interesting, and that she will be looking to see me next session.

The Toy Demonstrator judged that Mrs. Willard had been "verbally interactive" during from 16 percent to 30 percent of the session.

SECOND HALF OF YEAR ONE

"Year One" of the two-year Program was actually only eight months long, from October through May, with time off for school holidays.

Early in January, Myrtle Crawford visited Mrs. Willard to find out how she liked the Program thus far. Mrs. Willard had no complaints and even said that Carol liked her Toy Demonstrator. Myrtle wrote about the visit:

Mrs. Willard said she is quite satisfied with the Toy Demonstrator, the time and the days of the Sessions. She said that Carol asks her mother to read to her every day and then goes through the book by herself.

Mrs. Willard tends to be non-verbal in the Sessions. When she does contribute, she often seems to be nervous. I re-emphasized the importance of her participation.

A few weeks later the Toy Demonstrator described another Home Session:

Carol, Mrs. Willard and I sat on the livingroom floor with the VISM. [VISM is the acronym for "Verbal Interaction Stimulus Material"—the toy or book—which in this case was a large toy barn and its many inhabitants: animals, people, and implements.]

Mrs. Willard encouraged Carol to name some of the

animals, also to try to get the child to tell what the cow says and some of the things other animals do. Carol named most of the animals. She was counting along with her mother, how many people and how many animals were on the farm. Carol played mostly with the tractor and trailer. Pretending to bring food for the animals. Mrs. Willard also got the child to name colors of the animals.

The Toy Demonstrator judged Mrs. Willard to have been verbally interactive during from 30 to 45 percent of the Session.

By the end of Year One, Mrs. Willard had kept her appointments for forty-four out of forty-six possible Home Sessions. Thus she had participated in ninety-six percent of the Sessions.

Myrtle Crawford came around to Mrs. Willard's apartment to ask her some questions after the last Home Session of Year One. She wanted to get Mrs. Willard's reactions to the Mother-Child Home Program now that she and Carol were half-way through the two-year Program. She also wanted to find out what other intellectually stimulating experiences Carol had had. Finally, she needed to know whether Mrs. Willard intended to complete the Program by enrolling in Year Two of the Mother-Child Home Program in the fall.

Mrs. Willard was now used to the Program people asking her questions and noting her answers carefully on printed pages. Her Toy Demonstrator, after each Session, had noted down her answers to a few questions about the week's events. Now Myrtle sometimes just circled a number and sometimes wrote down exactly what Mrs. Willard said. It made her feel good that Myrtle Crawford took everything she said seriously enough to write it down, one way or another. In fact, that was the way Mrs. Willard had begun to feel in the Home Sessions: taken seriously. By the Toy Demonstrator and by Carol. Most of all, by Carol.

Myrtle checked off Mrs. Willard's answers to multiple questions: that Carol spent most of her time playing with her mother, or by herself, or with neighborhood children, or with her brothers and sisters. Sometimes she watched TV, and sometimes she just followed her mother around. Sometimes she went shopping or to the beach with her mother, and sometimes other children would take her to a playground or to visit people nearby. She never went on family outings nor to a library nor to church. Mrs. Willard (and no one else) read to Carol a couple of times a week (aside from Home Sessions), played with her for about a half-hour a day, and let her watch TV cartoons, her favorite programs. No other adults did these things with Carol. Carol was in no other preschool program along with the Mother-Child Home Program, and Mrs. Willard had no regular activities outside of the home. She thought the Program was "very good," adding, "She enjoyed the books and games." She was satisfied with the amount of her participation in the Home Sessions. In spite of the actually rather low amount of her verbal interchange with Carol, she was able to put into words, with fair accuracy, the Program's goals: to get her and Carol to talking with each other so that Carol would be more ready to learn in school later on. She felt that she had personally benefitted from the Program, commenting spontaneously, "We got closer—now I realize how to help her learn." Mrs. Willard hoped that Carol would become a nurse when she grew up and that she would go in school as "high as she can." She had no suggestions for the Program; she thought it was all fine exactly as it was.

To Myrtle's question about whether she would participate in the Mother-Child Home Program for Year Two in October, Mrs. Willard said "Yes," but hesitantly. It was June now. Who could tell what would happen by October? Even August seemed far away. Planning ahead from week to week within the Program was OK. A month was almost too much. Who could tell about October? Myrtle said she'd be back at the end of the summer. Mrs. Willard could make her final decision then.

Mrs. Carter and Jo-Jo: Year One
FIRST HALF OF YEAR ONE

Mrs. Carter made sure that her Program Home Sessions were arranged for when Dee-Dee, her six-year-old, was in school.

She gave the Toy Demonstrator, a college graduate volunteer, a warm welcome when she was brought by Myrtle for an introduction in October. Along with the introduction, came an unassembled toy chest that Mrs. Carter and the Toy Demonstrator put together, the two of them, the very first time they met. With neither of them skilled with a screwdriver, Mrs. Carter felt they knew each other pretty well by the time the toy chest stood finished. It seemed to stand for their promise of gifts of toys and books, since she had already been assured that she would keep the toy chest, to be filled by Program toys and books.

The small livingroom was neat, and Jo-Jo was in a little blue suit recently handed down from the child of a friend, when the Toy Demonstrator knocked at the door the following week.

Mrs. Carter sat on the floor with Jo-Jo and watched carefully, making a couple of enthusiastic exclamations when the Toy Demonstrator pointed out the shapes and colors of the blocks from a little cart to Jo-Jo. When Jo-Jo could show his mother the things about the blocks named by the Toy Demonstrator, Mrs. Carter smiled in delight and imitated the Toy Demonstrator's praise of Jo-Jo for following the directions correctly. She was only a little surprised when the toy ended up in Jo-Jo's new toy chest. They were keeping their promise!

She had picked up other cues from the Toy Demonstrator. By the second Home Session, she began to initiate praise as she read most of Jo-Jo's new book and talked with him as they sat together on the sofa.

The Toy Demonstrator wrote in her Home Session record some comments on another early Session, which focused around *Pat the Bunny.*

> Today was a very verbal visit with Jo-Jo. He was right at the door, holding his book, when I arrived. Mrs. Carter told me that Jo-Jo enjoyed showing his sister his book. We all sat down and began to look through the book. Jo-Jo's interest centered on the mirror, the peek-a-boo cloth (which needed to be re-glued) and the flowers. Jo-Jo insisted that these didn't smell anymore.

After five minutes of looking at the pictures, Jo-Jo asked if he could bring out some of his own books. Mrs. Carter said he could and I did not discourage him. They started with his dictionary. While looking through it and identifying the pictures, Jo-Jo became engrossed in finding pictures of the water and objects under the water. He found a picture of a sunken boat, Donald Duck, scuba diving, fish swimming. He really was quite excited and talked to his mother throughout the session about what he wanted and what he was looking for as they went through the books together.

The Toy Demonstrator (a volunteer with no prior experience as a mother in the Program) judged that Mrs. Carter's verbal interaction activity with Jo-Jo during this Home Session had occurred during 90 per cent to 100 percent of the Session.

SECOND HALF OF YEAR ONE

When Myrtle Crawford came back in January, she asked Mrs. Carter how she felt about the Mother-Child Home Program, now that she and Jo-Jo were almost halfway through Year One. Mrs. Carter was enthusiastic. Myrtle wrote:

The family was resting, as mother had been running back and forth to the hospital, due to her mother's illness. Talked with Mrs. Carter briefly while the children slept.

Program and Toy Demonstrator are working out fine.

Mother was enthusiastic, very involved with her children and indicated that she tries to expose them to as many learning and social experiences as possible. She continues to pursue higher educational aspirations for herself.

Re the Program, Mrs. Carter wondered if the change in her daughter's school hours would affect Home Sessions. She thought we would have to ask to have Dee-Dee excluded from Home Sessions, now that she would be at home when they took place. I assured her inclusion was all right with us if it's all right with her, but she could work it out with Toy Demonstrator.

Mrs. Carter had no criticisms and thought well of her Toy Demonstrator.

Some weeks later, Mrs. Carter's Toy Demonstrator wrote about a Home Session focused around the Toy Barn and its contents:

> Such enthusiasm! Jo-Jo loved the farm—every item. Mrs. Carter loved it too. She and Jo-Jo set up the farm immediately. The cow and horse bent their heads up and down while they drank from the trough. The dog moved his head back and forth. They all went up to the loft and jumped down. Just about every activity was labeled by Mrs. Carter.
>
> Mrs. Carter also encouraged Jo-Jo in imaginary play. They made up a story about the farmer's family going to town with the cart to buy supplies and food for the animals. We all had fun.

The Toy Demonstrator rated Mrs. Carter as having been verbally interactive with Jo-Jo during 91 percent to 100 percent of this session.

Jo-Jo Carter's last Home Session of Year One with his mother and their Toy Demonstrator occurred on June 2. It was Home Session #45. Out of a possible 46 Sessions planned for Year One, only one had been cancelled by Mrs. Carter. Mrs. Carter had thus honored 98 percent of her Home Session appointments in Year One of the Mother-Child Home Program.

The Toy Demonstrator did some reflecting in her Home Session Record notes on Session #45 with Mrs. Carter and Jo-Jo:

> Jo-Jo knew where Charlie was in all the pictures. In fact, he "read" the story to Mrs. Carter during the session. Mrs. Carter did her usual good job with the book. When we finished, she told me that Jo-Jo might

be going to Headstart in the fall. She is really a highly
motivated mother and she knows how to accomplish
her goals. In fact, I am sure she worked closely with
both her children before she became involved in the
Program. Both of them are well prepared for their
school experience.

And, as in most of the previous Home Session records for
Year One, the Toy Demonstrator indicated that Mrs. Carter's
verbal interaction with Jo-Jo was evident in no less than 91
percent of Home Session #45.

Mrs. Carter responded almost fervently to Myrtle Crawford's
interview questions when the latter visited at the end of Year
One. Mrs. Crawford asked her the same questions that she
had put to Mrs. Willard. Mrs. Carter's responses were, however,
somewhat different from Mrs. Willard's. Jo-Jo played with
others, and watched TV, just as Carol had. But unlike Carol,
"He daydreams, as if studying or communicating with nature
for long periods of time," said his mother.

Mrs. Carter took Jo-Jo most weeks to all the places named
by Myrtle: stores, playground, family outings, visits to neigh-
bors, churches, and to a library. In addition, Jo-Jo had been
taken by "another adult" to visit a local college and had played
in the college gym. She reads to Jo-Jo four or five times a week,
and "someone else" reads to him about once a week. She
played with him about forty-five minutes a day; other adults
played with him fifteen to twenty minutes a day.

Mrs. Carter watched "Sesame Street" and "The Electric Company" on TV with Jo-Jo almost daily. Still, Jo-Jo's favorite TV
program was "Mighty Mouse Cartoon."

Jo-Jo was in no other preschool program along with the
Mother-Child Home Program. Mrs. Carter, however, had been
in a part-time school program for a few months, leaving the
children's care to their paternal grandmother.

Mrs. Carter thought the Program was "very good," and, like
Mrs. Willard, showed almost full knowledge of the Program's
goals for children. She felt that she was given enough chance
to participate in Home Sessions and said that what she herself
had gotten out of the Program was: "I had lots of fun and

learned how to communicate with my son better." She could suggest nothing to improve the Program. She hoped that Jo-Jo would graduate from college and become a doctor.

There was apparently no hesitation in Mrs. Carter's mind about enrolling for Year Two of the Mother-Child Home Program, starting again in October; however, a moment after saying so, she looked worried. She explained that she wanted to start looking earnestly for a job to get off welfare, or to start college. But what would that do to her participation in the Program? Mrs. Crawford assured her that the Program would somehow adapt to her work or school hours—her Toy Demonstrator would come after or before work, even perhaps sometimes deliver the books and toys to her babysitter so that Mrs. Carter would be sure to have them. They could talk about it again at the end of the summer, when Mrs. Crawford would come again to arrange Year Two of the program for Mrs. Carter and Jo-Jo.

Mrs. Carter's face looked for a moment as if she were going to weep. Then she smiled, radiantly. "It's real important," she said. "Jo-Jo's learning, and I am too. He really knows what I teach him."

Myrtle Crawford recalled the written comment of a mother on an anonymous written evaluation of the Mother-Child Home Program: "What I have taught my two-year-old, he remembers very well."

This was, in fact, one of the major ideas behind the Mother-Child Home Program.

Second Year of Mother-Child Program: October to June

Mrs. Willard and Carol: Year Two

When September came, Mrs. Willard could look ahead to October. She told Mrs. Crawford, who visited her in September, that she had definitely decided to continue in the Mother-Child Home Program for Year Two. Myrtle noted some changes in Mrs. Willard and in the arrangements of the apartment. The previously backless chair had acquired a back, or perhaps it had been replaced by a different chair. There was less debris on the floor and none on the kitchen table, which was visible from the livingroom. Mrs. Willard was now wearing a dress rather than her usual bathrobe.

Mrs. Willard agreed to have only one Home Session each week in Year Two, instead of the two she had had in Year One since she was now an experienced Program participant.

Later in the fall Mrs. Willard's new Toy Demonstrator (Toy Demonstrators were routinely changed each year to prevent overattachment between them and the children) wrote about Session #5 of Year Two:

> When Mrs. Willard opened the door, she said there was no heat and that she didn't think we should have the Session. I said I didn't mind leaving my coat on. Mrs. Willard started looking for the book. She couldn't find it. I said we could use another book. They brought out "One, Two, Three for Fun."

> We sat on the couch. I talked about a couple of the pages and read the words. Carol didn't give any response to questions. I asked Mrs. Willard to do the see-saw pages. She read the words and then pointed to the see-saw and asked Carol what it was—no response. Mrs. Willard reminded Carol that she used the see-saw in the nearby playground.

> I suggested we get up and play Ring Around the Rosy to warm up. Carol got up reluctantly and the three of us went around twice. Carol did not sing with us.

The Toy Demonstrator (a college graduate volunteer) judged that Mrs. Willard's verbal interaction was present in 30 to 45 percent of Home Session #5, in spite of the probably discouraging effect of Carol's almost unyielding passivity.

Perceptibly more than in Year One, Mrs. Willard not only followed the lead of the Toy Demonstrator but sometimes initiated Program techniques she had observed or had read about in the Guide Sheets that accompanied each new toy or book. After Session #9, the Toy Demonstrator wrote:

> The Willards have their new oil burner, but it's work-
> ing sporadically and needs to be checked.
>
> Carol and her mother said they liked the book, 'Won-
> der of Hands.' We looked at the cover picture and I
> put Carol's hand on top of mine to see the difference
> in size. Carol said more words than usual today. She
> was interested in the picture of the man changing
> the tire. She said 'tire.' Mrs. Willard hasn't made a
> pie crust, Carol hasn't seen a rolling pin, but she said
> 'pie crust.' She hasn't been to the beach, but has been
> in a pool for swimming and has played in sand at
> a park. Carol said 'rabbit' and we talked about 'Pat
> the Bunny.' She said 'knee' when we looked at the
> hurt knee picture. Carol has used play dough. She
> said 'sewing' and 'guitar.' Mrs. Willard reminded
> Carol of someone they know who plays the guitar.
>
> Mrs. Willard says she can make string figures but
> doesn't have any string in the house. Carol has played
> dress-up and said 'hat.' She said 'dog' and 'cat.' I
> reminded her of the cat in the barrel she had last
> week. She did a good imitation of the little girl laugh-
> ing and clapping. I made a bird shadow. Carol
> counted the children playing Ring Around the Rosy.
> Carol said the girl was 'going to bed.' We pretended
> we were playing the piano. Carol said the mouse
> was a 'rat.' When her mother asked her which picture
> she liked best, she pointed to the girl trying on the hat.
>
> Carol was eager to see the Three Bears Game. I said
> the plastic bag was for the pieces after they were
> pushed out. Carol immediately pushed out the bears,
> etc., put them all in the bag. She put the board, the
> Bear book and the bag of pieces back in the box, all
> ready to take to her nap after I left.

Mrs. Willard's verbal interaction was judged to be present
in 46 to 60 percent of that session, possibly spurred on by
Carol's responsiveness.

Thus Mrs. Willard was active in more than half of Session #9 in Year Two. This was considerably higher than the usual amount of her session activity during Year One.

Her increased activity in Session #9 was not a flash in the pan. In many of her Year Two Home Sessions, Mrs. Willard doubled the amount of her Year One interaction with Carol in Home Sessions.

As she had done at the end of Year One, Myrtle Crawford came around at the end of Year Two to ask Mrs. Willard some questions, pretty much the same ones she had asked the year before. Mrs. Willard's answers were not much different either, except that Carol now watched TV less often. However, Carol's mother was more emphatic and explicit in her response as to what she herself had derived from the Program: "Yes—I did get something, a lot. I learned to sit down and give some attention to her, like reading to her and listening to her."

Mrs. Carter and Jo-Jo: Year Two

By the August after she had completed Year One, Mrs. Carter had not yet found a job or decided about taking college courses. When Myrtle came to see her about continuing for another year in the Program, Mrs. Carter expressed surprise and pleasure upon hearing that the Program staff thought that she was ready to dispense with a Toy Demonstrator in Year Two. She was now competent enough in Program techniques to conduct "Home Sessions" with her own child, without more help than the toys and books and their Guide Sheets. In fact, she had practically done so during most of the Year One Home Sessions, so that the Toy Demonstrator had faded more and more into the background. Therefore, the Year Two books and toys would be dropped off to her each week, along with their Guide Sheets, and she would not have to have a Toy Demonstrator, unless she wanted one.

Mrs. Carter was glad to accept. The new Year Two arrangement would allow Jo-Jo to have the Program materials, and she would have the Guide Sheets to remind her of how to use them with Jo-Jo. That would also make it easier for her to find work or begin college (if she could find the means for it). Buoyed up, it seemed, by the staff's confidence in her and by her own sense of accomplishment, she was able to find a part-time job doing clerical work. Jo-Jo's grandmother filled in with babysitting.

The Program's contact with Mrs. Carter during most of Year Two was through the delivery of the Program books and toys, along with their Guide Sheets. A Toy Demonstrator brought the toys, books and Guide Sheets to her on the usual weekly Program schedule. Mrs. Carter signed for receiving them, they exchanged pleasantries and then said goodbye.

Mrs. Crawford visited Mrs. Carter after Year Two ended to conduct a final interview with her. Like Mrs. Willard, Mrs. Carter responded to the questions much as she had done in the previous year, except for her answer that Jo-Jo watched less TV. She liked the "drop-off Program" and said, "I got a lot of pleasure from Jo-Jo's enjoyment of the books and toys." From her replies she seemed to have continued her frequent interaction with Jo-Jo.

It was evident that she derived at least equal pleasure from another piece of news she had been saving to tell Myrtle. She had just won a need-based scholarship to nearby Molloy College and was about to enroll full time!

Myrtle Crawford couldn't contain her pleasure either. She didn't know just how much Mrs. Carter's decision to try for the scholarship and to start college had to do with her Program participation. Mentally, however, she chalked up what she felt to be another score-point for the Mother-Child Home Program.

Evaluations after the Program

Mrs. Willard, with Carol, and Mrs. Carter, with Jo-Jo, returned to the Program office four more times for evaluations after the Program was over. This was so that the Verbal Interaction Project—the nonprofit research group that had developed and now ran the model Mother-Child Home Program—could measure the extent to which the Mother-Child Home Program had accomplished its goals. Thus the children were evaluated at approximately age two, four, six, seven and eight years.

Evaluations at Program Completion

The children's first evaluation had been in the August before the Program began. The second important one occurred immediately after the completion of the Program. Carol and Jo-Jo, now almost four years old, were given IQ tests with more challenging tasks than those they had been given at age two. This time each sat beside the mother instead of sitting in her lap. For this evaluation, too, both mothers agreed to be video-taped in ten minutes of play with their children. The taping had been explained, and their permission for it given, in a previous interview.

Follow-up Evaluations

Jo-Jo and Carol were almost six years old when they and their mothers returned to the Program office for the first of three yearly follow-up evaluations to test whether their Program gains had endured. It was two years since the last evaluation, and the children were now near the end of kindergarten. Once again, the mothers and children played together in front of the camera, and the children were tested with their mothers present, as in the post-Program evaluation just after the Program's end.

Mrs. Willard and Mrs. Carter agreed to have the Program staff drive Carol and Jo-Jo from their schools to the Program office for their second and third follow-up evaluations. These were to assess the lasting effects of the Mother-Child Home Program as the children advanced in grade school, first at age seven, toward the end of first grade; and then at age eight, toward the end of second grade. For these follow-up assessments, there was no videotaping. The children were considered to be too old for the play sessions with their mothers to be natural. Therefore Mrs. Willard and Mrs. Carter were not asked to participate in the evaluations.

The last two follow-up evaluations, occurring at first and second grades, were slightly expanded for Carol and Jo-Jo, now that they had actually started the serious business of academic work in elementary school. The evaluations included tests of the children's achievement in reading and arithmetic.

Reasons for the Evaluations

The purpose of all the evaluations was to measure, as objectively as possible, the impact of the Mother-Child Home Program on Carol, Jo-Jo, and their mothers. Had the children improved on their pre-Program scores? Were the mothers interacting more with their children? How did the scores of both compare with those of similar children and mothers who had never been in the Mother-Child Home Program?

The answers to these questions had important meaning for the well-being of the Willards and the Carters; but their significance also goes far beyond the benefits for these two families alone. To discover that wider significance, it is necessary to explain in much more detail the reasons for the Program's existence, and to tell more about the Mother-Child Home Program itself.

2

Mother-Love
and the
Underclass

Mrs. Willard and Mrs. Carter were, without knowing it, both members of what Swedish economist Gunnar Myrdal once called the "underclass." The underclass is composed of those people, usually without marketable skills, who seem to be permanently unemployed and who often end up as long-term recipients of welfare assistance (Myrdal, 1962). The underclass became a highly noticeable feature of American society after Myrdal first wrote about it in 1962.

In the decades since 1962, as Charles Murray (a specialist in social policy evaluation research) reported in his 1984 book, *Losing Ground,* the number of individuals receiving AFDC ("Aid to Families with Dependent Children," which is the chief federal source of welfare aid) has ballooned dramatically. By 1980, the AFDC rolls had exploded from two million recipients in 1950 to eleven million recipients in 1980. Put another way, in 1950 only 651,000 *families* were receiving AFDC, or 1.7 percent of all American families. Thirty years later, in 1980, the number of families on AFDC had increased six times, to almost four million families, or 6.6 percent of all families in the country.

However, James T. Patterson, a Brown University historian, has somewhat deflated the balloon by pointing out that the steep AFDC rise signaling an apparent fantastic jump in poverty was more likely a surge in the awareness of people already in poverty of their legal right to apply for AFDC (1981). Perhaps the surge was given its impetus by the civil rights movement of the 1960s. The fact that the largest part of the huge AFDC increase (to more than three million families) had occurred by

1972 tends to support such a conjecture. "For the first time in American history," Dr. Patterson commented, "the largest category of people eligible for assistance—AFDC families—was taking virtually full advantage of its opportunities" (1981).

Still, the truth is that about eleven million individuals are, and have been for several years, receiving AFDC. No one knows exactly how many of the eleven million have been the same persons staying on AFDC year after year. Studies have shown that most of those receiving welfare assistance are doing so temporarily. Families are usually tided over by welfare checks from the end of the bread winner's unemployment benefits to the beginning of his or her next job. Still, a troubling aspect of permanence does seem to characterize some of the AFDC recipients, and their long-term welfare dependency automatically admits them to membership in the underclass.

Ken Auletta, a political scientist turned journalist, estimated in his book *The Underclass* (1982) the number of individuals in the underclass at about nine million persons. This figure reflects the judgment of the Manpower Demonstration Research Corporation, the five-year federally supported work experiment begun in 1975, which specifically focused on the underclass. Patterson's report (1981) that 90 percent of 2.7 million families remain on AFDC for an average of four years tends to support the MDRC's approximation of nine million individuals, taking into account jobless people who are not on the AFDC rolls.

Experts' consensus about the underclass is that many families in it tend to be dysfunctional and at the storm center for some of our country's most serious social problems. They are less certain about which are the causes and which are the effects of poverty and its problems in such families. Some fall back on referring to a "tangle of pathology" in the most troubling underclass families (Patterson, 1981). It should be recognized that not many of the problems in that tangle are unique to poverty. Middle-class people, too, are vulnerable to some of the same problems; they even have a few of their own (e.g., "white-collar crime") that are beyond the reach of the underclass. Yet the intensity, prevalence, and intermingling of many serious social problems permeate the underclass more than any other segment of society. In the tangle of social problems, some are especially conspicuous.

Long-Term Unemployment

The lack of paid employment is the most obvious cause of poverty, and joblessness is, of course, the prime characteristic of the underclass. According to *Risking the Future* (the important 1987 report on teenage pregnancy and motherhood authored by the National Research Council) sixteen percent of white male 16- to 19-year-olds reporting that they were eligible for the labor force during 1985 were actually unemployed. The rate for black male 16- to 19-year-olds was still higher—41 percent were unemployed.

What explains these high unemployment rates among teenage men, particularly noncollege bound 16- to 19-year-olds who have dropped out of school and are supposedly ready to take jobs? The explanations range from Murray's contention that the blame rests mainly with welfare-encouraged indolence (Murray, 1984) to that of many experts who claim that the culprit is principally the elimination, by technology, of many unskilled and semi-skilled jobs. They are the jobs that could once be counted upon to absorb the young men and women who did not graduate from high school. Gunnar Myrdal prophetically remarked in 1962: "As less and less work is required of the type the people in rural and urban slums can offer, they will be increasingly isolated and exposed to unemployment, to underemployment, and to plain exploitation."

Senator Patrick Moynihan, once a Harvard professor of government, put it succinctly in his 1986 book *Family and Nation,* almost 25 years later: "Certain jobs are simply not there, while the people who once held them are."

As described in an October 22, 1986, *New York Times* article by John Herbers, Dr. John D. Kasarda, a sociologist at the University of North Carolina, supported this "structural" viewpoint of unemployment by information he supplied to the Joint Economic Committee of Congress. His statistics, mainly from the U.S. Census Bureau's March, 1985, *Current Population*

Survey, showed that the old industrial cities suffered huge losses in blue-collar jobs and white-collar population in the 1970s. Dr. Kasarda commented: "That there are increasing job opportunities for accountants, stockbrokers, corporate lawyers and other knowledge-intensive occupations . . . is of little comfort to the unemployed high school dropout" (Herbers, 1986).

The blow to self-esteem represented by the long-term unemployment of formerly employed male family heads cannot help but damage family relationships. For example, fathers sometimes compensate by either withdrawing psychologically or by trying to restore their injured pride through abusing the women and children in their families.

Unmarried young men who have never held a job are no less rudderless but are not burdened by the responsibilities of family life. Lacking the self-respect that might come from working at a satisfying job, some use, as a major source of personal pride, the fathering of children they cannot support either financially or psychologically. The cost of this is often suffered by the women who bear their children and by the children themselves, through the erosive effects of the dysfunctional families the young men have thus started and abandoned.

Criminal Alternatives to Jobs

The flip side of the problem of unemployment is the seductive pull of "The Street," with its glittering, peer-approved alternatives to legal—and scarce—jobs. "Hustling" is one such alternative, and violent crime is another. Hustlers are people who find their way adroitly through the labyrinths of the Street's underground economy. They sell drugs, stolen goods, and themselves. They learn and use the tricks of gambling. Perhaps most conspicuous among the hustlers are the prosperous pimps who serve as glamorous role models for young male school dropouts.

The hustlers' operations, however illicit, are still a long step removed from the violent crime that serves as another alternative to working at a job. It is true the victims of hold-ups, muggings, rapes, armed robbery, and murders are more likely to live in the criminals' own poor neighborhoods, perhaps as rival gang members, than to inhabit wealthy areas. However, wealthy people are equally vulnerable, and certainly much more profitable, targets.

The criminals themselves usually make a life career of crime. Many are often known to the police, since a relative few are responsible for the majority of crimes in big cities. Even so, few are caught, and even fewer are ever punished by imprisonment. Teenagers are well aware that their chances are good for getting away scot-free with a lucrative violent crime. This is one more factor that makes ordinary employment less than interesting. This is especially true for high school dropouts, for whom not many interesting or well-paying jobs are available.

In the last few years juvenile crime experts have become even more disturbed by a new development in the criminal careers of Street people. There has been an alarming increase in violent crime by *elementary school* students or dropouts, with a disproportionate number coming from the underclass. When Peter Applebome, a *New York Times* reporter, interviewed juvenile justice officials around the country, he heard from them that the age at which youngsters are committing serious crimes is declining steadily. Cases that seemed like bizarre anomalies a few years ago are now becoming much more common. According to Applebome's article (1987), the Federal Bureau of Investigation has reported that children of 12 or under were responsible in 1985 for 21 killings, 436 rapes, 3,545 aggravated assaults, and 1,735 robberies. Officials at the National Center for Juvenile Justice in Pittsburgh were quoted by Applebome to the effect that the rate of referrals of juvenile courts rose from 1978 to 1983 by 37 percent for 13-year-olds, by 38 percent for 12-year-olds, by 22 percent for 11-year-olds, and by 15 percent for 10-year-olds.

Most criminals are known by psychologists to have serious gaps in their cognitive and academic achievement, with reading disability the most common. However, juvenile criminals share at least two additional cognitive/emotional deficits: an inability to anticipate the possible future consequences of their acts (except for blind confidence in their own ability to evade the law); and an indifference to the suffering of others. This indifference comes less from callousness (which implies a former openness to compassion) than from a genuine, life-long absence of the capacity to empathize, to feel with the joy or pain of other people. They have spent their brief lives in families which were dysfuntional for teaching these most human of all emotions.

Drug Abuse by Children and Women

Of particular nationwide concern, Applebome continued in his *New York Times* article, is the growing involvement of elementary school children not only with crime but also with drugs. The favorite drug for use and sale among these children is "crack," a cheap and highly addictive form of cocaine. The comment of an official at the Pittsburgh Juvenile Justice Center that "Drug use used to be a decision of adolescence—now it's a fourth grade decision" was supported by Applebome's quotation from James A. Payne, chief of Family Court for New York City's Law Department. Mr. Payne said that Family Court has had an almost 50 percent increase in drug crime: "Crack is the main reason. We are seeing kids as young as 10 or 11. They can make $800 a week. They only stay in school because that's where their constituency is."

Indeed, starting as recently as 1985, cocaine, especially in the powerful form of crack, appeared to be swiftly replacing heroin as the drug chosen by addicts. The leap is documented in another *New York Times* article, this one by Peter Kerr (1987), who quoted statistics that demonstrate a recent change in people requesting help from Phoenix House, the largest operator of drug treatment centers in New York City. In 1984, 48 percent of applicants for help were addicted to heroin and only 11 percent to cocaine. In 1986 the figures were stunningly reversed: heroin was the drug of choice for only 13 percent, whereas 52 percent were addicted to cocaine.

Moreover, the number of women applying for treatment at Phoenix House increased by 43 percent between 1985 and 1986. This jump paralleled the marked increases in crack/cocaine casualties noted in hospital emergency rooms and psychiatric wards serving underclass women who were sometimes about to give birth. The immediate consequence for their new-born babies was a risk-related delay in their hospital discharge and often eventual referral to childcare agencies.

Toddlers and older children suffer neglect, child abuse, and even death linked to the drug abuse of their parents, who are usually poor, single, and female. "The effect [of crack] has been so dramatic in some neighborhoods that the heads of some drug treatment centers express fears about the drug's long-term impact on the already fragmented family structure of the under-class," Kerr commented.

Whether the serious drug situation in New York City is typical of other geographical areas can only be a matter for speculation. However, social problems noted in New York City are usually duplicated at least to some extent in other cities. The drug problems described here are likely to be typical of those in the rest of the United States.

High School Dropouts

The high school dropout rate in the country averages around 30 percent. In the low-income neighborhoods of large cities the percentage is much higher, hovering between 40 and 50 percent. Low-income teenagers appear to vanish from the school scene as soon as they are legally of age to do so, and sometimes even before.

Many young women drop out as early as junior high school, either when they are pregnant or during the year before the birth of their child, according to *Risking the Future*. "Although some are undoubtedly pregnant at the time, it also seems likely that many young women who drop out become pregnant within several months after leaving school . . . early childbear-ers are more likely to have reduced educational attainment than later childbearers. . . . Do high school dropouts catch up? . . . the answer is generally no" (National Research Council, 1987).

Young men almost always drop out for reasons other than the pregnancy of their girlfriends, but their basic reasons may at bottom be shared by both male and female students: profound dissatisfaction with school, starting with the humiliation and acute sense of failure engendered by their own poor academic achievement manifested in the earliest school grades.

The implications of the dropout problem are dismal for young people hoping to climb out of the underclass. As described in Peter Kerr's article quoted above, Dr. Kasarda, the sociologist, commented in regard to the increase in educational requirements for jobs in the central city: "In the last 14 years alone, New York lost almost 500,000 jobs in those industries where the average job-holder has not completed high school . . . So you can see the entry level jobs [are] disappearing."

The Feminization of Poverty

The social problems of the underclass and the tangle of pathology in underclass families are linked to the family dysfunction that often accompanies the conditions and stresses of poverty. In fact, the very formation of single-parent families can be in itself a cause of family dysfunction. As Moynihan commented in his *Family and Nation*: "A family is formed when a child is born. When an unwed teenager gives birth, a broken family is formed."

Since the family is the basic social unit for society, bad news for the family is bad news for society. In the same book Moynihan sounded a warning that should be heeded:

> The family is the cornerstone of our society. More than any other force it shapes the attitude, the hope, the ambitions, and the values of the child. When the family collapses, it is the children that are usually damaged. When it happens on a massive scale, the community itself is crippled (Moynihan, 1986).

In 1966, Alvin Schorr, Director of Research and Planning at the federal Office of Economic Opportunity, was already able to point out in his book, *Poor Kids,* that "hidden from view is a striking demographic fact—namely, that three out of four poor youths can make . . . [this] statement: 'I did not live with my father or even a man I could call father . . .'"

Twenty years later Moynihan found that the trend had accelerated: nine out of ten children born in 1984 can expect to live in a female-headed household before they reach the age of eighteen. It is true, as Moynihan noted, that "single parenthood is now a fact of life for all classes and for all races." But, as he also pointed out, "if the proportion of the poor who are in female-headed families were to increase at the same rate as it did from 1967 to 1977, the poverty population would be composed solely of women and their children by about the year 2000."

The immediate causes of this feminization of poverty are superficially simple. The dramatic rise in the AFDC rolls (however caused) has been paralleled by two relatively recent developments: the increasing percentage of first-born children conceived and born outside of marriage to teenagers from 15 to 19 years, and the increasing number of absent fathers—young men who either disappear or take only minimal responsibility for their own children. "Across race groups, the proportion of fathers aged 24 to 25 who have had their first child at age 19 was higher for absent fathers than for those living with their children" was the comment in *Risking the Future*.

The "feminization of poverty" thus starts with young women's inevitable feelings of rejection which stem from real causes. To further deepen their depression and accompanying loss of self-respect, their problems multiply:

Welfare Dependency

The National Research Council reported, in *Risking the Future*, that nearly 470,000 teenagers give birth each year, the majority being unmarried mothers from "severely disadvantaged" backgrounds, and nearly half under 18 years of age. About 10,000 of the births are to teenagers under the age of 15, a rate five times higher than for any other developed country for which data are available. Two consequences are that a teenager's dropping out of school is likely to be permanent, and that she is likely to have more children as an unmarried mother. Both effects will handicap her ability to work at a job and will probably prolong her welfare dependency. Looking for a job entails her encountering and overcoming some difficult practical problems.

1. If her pregnancy occurred in early adolescence, it curtailed the young mother's high school, or even junior high school, education. She had to drop out before she acquired saleable skills or had even had a chance to learn some of the most elementary entry-level skills needed for any job such as reliability, punctuality, and respect for supervision and for job standards.

2. Single mothers sometimes have no extended family willing or able to look after their babies and toddlers. They hesitate to entrust their children to unlicensed strangers to enable them to work at jobs that would free the family from welfare dependency. Decent, affordable daycare for their children, whether group- or family-centered, is unattainable for all but a lucky few AFDC mothers. It should be noted also that minimal federal standards for daycare are still lacking for the relatively small number of affordable facilities presently available although standards set by states may prevail where they are applicable.

3. When appropriate daycare resources *are* made available to single mothers in poverty, some women without job skills do enter work-training programs supported by the federal government that provide a stipend, like the federal WIN ("Work Incentive") program. Most who enter such programs are likely to succeed and to retain their learning (Moynihan, 1986). But when the training is over, private sector jobs are conspicuously absent or are considered undesirable in terms of pay or conditions. Women find that they cannot support themselves and their children on the minimum wages usually offered, and they are forced to return to AFDC.

Patterson (1981) summed up these women's dilemma in a brief paragraph:

> For them, welfare was grim, but preferable to leaving their children with strangers. The women who actually enrolled in WIN initially welcomed the opportunity to get off welfare, but before long were frustrated

by the irrelevance of their training, the inadequacy of daycare for their children, or the poor jobs that awaited them when they got out. . . . They were willing to undergo training for decent-paying jobs, but they could not get them.

Underclass Children at Risk

For the first time in history, Moynihan (1986) observed, "a person is more likely to be poor if young than if old." The rate of poverty in 1984 among preschool children (24 percent) was twice that among the elderly (12.4 percent) and almost twice that among nonelderly adults (11.7 percent).

Further, the poverty rate for children in female-headed families was much higher (54 percent) than that for children in all other families (12.5 percent). The children are often put at risk physically, emotionally and intellectually by membership in a family which is broken—and poor—from the start. As babies, they may be at risk for long-term health and developmental problems, especially if their mothers are in the youngest age groups, since these have the highest rate of pregnancy complications (National Research Council, 1987). As they grow older, they are likely to suffer from neglect, if not outright child abuse. The intellectual stimulation necessary for the child's academic achievement may be severely limited, mainly because of the young mother's educational limitations. The National Research Council's 1987 study confirms earlier research that among all of the family structure factors that have negative effects on children's cognitive development, "mother's education has been shown to be most significant."

Risking the Future also reports that children of poor teenage mothers are at risk for having social behavior problems and problems of self-control, perhaps because young single mothers can hardly cope with their own problems. Their children must sometimes shift emotionally as well as physically for themselves. Yet, as indicated above in the discussion of juvenile crime, the dangers of such neglect, for the children and ultimately for society, can hardly be overstated. Another quotation from Moynihan's *Family and Nation* is both apropos and sobering:

Family life not only educates in general but its quality ultimately determines the individual's capacity to love. The institution of the family is decisive in determining not only if a person has the capacity to love another individual but in a larger sense whether he is capable of loving his fellow men collectively. The whole of society rests on this foundation for stability, understanding and social peace.

Mental Health Problems of Underclass Mothers

Thus, inexorably tied to the reality-based problems, which are linked to welfare dependency and the problems of child rearing, are the attitudes and mental health of single-parent mothers. The depression and hopelessness that often characterize underclass mothers result in a kind of listless passivity which causes these women, often little more than children themselves, to lack motivation for beneficial change, to drift along on a tide of whatever support comes easiest.

Cause and effect are entangled, as is usual with the problems of poverty, but most observers have long agreed with Elizabeth Herzog that women receiving welfare over a considerable period of time are emotionally and sometimes physically damaged (Herzog, 1966). Typically, Norman Polansky's research found such women to be passive, depressed, hopeless (Polansky et al., 1972). Whether black or white, rural or urban, their lack of self-confidence and self-esteem is a conspicuous feature. This in turn weakens the motivation of these women to change their lives.

Remedies

That the effects of underclass status can be disastrous for the children of female-headed poor families, so recently documented by the National Research Council's 1987 study, was a conclusion reached some time ago by researchers from several disciplines (Bee et al., 1982; Bower, 1963; Burgess & Conger, 1978; Kohn, 1977; Sameroff, 1978; Sameroff & Seifer, 1982). The results of their studies all pointed in the same direction: when mothers are sunk in despairing conviction of their own limitations and have no practical and emotional support for child-rearing problems, their children's development may be stunted. The children lose out intellectually and emotionally, possibly not so much from the lack of a male parent as from the impact of the mother's problems linked to her single-parent state. The intellectually and emotionally supportive parent-child network developed by the mother and child is usually too rudimentary to support the children in their school tasks. The resultant "educational disadvantage" in early grades (school failure because of a child's poverty background) leads to dropping out of school and thus to more or less permanent membership in the underclass.

Various remedies have been proposed for ending this "cycle of poverty" and its accompanying tangle of pathology. One of the most recent, and surely the most Draconian, is that put forth by Charles Murray (1984):

> The proposed program . . . consists of scrapping the entire federal welfare and income-support structure for working-aged persons, including AFDC, Medicaid, food stamps, Unemployment Insurance, Worker's Compensation, subsidized housing, disability insurance, and the rest. . . . It is the Alexandrian solution: cut the knot, for there is no way to untie it.

Preschool Education

Others have sought somewhat less extreme ways of tackling the problem, in the direction of untying the knot rather than cutting it. Because of its close relationship to the cycle of poverty, the poor school achievement of low-income children has been of acute concern to educators and to other behavioral specialists for many years. In the 1960s the federal government, as part of its "war on poverty," began large-scale financial support for remedial programs in every school system that enrolled large numbers of poor children. These Title One programs (transmuted more recently into the similar umbrella title of "Chapter One") usually focused on *remedial* efforts like eight-year-old Vincent Willard's special class for "slow learners."

Excellent preschool educational television programs like "Sesame Street" and "Around the Bend" were launched at that time, with the idea of *preventing* school problems before they started. Influenced by the same aims, the federally funded "Project Headstart" took its tentative first steps in that period. However, several child development researchers had already begun during the early and middle sixties to develop and conduct longitudinal research on carefully designed programs for disadvantaged preschoolers.

Some of the earliest among the researchers (Kuno Beller, Martin and Cynthia Deutsch, Ira Gordon and Emile Jester, Merle Karnes, Phyllis Levenstein, Louise Miller, Francis Palmer, David Weikart, and Edward Zigler) combined their short-term and long-range results as the "Consortium for Longitudinal Studies" and published their individual research in a book, *As the Twig Is Bent* (Consortium, 1983). The combined findings were also published as a research monograph by Cornell University professors Irving Lazar and Richard Darlington (1982). Many of the Consortium programs had already been described earlier in *The Preschool in Action,* edited by M. C. Day and R. K. Parker (1977).

Mother-Love Fights Back

One of the Consortium programs, which was also one of those published in *Preschool in Action* (Levenstein, 1977), was the Mother-Child Home Program. This home-based preventive program was begun in 1965 by the Verbal Interaction Project. It had the same goal of preventing educational disadvantage as did the others in the Consortium. However, it broke entirely with the classroom model followed by most of them (as did the Consortium program developed by Ira Gordon [1977], and a nonConsortium program created by Earl Schaefer, with May Aaronson [1969]).

Further, the Mother-Child Home Program reached poor children at the early, pre-preschool age of two years and continued until they were nearly four. It involved their mothers—for example, Mrs. Willard and Mrs. Carter—as playful teachers of their own children in their own homes, using toys and books as curriculum materials. The mainspring of the Program was an age-old motivating force: mother-love.

Although there is much joking and a good deal of sentimentality about mother-love (Mother's Day comes close to being a religious holiday in the United States), it is indeed universally the most powerful and lasting of all infatuations. Whenever mothers are the primary persons taking care of their infants and young children and are thus exposed to the feedback and intense emotion that this nurture generates, there is likely to be a close bonding of mother and child.

Because of this bonding, mothers are willing to act as nurses and as civilizing agents for their children. Mothers' love for their young is the lure that leads little children to conform to whatever type of civilization prevails in their societies. The basic patterns by which adults meet the demands of their particular cultures are laid down by mothers in their children's earliest years. And as with all their child care, they usually do it for love alone. Seldom does any society pay a penny for the long work hours and exhausting labor which mothers contribute in the course of bringing up their children.

This applies as much to children's preschool education in the home as to their cultural-emotional socialization. In America, as probably throughout the world, mother is baby's first teacher of intellectual skills. For several years she is the child's most important one. She is as much responsible for getting the child ready for school learning as she is for preparing him for any other aspect of civilization. Mothers, of course, hardly ever think this out ahead of time. They just do what comes naturally in their interactions with their babies and toddlers.

Still, for most mothers, "doing what comes naturally" turns out to be just the preparation that children need for classroom learning when they enter school. These mothers usually take the time and exert the effort to encourage their young children's conversation and, if they are above the poverty level, to provide them with attractive educational books and toys. These mothers know, from their education and from their life experience, or are able to learn quickly (like Mrs. Carter), how to stimulate interests and ideas in even very little children. Such mothers can be called "Strivers." They are to be found among welfare mothers as well as in other groups.

To be a Striver, as we saw with Mrs. Carter, neither a college education nor a middle class income are prerequisites. But in most cases, it takes a special effort for low-income, less-than-college-educated mothers to become Strivers. They are handicapped not only by poverty but often by the mental health problems described above. Of the latter, perhaps a most pervasive and insidious combination for low-income mothers of limited education is low self-esteem and depression. The two join to deepen or cause other problems, such as inertia and a lowered ability to care for themselves or for their children. Consequently, *most* middle-income, college-educated mothers are likely to be Strivers, and *many* underclass mothers, like Mrs. Willard, are what we will call "Hesitaters": these are usually high school dropouts who are weakly motivated to move toward taking charge of their lives.

Hesitaters could be Strivers in regard to their children, but they are too bogged down in their own problems and too depressed to heed their children's intellectual, emotional, and sometimes even physical needs. As a result, it is the Hesitaters' children who tend to have the school problems like those of Vincent, Carol Willard's older brother. They are problems often thought to be typical of all low-income children but probably most characterisic of those whose mothers are Hesitaters.

The children of Strivers, although they may be from the underclass, still are more likely to show good school performance and, therefore, have a better chance of eventually escaping from poverty than do those of Hesitaters. Further, their mothers will reach out for *any* program that promises to help them or their children. Point Striver-mothers in the right direction and mother-love will go to work. If a parent education or a preschool or pre-preschool program of almost any kind is offered to the Strivers, they will enroll. (This doesn't guarantee, however, that they will stay enrolled if the program doesn't seem to live up to its promise.)

Ironically, it's the underclass Hesitaters who are least likely to join parent/early education programs although they are the mothers, and theirs are the children, who most need them. However, they love their small children as much as Strivers do. Because they do, it is possible to convince Hesitaters to put their mother-love to work on behalf of their pre-preschool children's intellectual development *provided the program they are offered has a number of basic features designed to appeal to all mothers, and especially to those of the underclass:*

- It approaches mothers as free, valuable individuals, respecting their dignity, independence and right to privacy.
- It requires no minimum level of education from the mothers.
- It is voluntary and explicitly nonintrusive, yet perseveres in reaching out to mothers without exerting pressure.
- It has built-in incentives, part of which are the no-cost, attractive program materials (books and toys).
- It is minimal, with no mandatory tasks or difficult concepts.
- It is nonembarrassing and sensitive to mothers' needs.
- It respects and, wherever possible, incorporates features of families' cultural/ethnolinguistic differences from mainstream culture.
- It makes mothers the main members of the program team, whose other members, including professionals, take a back seat as early as possible within the program.
- It involves mothers' easy participation without leaving home, at their convenience, even if they have jobs.
- Its goals are limited.

The Mothers-Child Home Program fulfilled these conditions and thus could win the commitment of Mrs. Willard, a Hesitater. It also captured the lasting interest of Mrs. Carter, who was a Striver, so that she could be supplied with "curriculum materials" (books and toys) and some childrearing guidance to support her efforts to prepare her son for later school. Both Strivers and Hesitaters could be served. Varying the intensity of the Program suited the differing amounts of support mothers needed for developing the parent-child network which, in turn, would support their children's development.

The Program's assumption was that its role in fostering the parent-child network was also supportive of mother's development. The Mother-Child Home Program could serve as a vehicle for improving the mental health of the mother, and indeed of the whole family through the mother's improved self-confidence. It could provide her with an entry level job as a Toy Demonstrator within the Program and thus enhance her employability for other jobs after that.

"Mental health" is a vague and often ambiguous label which specialists use to mean a state of well-being, a feeling of relative harmony with the world and with oneself that engenders attitudes and behaviors tending to produce a similar state in "significant others." The "significant others" are likely to be close family members, in particular one's children. As we have seen, the mental health of underclass mothers can be so impaired that child neglect may become one consequence of their problems (Bolton et al., 1980). Yet many studies have shown that even beneath some mothers' seeming indifference, deep maternal affection is usually present, especially in the years before the child starts to be drawn more to peers and playing in the street than to an increasingly unresponsive mother.

By tapping into the reservoir of mother-love, the Mother-Child Home Program's main strategy was to utilize one of poverty's greatest weaknesses—its feminization—as a strength against its own pathological effects, in a kind of psychological ju-jitsu. Mother-love would serve both as a motivation for the mother to enroll and stay with the Program, and as a powerful motivation for the child's learning to learn—and to take joy in learning.

As a deliberately minimal method that was planned to strengthen the mother-child network with each passing year to become a support against school failure, the Mother-Child Home Program dared to hope that it might interrupt, for some, the cycle of poverty. It proposed to start small changes in the lives of underclass mothers and children at a time in the children's lives when slight modifications of family dysfunction might widen in a few years into changes significant for the child's academic progress.

At the same time, it was hoped that fostering the frequent, happy interaction between mother and child in two of the child's most formative years would have a good mental health effect on the child. It could aid the child to develop into a happy, sociable human being, a little readier to meet the challenges of school, to empathize with the feelings of others, to resist the temptations of drugs, of dropping out and of The Street.

Ultimately, it was hoped that mothers' pride in their visible accomplishments with their children would raise their own self-esteem and ability to cope with the everyday world, perhaps enough to escape from the underclass altogether, to "get up from under." The Mother-Child Home Program could provide a ladder from livingroom into classroom for the child, and from livingroom into a new realm of self-competence and self-confidence for the mother.

3

Getting Up
From
Under

The Mother-Child Home Program was founded, as we have seen, on the proposition that a low-income child's best preparation for grade school, like that of other children, is a cognitively and emotionally supportive parent-child network started in pre-preschool years. The Program theorized that the network develops from positive interaction, especially verbal interaction, with a beloved parent, who is likely, for an underclass child, to be the child's mother. The interaction, it was believed, contributes to the mother's dignity and self-esteem as well as to the child's school readiness. The Program converted these beliefs into practical action by helping both child and mother to climb out of the underclass, to use the Program to get up from under.

A Thumbnail History of the Program

The Verbal Interaction Project (VIP) began the Mother-Child Home Program for pilot experimental research in 1965 (Levenstein & Sunley, 1968). The VIP, first attached to a private social agency, is now an independent nonprofit corporation affiliated with the State University of New York at Stony Brook. Its mission was to develop a pre-preschool, preliteracy program, research its effects, and then teach its replication to others if the research showed that the program was effective. Aside from a few generous personal gifts, the VIP's financial support has come almost completely from federal and private foundation funding of its research and training activities. Funds were

49

usually won by "competitive proposals"—that is, they were awards made to the VIP on the basis of a proposed work plan's technical merit and social relevance. Awards to the VIP between 1967 and 1982 totaled almost three million dollars.

In 1969 the original Mother-Child Home Program in Long Island began to serve as a model for Program replications (adoptions) throughout the country. By 1984 there had been eighty-four replications, scattered among sixteen states and Bermuda and Canada. All had found their own local funding. For many the funding sources eventually gave out, but eighteen of them still endured in 1985.

In the more than 5000 families served in the original Program and its replications, most had children at risk for educational disadvantage. All were of low income (with the exception of one adoption serving mentally retarded and autistic children). They were from many ethnic groups: Blacks, Cape Verdians, Eskimos, Hispanics, French, Italians, Native Canadian Indians, Native American Indians, and whites in many subcultures. They lived in a variety of geographical settings: Appalachian Mountains, rural prairie land, Louisiana bayous, suburbs, inner cities, villages, and small towns. Yet within this rich mixture of families and varying personalities served by the Program, two main categories of mothers gradually emerged: the Hesitaters and the Strivers. Mrs. Willard and Mrs. Carter were chosen to represent them.

The Program aimed to bring to all of the Mrs. Willards and Mrs. Carters the "curriculum materials" and guidance in using the pre-preschool "hidden curriculum" of parent-child interaction found so often in middle-income homes. It offered to mothers not only the quality toys and books they couldn't afford but some joyful ways of weaving the interaction around them into every aspect of their relationships with their children—of strengthening the parent-child network which was cognitively and emotionally supportive for both mother and child.

Now, 22 years after the VIP first tried out the tiny pilot version of the Mother-Child Home Program under the auspices of the Family Service Association of Nassau County, the VIP's remaining task as a nonprofit educational agency is dissemination of the Program. It assists school systems and social agencies everywhere to install the Program, assuring them of true replications in every aspect of its four major ingredients: curriculum, curriculum materials (toys and books), home visitors (Toy Demonstrators), and supervision (Coordinators).

Overview of the Mother-Child Home Program

The Program consists of a maximum of ninety-two home visits, over almost two years, to the homes of children and their mothers, when the children are aged two (Program I) and three years old (Program II). The visitors are called "Toy Demonstrators" to emphasize their nonteaching, noncounseling role with mother and child. The Toy Demonstrators are trained to promote a mother's "positive parenting" and to show the mother, during play sessions with her child in her own living-room, how to interact verbally with her child to enhance the child's conceptual and social-emotional development. The play-oriented interaction is centered around books and toys that are attractive to both mother and child and are gifts to the child. The mother is free to adopt the model of the Toy Demonstrator's behavior with the child, or not, as she wishes.

The Program parallels the school year, starting during October and ending in late May or early June. It observes the local school holidays, so there are actually only twenty-three weeks of the Program in each of the two Program years.

The mother-child pair (called a "dyad" in the Program, to indicate that mother and child interact with each other as a mini-social system) is visited twice a week for half-hour Home Sessions. The Toy Demonstrator brings a new toy or book to the first sessions of the week and shows techniques for conversation and other interaction around it. The second Home Session is used to "review" the toy or book introduced at the first Session.

Each Program year, twelve books and eleven toys, selected to fulfill a large number of criteria (including the opinions of mothers and Toy Demonstrators), are presented to the mother to give to her child. One week a book is brought, the next week a toy, in the same order for every child in the Program.

The main focus of the Program is on the mother rather than the child. Its touch is very light. The Program tries to convey that it respects the parent as the most important person in the child's life and does not want to take over from her. The mother is therefore required to be present at every Home Session and is put in charge of it as early in the Program as possible. In fact, the number of Home Sessions in the second year is routinely tailored to the growing skills of the mother. As with Mrs. Willard and Mrs. Carter, Home Sessions are either reduced in number or even completely eliminated. However, all dyads receive the same number of Program II books and toys regardless of Home Session frequency.

The operation of each Mother-Child Home Program adoption is supported by a large number of technical materials (record forms, letters to mothers, management schedules, curriculum guides, and so on) and three manuals (e.g., Levenstein, 1973), all issued free by the VIP along with its low-cost training for replication. The average annual all-inclusive cost of the Program itself, for each mother-child dyad, is about $1200.

The Mother-Child Home Program

First Program Ingredient: Curriculum

The Program's curriculum was unobtrusively conveyed by the Toy Demonstrators to the mothers, in their Home Sessions with Mrs. Willard and Carol, and with Mrs. Carter and Jo-Jo. The Toy Demonstrators' written records of their Home Sessions hardly reflected their own modeling of the curriculum. Indeed, the notes provided only the barest outline of what actually went on in the Sessions.

There was little hint in the records that along with their relaxed approach to child and mother, the Toy Demonstrators had been trained for the tasks of modeling the three kinds of parenting behavior which make up the Program's curriculum: *Verbal Interaction Techniques, Positive Parenting Behavior,* and *Fostering the Child's Social-Emotional Competence.*

VERBAL INTERACTION TECHNIQUES

This first part of the three-part curriculum relates mainly to nurturing the child's intellectual growth through conversation with his or her mother. It promotes mother-child talk around the toys and books. It encompasses the Program's techniques to stimulate the verbal interaction between mother and child—the most visible aspects of the curriculum.

The Verbal Interaction Techniques were made more tangible to Mrs. Willard, to Mrs. Carter, and to their Toy Demonstrators, through a Guide Sheet that accompanied every toy and book. Each Guide Sheet was complete in itself as a "curriculum" because it was a one-page summary of the main intellectually stimulating part of the Program's version of the "hidden curriculum." The Toy Demonstrators received a Guide Sheet for each week's new toy or book and kept it in their "Toy Demonstrator's VISIT Handbook." (VISIT was the acronym for "Verbal Interaction Stimulation Intervention Techniques.") They also received copies of the same Guide Sheet to give to Mrs. Willard and Mrs. Carter.

Two Guide Sheets used with Carol and Jo-Jo can serve as examples, one for a toy (the School Bus) and one for a book (*Ask Mr. Bear*). The little yellow School Bus looked very much like the real thing and even had some interesting passengers which could be lifted out and manipulated. *Ask Mr. Bear* (Flack, 1932) was a picture book about small Danny's quest among some animal friends to find a birthday present for his mother, which was finally suggested by Mr. Bear (a hug).

The Toy Demonstrators gave the Guide Sheets to the mothers when they brought the School Bus and *Ask Mr. Bear* for Carol and Jo-Jo during Program I, when the children were almost two-and-a-half years old. Mrs. Willard and Mrs. Carter were welcome to keep their Guide Sheets in a special folder provided by the Program, or to discard them, as they wished. The Program staff never questioned what the mothers did with them.

Each Guide Sheet contains down its left side a general list of verbal interaction techniques to use with both toys and books—the kernel of the Verbal Interaction Curriculum. Next to every Technique on the list are examples taken from the toy or book related to that Guide Sheet.

The examples for the School Bus and *Ask Mr. Bear,* which the Toy Demonstrators named, and encouraged the children to name, were:

They named	About the School Bus	About *Ask Mr. Bear*
Labels:	Bus	Grass
Colors:	Yellow bus	Green Grass
Shapes:	Square window	Round wheels
Sizes:	Little Children	Tall Trees
Relationships:	Up the stairs	In the center
Categories:	Children	Animals
Numbers:	Three girls	Two Birds
Causation:	"If you pull the bus, the head will move."	"When Danny looked for Mr. Bear, he found him."

However, after that, the techniques on the Guide Sheets were different for the School Bus (a toy) and for *Ask Mr. Bear* (a book).

On the Guide Sheets for the book, there was practical advice for how the Toy Demonstrators (and thus Mrs. Willard and Mrs. Carter) should read *Ask Mr. Bear* to Carol and Jo-Jo:

- Invite the child to look and listen.

- Try to sit with the child between you and the mother.

- Show and read the title page of the book.

- Show and describe how to turn the pages and treat the book.

- Read in a clear, easy voice. Don't go too fast.

- Stop at most illustrations.

- Invite the child to tell about personal experiences: "Can you hop too?"

- Ask questions about the illustrations to help the child reason things out: "Why is Danny sitting on the step instead of playing?"

- Encourage the child to join in on familiar words.

- Enjoy the book yourself.

- Invite the mother to take over the reading.

For the School Bus there were many additional techniques listed on the left side of the Guide Sheet. First, the Toy Demonstrators helped the children describe their actions:

- General: "The children are climbing into the school bus."
- Matching: "The girl in the red dress should go in the red seat."
- Fitting: "The round child fits into the round seat."
- Sounds: "Listen to the bus as it rolls along."

Second, the Toy Demonstrators reminded Jo-Jo and Carol to think about what they were doing, to be reflective, as they played with the School Bus:

- To give their attention: "Make the bus driver watch the road!"
- To make a choice: "Will you put the children in from the top or through the bus door?"
- To have self control: "Slow down or the bus will crash!"
- To remember experiences: "Have you seen the real school bus?"
- To pretend: "Let's drive to the children waiting for the bus."
- To do things in the right order: "First stop the bus, then let's have the driver put out the Stop sign."

Three kinds of general reminders were on the Guide Sheets for the School Bus and *Ask Mr. Bear,* and they are on each of the forty-six Guide Sheets used for all the toys and books in the two Program years. The Toy Demonstrators (and thus Mrs. Willard and Mrs. Carter) were reminded to:

- Encourage the child to talk: Ask him questions, listen to her answers, answer his answers.
- Encourage the child to want to learn: Praise him when he does well, try to ignore her mistakes, help him when he really needs help.
- Encourage his or her curiosity and his or her imagination.

These general suggestions were the same for both toys and

books. They were there to remind Toy Demonstrators and mothers of the most fundamental features of the mother-child verbal interaction.

For the second part of the curriculum, the Toy Demonstrator was to model, as often as she could do so appropriately, twenty items of "Positive Parenting Behavior" (Baumrind, 1967). Usually the Positive Parenting Behavior was directly related to the toys and books but occasionally it was not:

1. The Toy Demonstrator *responded verbally* to the child's verbal or perhaps nonverbal requests for her attention. She used words to show that she was aware of what the child wanted and that she would either grant the request or not do so. In either case, she was careful not to ignore a bid for attention. Example: She said, "Yes, I see the dog," when Carol pointed or exclaimed "Dog!" while looking at a book illustration. Or she said, "Not now—mommy says you'll be eating lunch soon," when Jo-Jo indicated that he was hungry and wanted a cookie.

2. She *verbalized affection* toward the child. She used words to express a feeling of warmth toward Carol or Jo-Jo. Example: "Jo-Jo, it's fun to build block towers with you!"

3. She clearly *verbalized to the child the expectations* she had from him. She put into words exactly what she wanted Jo-Jo or Carol to do, or not to do, so that they were sure about what she really wanted. Example: Instead of just saying generally to Carol, "It's time to clean up," she said, "It's time to put the blocks back into the block can!"

4. She *verbalized her approval* of the child. She praised Carol in words. She made comments that let Jo-Jo know that she liked what he was doing (or refrained from doing). Example: She said, "That's it!" or "That's good!" when Carol did start putting the blocks back into the block can.

5. She tried to *converse with the child.* That is, she tried to conduct conversations with Carol and Jo-Jo. She responded to their

utterances (whether or not they were questions) with a question, or with a comment on what they had said. The conversation might be more of an accompaniment to a child's actions than an actual verbal give and take. Example:

Jo-Jo: "Green!"

Toy Demonstrator: "Yes, it's a green block. And something you're wearing is green, too. Maybe you can tell me what it is."

OR

Carol: "I'm building (tower of blocks) up, up, up!"

Toy Demonstrator: "Yes, up it goes—up, up, up!"

Carol: "Gonna crash!"

Toy Demonstrator: "Bang!"

6. She *verbalized the reasons for the child's obedience.* She explained why it was necessary for a child to perform, or desist from performing, a particular action. Example: When she suggested that Carol put the blocks back into the can she added, "In that way the pieces won't get lost."

7. She *tried to enforce her instructions* to the child. She continued an attempt to get the child to comply when she directed her to perform, or not to perform, a particular action. She didn't let the directive drop without trying to follow through with it. Example: She would tell Jo-Jo to bring a toy for review from his Toy Chest, wait for him to bring it, and then repeated the directive a few times before giving up on it.

8. She *discouraged the child's overdependence.* She did not help with tasks she knew the child could do for herself. Example: When Carol asked her to put her shoe on, the Toy Demonstrator told her to do it for herself. Or when Jo-Jo gave her a puzzle piece to fit in for him, she returned it and suggested he do it himself.

9. She encouraged the *child's understanding the reasons* for her instructions. She tried to feel pleasure, rather than impatience or boredom, when a child showed curiosity about the pros and cons of a directive. Example: When Carol asked why it was time to put the blocks away, she patiently

explained in a way Carol could understand, "We have to put the blocks away because it's time for lunch."

10. She tried to show *respect for the child's reactions* to a directive. She took into consideration Jo-Jo's ideas and feelings, and she listened to what he had to say. She might either change the directive, or stand firm with it, but the child had had a chance to express his feelings or thoughts about it. Example: When Carol indicated that she didn't want to gather up her blocks and thus delay playing with the Truck, the Toy Demonstrator said, "OK, I know you want to play with your truck, but first you have to put the blocks away."

11. She actively *encouraged the child's independence.* She suggested activities which Carol was able to do for herself. Example: She would say, "Now it's your turn to decide what you will make on the Magnetic Form Board—find the pieces for it yourself."

12. She tried to *train the child for self-direction.* She gave Jo-Jo information, in a way he could understand, that would enable him to carry out age-appropriate tasks for himself, without any help. Example: She showed Jo-Jo how to turn the pages of a book without tearing them. Or she showed Carol how to put blocks on top of each other for good balance.

13. She expressed some *warmth toward the child.* She showed by her facial expression or some small act that she felt affectionate toward Carol or Jo-Jo. She smiled, touched Jo-Jo or Carol's head, or even hugged the child, but hugging was left mainly to the mother so as not to intrude on the mother-child relationship.

14. She tried to *satisfy the child's needs,* whether signaled verbally or nonverbally. She was alert to a child's request for something he needed, however the request was shown ("signaled"): by a child's words, facial or vocal expression, or actions. She tried to make sure that the need was real, rather than a passing whim, and then tried to satisfy it. Example: When Carol began to rub her eyes, yawn and seem weary, she suggested that the Home Session draw

to a close. Or when Jo-Jo pointed at something in a book illustration and looked at her with a questioning expression, she would name whatever he had pointed at.

15. She tried to be *comforting to the child*. She sympathized by word, expression or act with a child's distress and made some attempt at consolation. When either Carol or Jo-Jo seemed sad, she would divert their attention by reading to them or (more likely) suggest that the mother do so; or she diverted their attention by pointing to a toy.

16. She used *positive reinforcement* a great deal. In other words, she praised Carol verbally or showed nonverbal approval for behavior she wanted to encourage in Jo-Jo. Example: she smiled and nodded and told Carol she had done a good job when Carol cleared the floor of blocks in preparation for playing with the Truck. Or she clapped her hands when Jo-Jo fitted a puzzle piece into the right place.

17. She *refrained from scolding* the child. She never used nagging, hurtful words or yelling, no matter how exasperating Carol or Jo-Jo might be. Example: When Jo-Jo started to throw a block at his sister, she said, "If you throw blocks at Dee-Dee, you might really hurt her. Let's build with them instead."

18. Her directive *gained the child's attention*. She made sure that Jo-Jo was listening to her request or instruction. She would not accept Carol's appearing not to notice what was being said. Example: She would say, "Carol, are you listening? I said it's time to put the blocks back into the Block Can."

19. She would *persist* in enforcing directives. She not only tried to get the child to comply but continued the attempt until the child actually did so. Example: She told Jo-Jo to bring the School Bus, the toy chosen by him for review, from the Toy Chest. She then waited for him to bring it and kept reminding him to bring it until he actually did so.

20. She was *firm* with the child. She usually took a definite position, and she stayed with it, in giving a directive to the child. She tried not to waver or give an impression of uncertainty. Example: She told Carol it was time to end a Home Session (Mrs. Willard having shown her readiness)

and brought the Session to a close, even though Carol protested. Or she told Jo-Jo he was not allowed to throw blocks at his sister and physically prevented him from doing so when he persisted (took the block out of his hand and put all of the blocks away).

No Toy Demonstrator could show all twenty items of "Positive Parenting Behavior" during any one Home Session, or possibly even over a few months. It was hoped that they could all be shown to the mother several times during the first and second Program years. Some Striver mothers were already practicing many of them and seemed to need less demonstration. Their intuitive skills supported the items' selection from what I had learned about parenting in almost twenty years as a mother, clinical psychologist, teacher and social worker. My own experience was greatly augmented by that of VIP staff members and by a study conducted by Dr. Diana Baumrind, University of California, Berkeley (1967). Dr. Baumrind found that parenting practices like most of the "Positive Parenting Twenty" were carried on by the highly educated, middle-income parents of four-year-olds observed to be well-functioning in nursery school. Similarly, Program mothers' Positive Parenting skills correlated significantly with their children's social-emotional competence at the age of four years. More important, many of these skills were found to form a supportive network for Program graduates' school competencies when they reached first grade.

Very likely, the Positive Parenting Twenty are sensible ways for all parents to interact with their children. They are likely to be as appropriate for six-year-olds or eight-year-olds or twelve-year-olds as they were with two- and three-year-olds.

FOSTERING THE CHILD'S SOCIAL-EMOTIONAL COMPETENCE

The major aim of the third part of the curriculum is to help children develop not only intellectually but also in their attitudes toward social relationships; toward their inner selves; and toward the world of work, play, and ideas. In short, this Program goal, achievable mainly through the practice of Positive

Parenting, is to foster children's social-emotional competence. That competence at any age level, starting at about the age of two years, should be such that each Program child:

Is Emotionally Stable

- *Seems generally happy and content.*
  Gives an impression of being satisfied and even happy most of the time. Seems tension-free, and negative feelings such as sadness, fear, anxiety generally appear to be minimal.

- *Is spontaneous without being explosive.*
  Can freely express strong positive or negative feelings, but knows when and where to stop an outburst. Appears to exercise sufficient control over emotional behavior to avoid overintense extremes inappropriate to the situation.

- *Seems free of sudden, unpredictable mood changes.*
  Moods (happiness, sadness, anger, and so on) are usually obviously related to the situation at hand. Reactions follow a rather stable pattern. It is thus possible to forecast what the child's emotional behavior will be under most conditions.

- *Tolerates necessary frustration (like awaiting his turn at a game).*
  Can control the need for immediate satisfaction of a wish, whether involving physical, emotional, social or cognitive satisfaction. Appears to understand that at times it is necessary to wait to get something, and is willing to wait when necessary.

Has a Willing Attitude toward Tasks

- *Is attentive and concentrates on tasks.*
  Focuses with eyes and ears, quietly, first as a task is explained, and then in carrying through its accomplishment. Appears to be intent on reaching the goal set by the task and is not easily distracted by outside sights and sounds.

- *Understands and completes tasks without frequent urging.*
  Seems to understand directions and goes about what has to be done in a self-directed manner. Continues a task until it is done, at a fairly steady pace, with only occasional pauses. Does not have to be reminded frequently to finish.

- *Enjoys mastering new tasks.*

Shows pleasure in mastering a new activity. May show or express a sense of accomplishment ("efficacy") at completion of the task.

- *Initiates nondestructive, goal-directed activities.*
Shows independence, and sometimes thinks up and begins activities which will not hurt others and will have some constructive aim, however limited. The activity may not involve much creativity but does demonstrate initiative and direction toward a goal.

Thinks Ahead

- *Is well organized in work or play.*
Thinks through ahead of time the materials or activities that will be needed and then uses them to go ahead with accomplishing the task or play in orderly sequence. Appears to be reflective about the task.

- *Expresses ideas in language.*
Uses words and/or sentences to convey thoughts instead of just gestures, tone of voice or facial expression.

- *Is creative, inventive.*
Uses materials or ideas in original ways which may be different from those initially intended. The results may be interesting, attractive, even exciting.

- *Seems to know the difference between fact and fantasy.*
If "making believe" in play, the child clearly understands that the pretending is a game, a fantasy. Seems firmly based in reality.

Cooperates in Social Situations

- *Refrains from physically aggressive behavior toward others.*
The child does not direct physical force against people, and is able to channel hostility into appropriate angry language or other nonphysical activity.

- *Can put own needs second to those of others.*
Understands that at times others have rights that transcend one's own. Shows consideration for the physical, social, and emotional requirements of other people.

- *Follows necessary rules in family or school.*

Complies with directives devised for social group harmony at home or school (but feels free to question the general necessity for a particular rule).

- *Is cooperative with adults.*
Is generally willing to follow the suggestions or directives of responsible adults, without arguing, objecting or balking.

Is Responsibly Independent

- *Seems self-confident, not timid.*
Is not shy in social interaction. Initiates interaction or responds to others with little hesitation. Shows self-esteem and does not seem to fear people or tasks.
- *Accepts or asks for help when necessary.*
Permits or requests help from adults without seeming to need help for everything. Usually tries at least briefly to understand or master the task before asking for help.
- *Protects own rights appropriately for age group.*
Tries to defend self or property from physical attack by others without overreacting or carrying hostilities beyond the actual attack.
- *Refrains from unnecessary physical risks.*
May enjoy physical challenge, as in sports, but does not expose self to danger without good reason.

These skills, so closely related to the "Positive Parenting Twenty," echo most parents' goals for their children's social-emotional competence. They add up to children's being happy, civilized and intellectually well functioning young human beings, whether they are aged two years or eight—or even close to teen years and well along the way toward maturity.

Second Program Ingredient:
Toys and Books (Curriculum Materials)

The "curriculum materials" which comprise the second Program ingredient in each Program year are a toy chest, followed by twelve books and eleven toys. All are of good quality—sturdy, attractive and available at most toy and book stores. As the second Program ingredient, they are gifts for the child, to provide a focus which is enjoyable to both child and mother in sparking verbal interaction between them.

To put it more simply, the toys and books supply mothers and children with natural, intrinsically interesting subjects for conversation. The Toy Demonstrators use the toys and books to model and encourage verbally oriented play activity within the mother-child dyads.

By furnishing picture books and playthings as gifts, the Program puts the stamp of approval on what is too often considered an unnecessary luxury by harried low-income mothers: conversation between mother and child playing together and enjoying their play with each other. In fact, an important reason for the "permanent assignment" of the toys and books, as if they are indeed school curriculum materials, is to insure that the dialogue will continue between Home Sessions and long after the Program is over.

Another reason for making the toys and books the focus of the Program's verbal interaction is that they provide a steppingstone from the infant world of perception and action to the adult world of words. The books are profusely illustrated and thus have a rich potential for stimulating conversation. They are an inviting introduction to literacy and a bridge to school. Often children bring Program books to show their kindergarten and first school teachers.

A different set of toys and books is used with each age group, one for two-year-olds and one for three-year-olds. They come to a total of 46 books and toys over two years. After the presentation of an unassembled Toy Chest (put together by mother and Toy Demonstrator in a meeting before their first Home Session, a good get-acquainted device), a new book or toy is brought for the child each week, one week a book and the next a toy.

The first of the week's two Sessions is centered around the new toy or book. The second is a "Review Session" at which the new toy or book is again the center of attention. Sometimes the child brings out material from much earlier in the Program. Whatever interests the *child* is the subject of that Session. The books and toys are brought in the same order for every child in the Program, so that the demonstrations of verbal interaction techniques around them in the weekly Toy Demonstrator Conferences can be applicable to the work of every Toy Demonstrator.

It should be emphasized that although the toys and books may be educationally valuable in themselves, and the books serve as a bridge to future reading and school, their main value in the Program lies in their providing an abundant source of possibilities for verbal interaction between mother and child. As previously noted, their Program acronymn is VISM (for Verbal Interaction Stimulus Materials).

The Program's list of toys and books changes from year to year, in response to new materials coming on the retail market, to past ratings of the books and toys by mothers and Toy Demonstrators of how much the children liked them, and of course, to the children's advancing ages. They are chosen initially by how well they fit into the following sets of written criteria.

Criteria for Choosing Toys

- *Verbal:*
  —should induce or permit verbal interaction.
- *Perceptual: has*
  —strong primary and secondary colors;
  —possibilities for size discrimination;
  —simple geometric shapes, varied but not confusing;
  —form-fitting possibilities;
  —spatial organization possibilities;
  —simple sounds when manipulated by the child;
  —varied and pleasant tactile qualities.
- *Motor: allows for*
  —large and small muscle activity;
  —possibility of much manipulation;
  —challenge to finger dexterity;
  —development of specific motor skills;
  —outlet for diffuse motor discharge (banging, pushing).
- *Conceptual: possesses possibilities for*
  —imaginative play;

—challenge to problem solving;
—self-rewarding activity;
—gender and ethnic neutrality;
—promoting sociability;
—purpose understandable and interesting to a young child.

- *Other: has the features of*
    —safety;
    —durability;
    —low anxiety potential for child;
    —easy care for mothers.

Criteria for Choosing Books

- *Content*
    —geared to child's age and interests;
    —interesting to mothers;
    —widens child's experiences;
    —leads to associations with child's experiences.

- *High literary standards*
- *Language simple, with some repetition*
- *Illustrations large, colorful, profuse, rich source of conversation*
- *Attractive to both sexes and any ethnic group*
- *Low anxiety potential*
- *Durability*
- *Reading level within ability of most Program mothers*

Appendix 3 summarizes the criteria for the Program VISM, using as examples some of the books and toys used with two- and three-year-olds.

Third Program Ingredient: Toy Demonstrators

The Toy Demonstrators are the Program's home visitors, like those who came to the Willard and Carter homes. They can be either unpaid volunteers, usually college-educated women; or paid "paraprofessionals," especially former Program mother-participants, of high school education or less. Both types of Toy Demonstrators are trained together in an initial eight-session Training Workshop and in weekly Toy Demonstrator Conferences throughout the Program. They are trained not to be a friend, counselor, or teacher but to *model* for a mother how to utilize the three parts of the curriculum while playing and talking with her child about the toys and books.

Paid Toy Demonstrators seldom have had previous work experience and so have had little opportunity to acquire basic work skills. They are of low income, usually a prerequisite for receiving payment in the Program. Volunteer Toy Demonstrators often have had previous work experience in teaching or in similar professions, and they do not fall within the low-income group. All Toy Demonstrators are trained and supervised in the same groups, paid and unpaid together. The resulting valuable interchange of life experience helps them to give better service to mothers and children. It also aids the personal growth of many Toy Demonstrators, paid and unpaid, or so they indicate on their anonymous written end-of-Program Evaluations of themselves and of the Program.

The Toy Demonstrators meet weekly, each Program year in 23 Toy Demonstrator Conferences with the Coordinator. They learn the Verbal Interaction Techniques for each new toy or book, studying the Guide Sheets for them and putting the Guides into a cumulative "Toy Demonstrator's VISIT Handbook." (VISIT is the acronym mentioned earlier for "Verbal Interaction Stimulation Intervention Techniques.) They also get support and counsel for the problems that they face in Home Sessions and which they have noted in their Home Session Records. The Coordinator is able to be of special help because she herself has recruited all the dyads for the Program, has interviewed every mother, and has introduced the Toy Demonstrators to the mothers, as Myrtle Crawford did for Mrs. Willard and Mrs. Carter. Each Toy Demonstrator also had two individual supervisory conferences with the Coordinator, near the beginning and near the end of the Program year, focused around an audio or video tape recording of one Home Session.

Mothers want Toy Demonstrators to be adult women, according to a VIP survey. They (or their mates) seem reluctant to have regular visits from a male Toy Demonstrator during daytime hours when they and their children are alone at home.

Also, the important modeling aspects of the Toy Demonstrator's role require that she be old enough to be respected in the mother's eyes. Otherwise, the Toy Demonstrator need have little more than the knowledge and attitudes which she will learn from the Program itself. She must start off with some degree of flexibility and warmth toward children and mothers, but she may have a wide range of education, from below high school and up, and she need not have any vocational preparation for the job.

Thus the Toy Demonstrator is not expected to enter the Program with any particular skills. However, by the end of her first year in the Program she is expected to have at least modest competence on 50 skills divided among four major areas and formally rated by Toy Demonstrator and Coordinator together in their two individual conferences:

• the Toy Demonstrator's Program knowledge and work skills;
• her attitudes toward her mother-child dyads;
• her dependability;
• and her ability to utilize supervision constructively.

The Toy Demonstrators are not expected to acquire counseling or teaching skills. In fact, they are carefully trained to abstain from direct teaching and to resist the temptation to counsel mothers even when their advice is sought. The brief Training Workshop and weekly Toy Demonstrator Conferences are sufficient only to equip Toy Demonstrators for their relatively limited functions. Limiting the Toy Demonstrator function also protects the mothers from a "service overload" which they might consider intrusive. However, the Toy Demonstrators are taught to alert their Coordinator to mothers' requests for help (sometimes unspoken). The Coordinator then immediately visits the mothers to explore whether they indeed wish help, either directly from her or from a community agency.

The modest on-paper requirements for the position of Toy Demonstrator hardly reflect the diversity among the Toy Demonstrators in practice. Their differences sometimes appeared through their individual ways of describing Home Sessions (from the original model Program):

Yolanda spoke little—speech not intelligible except for single words. Mother does not comprehend either. Child quite infantile: throws or drops pegs wherever hands are, rather than putting them somewhere convenient for next usage; goes to get bottle; self-absorbed in solitary play with little use of suggestion, direction or social play. Learned mechanics of toy very quickly and enjoyed toy manipulation. Mother joined TD in describing child's activity, was inventive in using wagon stick to point out longer from shorter pegs. TD made clear there is no expectation from child's performance, reassured mother re child's "poor" performance.

* * * *

Child wasn't too interested in book other than the pictures. Asked questions about the pictures. I couldn't understand her, nor could mother, so we just said yes or no, whichever one was satisfying.

* * * *

Gary didn't like to use the hammer, he just wanted to push it down with his finger, but he did repeat everything after me like his colors, and what he was doing, and he enjoy seeing the pegs coming out of the round hole, like "guess what coming out next." He is also getting to be very close to me, like happy to see me when I come in. Mother seems to be very interested in what Gary is doing, like she always ask him the color after me if he don't repeat it.

* * * *

At this session I introduced Ann to the color-roll wagon. She was very excited about it. She wouldn't look up when I tried to show her anything so I began describing what she was doing. She counted the sticks, built a tower and rolled the blocks. After playing for about 20 min. she ran and got *Pat the Bunny* and read it to mother and me, she also played her music box and sang to me as I left.

* * * *

Sammy was fantastic—in comparison to what had gone before, he practically made a formal address regarding page 1 of

Good Night Moon. Identified phone, stars, moon, rug, light, window, "light on." He then climbed up on a stool and turned the living room light on. He and I noticed that the pink blanket was the same color as his, and "talked" about how the toy house roof protects everyone, like his roof. We all had a wonderful time, and I hated to leave. I'm always so glad when he says a word, but he is so unintelligible much of the time that I'm not sure how to respond to what he's saying. (I'm slowly getting a little more attuned to him, I hope.)

*   *   *   *

We started out reading *All Fall Down*. Tommy wasn't talking today, which he usually doesn't talk much just every now and then. Today I decided to talk less and play more. In the story I called a cat a boy, then Tommy said "no-no, that's a cat!" And I continue things like that, and I discovered that he knew what the following is: dog, cat, flowers, girl. The lady with the carriage he called a Mommy and he knew man and boy. It was very funny when I called the snow, ice-cream falling down. Tommy just laugh and laugh then, said that's not ice-cream, that's snow, silly!

*   *   *   *

I debated whether or not to review the rubber puzzles. My decision was difficult simply because, as a creature of habit, I have reviewed all of the toys and books. Candy seemed to have had mastery of the puzzles the first time we played. However, I did want to see if she had retained the names of the shapes. It was and has been extremely exciting for me to watch Candy in her learning process. She did retain a great deal and the session was very relaxing for mother and child alike.

*   *   *   *

Ruth was very happy today. She played and laugh every time she name a color and she knew it was right. She clap and yell, she was very very funny. I ask about the new baby and she talked about something else. Each time she did something right and I said "very good" she would say "yep—very good!"

Trained social workers with Master's degrees (Helen Roth Adelman and Arlene Kochman) were chosen to be the first Toy Demonstrators in 1967. Their professional skills were utilized, paradoxically, to test out the acceptability to mothers, and the workability, of employing untrained people in the role, people who might not even have an undergraduate college degree. They deliberately confined themselves to nonteaching, noncounseling behavior during Home Sessions while observing mothers' acceptance of their simply modeling the curriculum. The mothers seemed to welcome this role limitation, thus opening the door to the use of paraprofessionals as Toy Demonstrators. Nevertheless, the actual complexity of the Program's apparently simple delivery system required a college-degreed person to direct it as a Coordinator. The social workers who pioneered the Toy Demonstrator role became the Program's first Coordinators in the years that followed.

Fourth Program Ingredient: Program Coordinator

The Program Coordinator carries responsibility for the total operation of the Mother-Child Home Program, often establishing it as a brand new function within a sponsoring agency or school system.

As background for the job, the person chosen to be the Coordinator has achieved professional status in a field closely linked to the method and goals of the Program, perhaps education, nursing, psychiatry, psychology or social work. Either as part of his or her own professional training, or in addition to it, the Coordinator must be "family oriented" (knowledgeable and caring about interpersonal behavior, values and attitudes in families). Within that framework, the Coordinator is able to be responsive to families and to teach that responsiveness to the Toy Demonstrators. The Coordinator should also be prepared to work with relative independence and yet within the philosophic and structural framework of the sponsoring organization.

A Program Coordinator (for brevity to be referred to as "she" since most, in practice, are women) can work with an Assistant Coordinator, or by herself. Her main job is to pull together the three other elements of the Program—Toy Demonstrators, books/toys, and curriculum—to form a smoothly working and effective whole. Her tasks are manifold and sometimes not easy. After she herself has been trained by the Verbal Interaction Project, she enrolls the mother-child dyads; recruits and trains the Toy Demonstrators; purchases the Program toys and books; utilizes appropriately the large kit of technical aids for running a Program that she received as part of her own training (the *Index to Technical Materials for Operating a Mother-Child Home Program* is in Appendix 1); and works as a Toy Demonstrator herself for a year or longer.

The Coordinator is known to all mother participants in the Program. She has made the initial recruiting visit to them, has introduced the Toy Demonstrator, and returns at mid-year and at the end of Program year for home interviews. She gives every mother a chance to speak her mind about any aspect of the program or relations with her Toy Demonstrator. During the introduction of the Toy Demonstrator to the mother, the latter is invited (in the Toy Demonstrator's presence) to get in touch with the Coordinator whenever she wishes to do so. Thus the ongoing nature of the mother's relationships with both Toy Demonstrator and Coordinator is clearly defined. If the mother continues on to become a Toy Demonstrator herself, her previous experience with the Coordinator is an asset in her future working relationship with the Program.

The Coordinator seeks and heeds the wishes and opinions of mothers in regard to their participation in the Program. When Toy Demonstrators report verbal or nonverbal signals suggesting that a mother may want help of some kind, the Coordinator visits the mother at once. If the mother does wish aid with a family problem (possibly relating to a child's schooling, or medical, emotional or legal questions), the Coordinator helps her to obtain counsel from appropriate community agencies if she judges that she herself is not qualified to give it.

A Sampler of Home Sessions

No two Home Sessions are alike, and few reach an ideal

standard. But, although enormously varied, each has within it some element of the ideal. Moreover, some common emphases emerged among the thousands of Home Sessions described by the Toy Demonstrators in the original Program.

Individuality of Children in Home Session

Robert knew every picture in the book. He calls the bear a teddy. He name the rabbit, telephone, clock, etc. When he name out the telephone, he pretend to talk to the rabbit. He said, Hello rabbit, are you there? Do you see that balloon and big rabbit sits in the chair?

* * * *

Most of Teresa's board-game toys were lost and she insisted that she get a new one. She wanted me to go home and get her some more toys for the game. She started crying and her mother got after her. I told her to get a book and I would read to her. She said "No" and went into the bedroom. Her mother couldn't get her to come out.

* * * *

Tim brought out his rubber puzzles. We put the pieces together and he did a very good job. Then I give him the book. We sat together on the floor and his mother read the book and show him picture of Peter's high chair and Peter when he was a baby. Then Tim show me his own crib and his high chair. He told me to get in the crib but I told him I was just to big. Then it was time for me to go, and for the first time he didn't want me to go.

* * * *

At first the session started off OK, then Lena and her mother started fighting. Lena had a spanking just before I came and now she got another one. So she just put the puzzle colors together and we didn't try to make anything. She was crying but she repeated well and knew a few colors and shapes.

* * * *

Steve greeted me with bubbling enthusiasm, and tried very hard to tell me several things during the session. I was unable to understand (his mother made no attempt) but he was very earnest about trying to communicate.

*   *   *   *

For the first time since the Program started I was unable to do anything with Terry. She threw the drum at her mother and then she wanted to put on her new coat. I believe that was the problem. I started singing and she kind of cool down. The session ended much better than it started.

*   *   *   *

Earl was happily excited and enthusiastic when I arrived, told me he had made a Christmas wreath in preschool and showed it to me. His speech requires close attention; the words are imperfect but he seems to have a vocabulary large enough to express himself when he wants to. Usually he speaks very little—one or two words at a time, but today he used whole sentences. "I made a Christmas wreath." "I made it in school." "We used pine cones."

*   *   *   *

Simone did the puzzle twice with me. She stuck to it, enjoyed it thoroughly—learned with each try and seemed determined to master it completely as I left, refitting each piece over and over.

*   *   *   *

Cathy was very sleepy today. As soon as we all sat down in the living room, she lay down on the rug and looked as if she was ready to go to sleep. This happened once before, so I decided to do as I had the last time. I suggested to Mrs. Hopkins to let her rest. We chatted for about 15 minutes, then Cathy woke up and we began our session.

*   *   *   *

Karen was good today, really great, fit circle and square by herself. She talked and talked, fit pieces in the spaces like a champ, turned mat around to put pieces in the right place, she mix the colors, knew green and blue, triangle. Karen didn't like rough sides, place all the pieces on the smooth sides. Was very happy while working with her Fit-a-Space puzzle pieces, jump up and down when she did them all right.

Striver- and Hesitater-Mothers in Home Sessions

Great session! Warren and mother both asleep when I arrived but got up right away and Mrs. B. apologized quite profusely for being asleep. Warren brought out Mail Box, assorted blocks, peg bench and Mother Goose. He talked a great deal more, imitating or repeating what I or mother said. Used blocks with big holes as a spy glass, mother did too. She read a couple of rhymes also. At end Mrs. B. apologized again for sleeping. We discussed her fatigue a little—natural as a result of working at night. She seems much more relaxed about sessions—very cooperative. We all had fun.

* * * *

Mother had just finished spanking Cora when I came. She cried for half the session. Then her father came home for lunch and she stopped crying. Mother just sat while I played with Cora and showed her how to lay the forms flat and mix colors.

* * * *

The mother spent a large amount of time with Simon in filling the boxes and naming, as well as counting, the toys. He named only a few and we had the usual detour of his madly wheeling the car back and forth and making motor noises. Mrs. Deacon carefully counted the pegs and named their colors and explained the game very well, keeping it extremely simple and step by step. She seemed to enjoy the idea of the game's long term value and being a group activity.

* * * *

We reviewed *Good Night Moon* today. Mrs. Haywood seems to have a very high expectation of Carla. Carla simply wanted to leaf through the pages and identify the familiar objects over and over again. Mrs. Haywood seems anxious about this. She began picking up the incorrect answers but did try to correct rather than reprimand Carla.

* * * *

When I arrived mother and child had just woke up. Mother gave us the two telephones and sat down on the couch by us and began falling back to sleep. When I asked for the toy dishes, mother told me that the child had made such a mess playing with the dishes in water, that she told the child that the man had come and gotten the dishes (which she had really put up in the closet). So we wasn't able to play with them. Anna didn't want to play with the telephones by themselves. I think she was kind of upset by not being able to play with the dishes.

*   *   *   *

Again, Mrs. Roddick's reading and usage of the book was great. I really had very little to add, except to get her back to the book itself when she would overdo one page with David. He like it enormously and said many, many things, including "Chick come out of the egg" and "On top of his head." Mrs. Roddick was excellent in stressing what was happening and continually asking, "What will happen now, David?" She confessed to some "self-conscious" feelings, as she put it, in reading, and I assured her that she is well ready to read, play, and enjoy herself with David.

*   *   *   *

Child delighted with School Bus. Still mixes up colors and guesses, but cheerfully repeats all info TD gives. Easily matches children to same color seats. Delighted with dramatic play. Named all children and fed and took back and forth to school. Mother was silent—enjoyed Nancy's pretend play with a smile and slight embarrassment.

*   *   *   *

The story had been read to Cassy during the week so she now could understand it, whereas when she first received it, she seemed unable to comprehend the sophistication of Peter's feelings toward his sibling. However, during this session today she really seemed able now to grasp the idea and even related her own experiences as they related to the book, *Peter's Chair.* Mother and Cassy virtually did the whole session.

*   *   *   *

We didn't spend the whole time with *A Letter to Amy,* since

Michael didn't seem too involved with it (he was tired). The important thing to me about this visit was Mrs. Walker telling me that Michael was a) more interested in *Letter to Amy* than he let on when we first read it and b) he memorized the action and objects in the pictures fairly quickly and insisted on telling Mrs. Walker the story, rather than vice versa. I was really pleased to hear not only of his initiative but of her recognition and pride in what he is doing and in letting him do it.

Twins in Home Sessions

The twins seemed to enjoy this toy very much. Angela repeated words after their mother and me, and she answered questions, but Alexandra wouldn't say anything. They both built towers out of the blocks and sticks, but Angela had more trouble because she just couldn't leave the stick on the floor when placing a second block on top of the first. Every time the blocks would fall down the girls would put them into the wagon and take them for a ride. In fact, that's the only thing that Alexandra would say: "Blocks going for a ride now!"

*   *   *   *

Mother had been teaching the girls how to set the table with the tea set, where to put the knife, fork and spoon. They had also been eating their real food out of the dishes. Angela wasn't feeling well, she had a very bad cold. It didn't make her any less active, though. We talked to each other on the telephones, each pretending we were someone else. We had a party, the girls cooked chicken. Afterwards they washed the dishes, and mother and I dried them.

*   *   *   *

Mother wasn't at home, but Grandmother was there to be in the Home Session. The twins were very verbal. After I read the book, each one read it back to me, first Alexandra and then Angela. They told me what Peter was doing on every page. They tended to copy what each other said. Grandmother did more listening than talking.

Fathers as Home-Session Participants or Observers

Mother wasn't home today, but the father was there. He didn't participate but he sat and watched. Today was the first time that Amy didn't run and get *Pat the Bunny*. Instead, she got *Good Night Moon*. We went over the book a couple of times. I then asked her if she would like to play with her col-o-rol wagon. She went and got it but after playing with it for a few minutes, she went back to the book. But first she showed it to her father, then sat to read it with me. At the end, I asked the father the questions about what has happened in the family during the week.

* * * *

Today I got there ten minutes before Mrs. Jones came from work. I was let in by Mr. Jones. He introduce himself and call Tommy to play with me. Then he started to leave the room, when I asked him to join Tommy and me. He did, he read the book to Tommy. Then Mrs. Jones came in. Tommy jump up to greet his mother. Then Mrs. Jones start reading (after she got settled). Tommy was more lively and point out cat and said "the cat" and then the dog. He said to his mother, "The apple falling down!" Then it was time to leave.

* * * *

With slight assistance from mother, and following suggestions of removing one piece at a time, Jeff finished puzzle. Many of the objects were not recognizable to him and some not to his mother. No wonder his patience was exhausted the second time around. However, at this point I interceded to avoid verbal displeasure from the mother. During the session Mr. Westminster was upset—couldn't find his pen—showed his upset. Then he saw that Jeff had a loose piece of skin on finger. I suggested a band-aid. Father ordered him to leave it alone or be taken to the doctor for an injection. Mother appears less tense when father is not present. He frequently issues directives to the children to "shape up!" Mrs. Westminster mentioned her concern about Jeff's stammering.

* * * *

Dick loved the drum. Joe helped him name primary colors. Dick went to get a second stick from the block cart on his own. He loved the singing, tapping and marching. Did the "Indian" song for me by himself. Very good control over noise, as mother requested. Showed the drum to his father on father's entrance as I left.

*   *   *   *

Father and friends sat at kitchen table with backs to us, talking. Not until end, when Billy was finishing the session, did father turn around and smile, talked of how well Billy seemed to be doing—showed definite pride, though embarrassment at being present at Home Session with his friends.

*   *   *   *

In the book *Good Night Moon* he only wanted me to read a few pages to him. He wanted to show me all the thing on the page with the bunny going to sleep. And then he would walk to the back with the book and show it to his father. With every page it was the same and I never did get through reading the whole book to him.

Brothers and Sisters in Home Sessions: Helpers and Hinderers

Osbaldo's brother Cessy is impossible. He threw things, tried to break toys, cursed, etc. When I praised him for being able to stand animals on their heads (after their mother yelled and hit him in face) he showed O. how to do the same thing. O. tried to listen to the book, to show his mother the pictures and compare them to the toy barn animals. But he gets caught up in Cessy's acting out and session is not as valuable to him as it could be.

*   *   *   *

Lisa thrilled with the Toy Barn. She allowed her mother to finish fixing her hair while her brother Barry and I opened up packages and set up figures. Then Lisa started to play. As usual her play was rather frantic, shoved every figure in Barn as Barry named them for her. Sister Wendy spent most of the time feeding the animals, filled the trough with "cereal" and fed them. Lisa repeated names—tried to manipulate animals' limbs. Barry pleasant, warm, good to his sisters.

*   *   *   *

Chantra and her mother were ready with the Earth Puzzle. Chantra was eager to "perform." She and her sisters had really been working with the puzzle during the week. The mother commented on how well the girls played together. In this family it seems that the girls have a tremendous learning influence on each other, i.e., the older children really teach Chantra quite a bit in their play.

*   *   *   *

When I entered the Whites' apartment, the TV was on and the girls (Linda and her sister Carolyn) were watching a show. Mrs. White quickly told Carolyn to go into her room because Linda's teacher had come. The 5 year old did not make any effort to go. In past sessions when Carolyn was there, a tug of war ensued between mother and child. This time I took the initiative and asked Mrs. White could Carolyn stay, providing she helped Linda play and did not grab the toy from her. (Carolyn is the middle child and I believe she feels just like the one in the middle). The Knock-Out Bench was a huge success with both of them!

*   *   *   *

Tracy took the book, as always, and turned the pages. Andrea, her baby sister, was restless and distracting to Tracy, and after a few minutes Tracy was ready to forget the book. The mother sat with us, Andrea on her lap, and she loved the story and pictures, found them amusing, and wished Tracy would appreciate the book. When Andrea howled, she told Tracy that Andrea looked like the little bird in the book with his beak wide open.

*   *   *   *

The toy was moderately successful. I believe this can be attributed to the fact that there was too many distractions, i.e., the older sisters wanted to take over, which Dorothy resents bitterly. Mother stepped in and was able to interest the big girls in another activity (outside play). Unfortunately, when everyone had finally settled down, Dorothy was just too upset from the preceding events to be able to enjoy the toy.

*   *   *   *

Mrs. Burke seemed pleased to see me, and Darrell and Charlie could hardly wait to see what I brought them. I think they all enjoyed it. The older boy, Darrell, tended to take over quickly, naming everything before I even got to read. The mother was focusing on Charlie in a demanding tone. She tried to get the 5 year old, Joseph, to go inside and watch TV. When he was inside crying, I told her I didn't mind if [he] was here with us, so she let him come in. He too became interested and participated, so there was good interaction among Charlie, Darrell and Joseph.

*   *   *   *

All siblings were present, interested, vocal and aggressive. Extremely high noise level so it was difficult to be heard. Eddie enjoyed the School Bus, played well with it, involved two of the other children. Knows colors and numbers but is confused on shapes, had to be helped by a sister. Was eager to be read to, left the Bus willingly and climbed up on the couch without hesitation, followed by two of his brothers. All participated in listening to the story with a good interchange of information about the pictures. Mother was much more passive than any of the five children.

*   *   *   *

Jerry's six year old sister was present. Mrs. Grant wanted her away but we helped her join in, and she helped Jerry pick up cues from me, teaching him.

Books in Home Sessions: Listening, Looking, Talking

Nicole likes the books very much. *Good Night Moon* she enjoys. She likes to put her hand on the picture of the fire and say "Hot!" She repeats if you ask her to.

*   *   *   *

Barry sat very quietly and listen to me while I read the book to him, then I invited Mrs. Summers to read to him. Mrs.

Summers asked Barry was the kitten and dog the baby bird's mother? He said no. And when she got to the cow, he took the book and said, No, Mommy, thats not his mommy. And he turn to the back of the book and show us the baby bird's mother! I asked Barry where is his mother. He put his hand on his own mother.

*   *   *   *

Mother read the book for the first time. She did well with the book but still constantly spoke of how bad Yvette is. So quite naturally the child acted up. Hitting the book and giving the wrong answers to questions. Yvette said the Mailbox was a garbage can. But when her mother went along with her and said that Peter was mailing the letter by putting it into the garbage can, she corrected her mother by saying, "No, he's putting the letter in the Mailbox!"

*   *   *   *

Kathy sat and listened to the story for 15 minutes today. The first thing she said when I open the book was that the Mail Box on the first page was like the one Kathy had. She brought her Mail Box out. She sang "Happy Birthday" to Peter in the book. Then she brought out *Are You My Mother?* and did a great job telling me about the baby bird in it.

*   *   *   *

Nancy asked her mother for *Wake Up Farm*. She doesn't usually ask for a book to read. I ask her to read the story to mommy and me. So she did. On the cover she pointed out everything. Then she showed us Daddy with the milk pails. She says "He's going to put milk in the baby's bottle." She says "The chickens are hungry!"

*   *   *   *

Bobby talk very much during the session. He wanted to know why Peter Rabbit didn't eat before he went out to play. He named some colors, but he didn't keep his mind on the book because the TV was on. His older sister was in and out. Mother wasn't too pleasant. When asked to show his mother book, he told her everything he heard me say, like: Snow falls on Peter's head. Peter's mother took his clothes off for a bath. Why didn't Peter have on his shoes?

* * * *

Karen didn't say a word when I read the book to her. I kept reading it over and over again—but not a word. When I told her to take the book over to Grandma and show it to her, she told her Grandma almost everything I had read! I praised her, and we clap, she said, "Thank you!"

Toys: Playing and Talking in Home Sessions

Bobby loved the Mail Box but he seem to have a hard time fitting the block in the holes. He tried very hard, but he hated the idea of stringing the blocks like beads, he said blocks didn't go on a string. He worked very hard with the Mail Box—naming colors, mailing letters. Talked about the big Mail Box on the street and how he could climb on one. He knew the shape of some blocks and kept repeating "triangle" over and over.

* * * *

The School Bus was not new to Tony, as one of his friends had this toy before he did. He loved it, and so did his mother. He pulled it, played with the stop sign, loved giving names to all the children. He put them in the right color seats without my suggesting it. Mrs. Brown was delighted, and again impressed. She says she didn't realize all the possibilities the toy offers when she saw it at a neighbor's house.

* * * *

Darcy loved the School Bus. Was good at matching children to their seats even though the colors aren't very similar. Was too busy to answer questions, which upset his mother. Favorite trick was to overturn bus, almost "killing" the children, then loading them into ambulance (cart) to take them to the hospital where they received a great many shots. We finally got the Bus to "school" by being strict with the reckless driver, and we made desks of blocks, for the children to sit at.

* * * *

Martin concentrated for 20 minutes on the Magnetic Board.

His main focus was on creating birthday cakes, but he allowed me to start a boy, and he helped with the parts (he's got a fairly good conception of body and facial parts). He also made a circle from two halves, and a square from two triangles. In addition he tried to stick the magnets on to everything but the Board. He named almost all the objects on the Board. After 20 minutes, he was messing up the pieces and had lost interest.

*   *   *   *

Gerald listened for a while to the reading of the book. Then he got down and got out the Magnetic Form Board, and we played with that. He showed me how to make a fish, and that you eat fish. He also made items which he said was me and his mother. Mrs. James made a boat and told him what colors she used.

The Toy Barn: A Favorite Toy in Home Sessions

Terrence was very happy to see me, he took me by the hand and said, "Come on in, teacher!" I gave him the Barn and he said, Thank you. I told him it is a barn and I went on by telling each piece I took out to put together. I told him what it was, he seem to be very happy. He named every animal after I did. Knew the dog, horse, chicken, cow. He didn't know the sheep. We put the barn together and pretend to feed the horse and the cow. Mrs. Johnson said she was very tired but she sat and watch.

*   *   *   *

The mother thinks that the Barn is too complicated for the children to learn all the things in it. I tell her, as with all the toys, at first it isn't easy but children learn faster than we sometimes realize. May played well with the Barn and the animals and people. She said, "The mother cooks and the daddy works."

*   *   *   *

Pamela ran for the Toy Barn with great excitement when I arrived. The *Wake Up Farm* book was already on the table. We put the Barn on the table and started with the book—showing her how the Barn looked a lot like the barn in the book, etc. Loves the noises of different animals. Still has trouble knowing the name of some of them—the pig, cow, horse, sheep. After going back and forth between barn figures and the book, we played with the Barn. Incidentally, her five year old sister Cammy came over to the table and stood and watched during this part of the session—even pointing out which figure was the cow, the horse, etc., to Pamela. She stayed with us until Mr. Nolan called over to her and asked her to get something. As we played with the Barn, Pamela wanted to play the "Farmer in the Dell," with the farmer figure picking out each animal as we sang. I try to get her to pick the right figure. She loves the song, loves all songs. Mrs. Nolan seems to enjoy the singing too, and although she doesn't join in with the actual song, she helps Pamela pick the right animal.

Toy Demonstrators' Criticisms of Toys and Books Used in Home Sessions

This game is a bit too much for Nancy. I wasn't able to play it with her. She wants to take all the toys out of the boxes. We just talk about the objects and let Nancy do as she wanted. She wouldn't let me touch any part of the game. Every once in a while she would give me one each.

* * * *

The book appears rather colorless and when I first brought it out Darin looked depressed and then darted away to find something else to play with. After we persuaded him to have a look, it turned out to be the most successful book so far and we all had a lovely time.

* * * *

I really think the tea set and telephone were too much at one time. Karen did not respond to the telephone in the beginning. After I was there for a few minutes, she said she was going to call the police—not a word about inviting anyone to her tea party. She gave all of us in the room tea but didn't seem very happy about it because grandma ask her to use the telephone. She was upset for a while but later she had a ball serving everyone tea, coffee and Koolaid.

Bilingual Home Sessions (Spanish and English)

Lisa vacillates between repeating English words for objects in book (*Good Night Moon*) and saying a Spanish word if I give the English word. Child delights in "telephone" and "curtains." Loves seeing bunny go to sleep. "Shh—bunny is sleeping!" she whispers, holding her finger across her mouth. I name colors, objects, body parts. Lisa tirelessly leafs through book. Sister Rochelle looks on and repeats also.

*   *   *   *

Arturo gentle, quiet, interested. Luis (brother) close, loved book, repeated everything in English. When he told me what something is in Spanish, I told them I don't speak Spanish. The mother liked this. Arturo answered in English, jealous when I spent time with sister Rochelle.

*   *   *   *

Maria at first shy with me, naturally. Carried the book to mother. Told me to sit (in Spanish). Smiled with joy when we played "This Little Piggy" and "Ring Around the Rosy." Repeated cat, dog, boy, girl. Mostly enamored of pictures in front of book—not interested in words. When Mother left room, Maria ran after her. I explained to Mrs. M. about staying. Father came in and sat in on session, astonished at Maria's saying English words. I don't think English is ever spoken in the home, only when I come.

*   *   *   *

Carmen as usual repeated color names for mother but seemed to make no real connection of word to color. Her mother asked me to write the English names of objects, shapes and primary and secondary colors on a piece of paper for her.

*   *   *   *

The book *Snowy Day,* was difficult since a story about snow was incomprehensible to a child who had never seen or heard of snow. The mother helped by roughly describing each picture in Spanish. Then I explained in English. Susana got "snow" down pat and also "Peter" as the name of the boy. Susana played with my ring and metal belt. Got into naming body parts.

*   *   *   *

Elvira identifies many objects by name as she leafs through the pages. She seems to use English and Spanish interchangeably in naming. Comments, though, are always in Spanish.

*   *   *   *

Mellisa knows why Peter's building fell down and exclaims "Dog!" in Spanish. She does not seem to comprehend story content, but she does get Peter's joke on his mother (shoes under the curtain) and knows a baby is in the lacy crib. The mother is good at explaining my sentences into an easy Spanish explanation of the story action for Mellisa.

*   *   *   *

Child imitates but has almost no comprehension of the connection of English words to an object. Does use Spanish quite freely. Imitation and absorption in play is quite variable. Attitude toward TD is neutral to negative except for an occasional smile or non-verbal overture. She participated in tea party only on mother's lap.

*   *   *   *

Yalira was very distracted today. Her mother at my suggestion pointed out pictures, mostly spoke to her in Spanish. Yalira wanted only to kiss the mother and baby in the book and did so continuously. Then her mother had to start cooking lunch. Yalira got a blanket, climbed into the play pen with the baby, and went to sleep.

*   *   *   *

The three girls, the mother and I sat around the table together, Rita on my lap and Vera on her mother's, and we read the book. The girls are beautiful—interested but shy—very little English. The mother is wonderful. She uses Spanish and English in describing books and uses illustrations to help the girls use the English words, which they do. She is patient and gentle with them. Rita responds less than Vera, who is more verbal and seems more outgoing. The mother said the Program is wonderful, perfect for her family. They are learning so much, she is working with them and loves it.

Family Problems Reflected in Home Sessions
ILLNESS

Mother had epileptic attack since last visit. Aunt apparently helps. Anna was dressed especially well. Aunt dressed her. Mother seemed ill—absented herself from part of the session. As a matter of fact, she just walked in and out, did not join in on floor. Mother would like to discuss her ills. Mother mentioned that everyone was surprised that "Anna didn't read her book to me." Very little verbalization on Anna's part. Apparently she has been exposed to colors and concepts. Shapes and textures appear strange. Liked playing as ice-cream man with truck—delivered ice cream to mother seated nearby.

*   *   *   *

Child had just awakened and had a fever. Last night that necessitated a trip to the hospital emergency room. He was listless and only half listened while tapping with a stick. I sang and asked the mother for the Mother Goose book but ended the session early.

*   *   *   *

Mother, Steven and Erik were all suffering from flu or colds (particularly mother) and I feel that I did not use good judgement in holding this session. But mother seemed to expect and want it, perhaps partly to let her sister-in-law observe. Erik related well to the book and responded better than usual, but Steven was restless and inattentive, went to the kitchen to get food and just wandered around the room eating crackers, carrying the book with him. Would not sit on Mommy's lap nor allow her to read the book. He was miserable, wailed a little for no obvious reason; finally, toward the end of the session, Annabelle (the sister-in-law) captured him, held him

on her lap did what Mommy would do, pointed out the pictures
to him, whispering in his ear as I read, and talked with Erik
and Lucinda. She is apparently more verbal than Mommy but
will be moving out in the morning. Steven did not say a word,
so far as I remember. This session was ATYPICAL.

*   *   *   *

The two books were in good condition, and I commented
on it. Patty was pleased. She "read" both books, telling the
story well and describing each picture. Her grandmother was
very proud. Jimmy brought a book and sat with us, pointing
out "apple," "car," etc. Patty was rather annoyed by his inter-
ference and my attention to him, but she was controlled. I
told the grandmother that it is clear that time is spent with
Patty and her books, and I gave much credit to the grandmother.
The mother is still in the hospital and may need a hysterectomy.
The grandmother feels that the period of recovery needed after
such surgery will be good for the children, as the mother "will
have to stay home with them."

EMERGENCY NEEDS

Patty and Jimmy listened to the story. Patty liked it and
practically read it back, word for word, to her grandmother's
great pleasure. She said that Patty is ready to read, points to
words and asks what they are. The mother is still in the hospital
and the grandmother's strength is beginning to wear out. Her
own doctor told her to get away for a while and she needs
someone to care for the kids 8 hours a day. She will speak to
the hospital social worker this afternoon about this need. If
they cannot help her, she will talk to our Coordinator, who
will try to do so.

CHILD'S ATYPICAL BEHAVIOR

It seemed very hard to get through to Rena with "Peter's
Chair" today. I read the book over and over before Rena said
any colors. Then she said "green." Usually when I would ask
"What color?" she would say "count." If I said "red," she would

say "Three." If I said "Orange," she would say "Eight." Each time, for a color, she would say a number. I spoke to the mother about it, and the mother said the child was doing it to be funny. But it has happened too many times for it to be funny.

MOTHER'S GRIEF

Mother participated only a few minutes in the session. She not only needs rest but is still depressed over loss of the baby. She told me of the whole unhappy event (stillbirth) and that she is on a lot of medication to build herself up after this ordeal. She wanted the session to continue. Howard was excited by the telephones and we immediately "called each other"—he then phoned his mother and spoke with her about having a party (make-believe).

MULTIPLE PROBLEMS

Child silent except for word "truck." Ignores directions and suggestions. Solitary manipulation of the toy. Only 3 trucks and the garage minus the tires were left to play with. Mother was rather withdrawn, preoccupied. House messy. Father has removed self. Mother has trouble organizing herself and coping with children and housework. Seems exhausted. Asked me to come at 2:30 PM instead of later when the other children will soon be home.

*   *   *   *

The mother was stretched out on the couch falling asleep. The house was in complete disorder. Debbie has been ill, rather lethargic. Showed me her School Bus, all the people were missing. Debbie said Arthur took *Snowy Day* outside and gave it away. All her other books are gone. She took me into the room she sleeps in to try to find the children which belong to the Bus. The room is incredible: there must be 6 months accumulation of laundry on floor, in corners, on dresser, boxes. So much junk, impossible to find anything. Debbie said she is going to hold on tight to her new book (*All Falling Down*)—so she has it! She likes it but prefers books "with more story to it," however she loved the pictures and seemed to grasp the concept of falling down. She took the book to her mother, who had fallen asleep, woke her to read the book to her. Mother said, "Wait till I wake up" and did—and did read!

The Boy Who Went to MIT

No formal VIP research followed children to college years, but by chance there has been occasional news of Program children having entered college. Brian Gordon was one such child. He recently entered the Massachusetts Institute of Technology (MIT). Since his competence when he became a teenager was thus obvious to MIT, a few of his Home Sessions when he was three-and-a-half years old may be of particular interest. His imagination, creativity, verbalization, and sociability were so evident in Home Sessions that, to provide a full description, his Toy Demonstrator's notes on him by the age of almost four years were unusually lengthy and detailed.

HOME SESSION #30: BOOK—ARE YOU MY MOTHER?

Both Brian and his mother were ready and eagerly waiting for me. They both were outgoing and friendly and volunteered many comments. Brian was very observant and verbal. He was very knowledgable about the birth of baby birds though he occasionally called the baby bird a chicken. Brian knew most of the objects and relationships. When I said the baby bird looked up and then the baby bird looked down, and pointed to the picture, he was puzzled. He called the steam shovel a tractor. Otherwise he was well informed. He mentioned that the half-drawn nest was broken. When the little bird was running fast, he remarked that he had learned to fly because his feet were off the ground. At the end he commented that the little bird had eaten the worm. When I asked how he knew, he pointed to the long tail which he mistook for the baby's tail and said he'd gotten bigger.

HOME SESSION #33: TOY—MUSICAL INSTRUMENTS

Brian was very enthusiastic and cooperative throughout the session. Younger brother Danny was quiet and insisted on watching most of the time. I felt that Brian showed a great deal of imagination and initiative and a willingness to pick up and amplify suggestions. He used the drum to beat out rhythms in great variation with the stick ends, the middle of his fingers, alternating sides, etc. He danced to the beat and marched to the beat and discussed and participated in various types of parades—marching, waving a flag (scarf), pushing a large truck and pretending he was a Superman balloon. He also invented a game which involved hitting the drum before his mother moved it out of the way. We discussed musical instruments and how they make music and he brought down a toy guitar which we all used in the parades. He was intrigued with the loop on the drum and experimented with having it hold the stick and using the loop to hang the drum up. We discussed the string loop and string holding the drum together. He and Danny talked about the parades they would have when Danny received his drum. Their mother is imaginative and obviously enjoys Brian. She participated very effectively verbally and physically. She is very friendly and seems to enjoy talking about a great many things.

HOME SESSION #35: REVIEW

Brian was outside when I arrived. When he came to the door and saw me, he playfully hid. When I asked what he wanted to do, he said he'd like to build a castle. He built a tall tower, and then we all built one together, seeing how high we could make it. He put some of the children from the bus on top of the tower, and I showed him how he could make a bridge for the children to walk under. He liked this—and then he made a structure and placed three children on top of it. He decided to go get the School Bus, and while he was gone, his mother took one of the children "to see if he would notice it was missing." This action seemed significant in view of the fact that she had expressed concern about how much

Brian teases. Brian discovered where the child was, he told his mother he didn't want her to do that any more. Brian became involved in imaginative play, taking the Bus children on a trip to a mountain which they climbed and slid down.

HOME SESSION #36: TOY—MAGNETIC FORM BOARD

Brian unpacked the Magnetic Form Board and asked how to detach the forms from the sticks. As he detached them, he matched them with comparable shapes on the board. He made a castle with wheels, a wagon, a train, Peter, buildings, trees, cheese (in wedges and in oblong pieces), stairs, a rocket, the moon, Humpty Dumpty (he insisted the H. D. had to have legs), various kinds of hats, etc. He tried sticking the magnets to each other and tried sticking the sticks to the board. He was fascinated by the semi-circles and kept manipulating them—putting them together and taking them apart. He made a design and stopped to study it, then added semi-circles to several of the shapes. When he put them next to the rectangle, he said it was bread. He named the pictures, except the tank and the fish. He called the fish a helicopter and couldn't seem to accept it as a fish. He identified colors, shapes and relationships. The mother played with the forms and made suggestions and asked questions throughout the session.

HOME SESSION #40: REVIEW

I have noticed that Brian carries on more mature conversations with me which are not always related to the VISM. He doesn't tease like he used to and relates to both his mother and me in a more mature manner. Brian has been playing a great deal with the toy Barn. The children from the School Bus were all in the Barn. Brian was interested in manipulating the legs of the animals and took a great deal of care to balance them on two legs, then at my suggestion he stood them on their heads. We decided to have a show with performing animals. The children were all lined up as the audience and Brian provided the voice for the ring master. Without any instructions as to what he should say or how he should say it, he sang

out "Presenting—the one and only dancing dog!" He also introduced a tight rope act (using the fence, which he discovered
had parts that fit into the holes in the bottom of the Bus
children), a trapeze act using the handle of the barn, and various
animal tricks. At one point he picked up the rooster by the
tail and tipped it like a pitcher, asking if anyone wanted any
milk. He pretended to give the animals a drink from the trough
and wanted to know how their legs went when they ran, as
he tried to move them in the proper way. Though he is very
receptive to suggestions, he has many imaginative ideas and
a great deal of self-confidence. He corrects me if he thinks I'm
wrong. For example, he told me "That's not a lamb, it's a
sheep." He seems to have a very comfortable relationship with
me and his mother.

Preventing a Dream from Becoming a Nightmare

A few years after the Verbal Interaction Project launched the
development of the Mother-Child Home Program, a professor
speaking at a national conference called it "a nightmare of the
future." His concern was that the Program, because it is home-
based, has a serious potential for infringement on the privacy
and rights of families.

This aroused some indignation within the Verbal Interaction
Project, where it was felt that safeguards against such risks had
been built into both the research procedures and the Program.
In addition, the research of the Program already indicated that
it might be a dream of effectiveness and social feasibility.

Nevertheless, the echo persisted of what we gradually came
to recognize as a socially responsible warning against the possibility that our Program could indeed become a nightmare of
coerciveness and intrusiveness to families like the Willards and
the Carters, in spite of our good intentions. The prime obligation of any social intervention program within our democratic
society is vigilance to make certain that the program and its
evaluation research are consistent with democratic values. This
is especially true of home-based, intervention programs. In
preschool programs located in a classroom ("center-based") the

mother and child can escape the program by simply remaining at home. In the home-based, Mother-Child Home Program, the Willards and the Carters *are* at home; they have no place to retreat to.

Since home-based programs are not readily accessible to public scrutiny, abuses can range from human error (for example, home visitors reporting misinformation to their supervisors, perhaps exaggerating the number or content of home sessions because it puts the visitors in a better light) to the near criminal (perhaps a program not delivered at all or delivered in a way that insults or otherwise hurts the family).

Another issue of crucial importance is that of confidentiality. In their contacts with family members, home visitors almost inevitably pick up details about a family which should be kept confidential in the interests of family privacy. To divulge such information is an indefensible breach of trust.

Further, home visitors can be tempted to be intrusive, to give uninformed advice and opinions, to insist that families conform to a particular visitor's version of mainstream language and culture, even to gossip about other families. There is a real danger that a home-based program *can* become a busybody nightmare. Our prevention of the nightmare rests on some of the Program's basic beliefs:

- That people using home-based programs should have the same rights as people who use center-based programs, or indeed, people in general, to *quality* services, to the *freedom of choosing or not choosing* to use those services, to *freedom from overt or subtle coerciveness* and *from invasions of privacy;*

- That people are uniquely *vulnerable in their own homes* to violations of those rights;

- That once a do-gooder has entered a home, it may take too much courage and initiative on the part of a host to terminate the relationship and ask that person to leave.

These beliefs have entered into every component of the Mother-Child Home Program, in the form of special care taken to safeguard the rights of families (Levenstein, 1980). The safeguards are explicit:

- Every detail of the Program was created and is monitored to be of the highest quality, whether tangible (like the toys and books) or intangible (like the Home Session procedures).

- The Toy Demonstrators and all other staff members are trained to preserve confidentiality about any family detail, including a ban on using participants' last names even in the Toy Demonstrator Conferences. Records of family contacts are kept in locked files.

- The Program is delivered to a mother only if she clearly states her wish for it and displays no contradictory signals that it is actually unwelcome (perhaps retreating to her kitchen during Home Sessions).

- A Toy Demonstrator may enter a dyad's home only when admitted by an adult (a two-year-old's enthusiastic welcome is not enough).

- Any kind of intrusiveness is avoided. The mother is not even helped to find apparently needed community services, like medical help, unless she asks for them. The Toy Demonstrator is trained to fit into the family's subculture as far as possible, whether it is unique to a particular family or part of a larger cultural/ethnolinguistic group within mainstream society. Neither Toy Demonstrator nor Coordinator takes over in any way.

- The Toy Demonstrators provide only the Home Session services in which they were trained (no counseling of any kind—psychological, nutritional, educational, medical, or whatever).

- To avoid competing with the mother for her child's affections, or creating in the mother herself feelings of dependency or of obligation to Program staff, the Toy Demonstrator is taught to be friendly but not to be a friend to mother or child.

- The Program does not interfere with a family's way of life but tries, wherever possible, to provide toys, books and verbal interaction designed to enhance the child's pride in his or her own subculture. Even when mothers insist, as they usually do, that the sessions be conducted in English, the Toy Demonstrator is alert for opportunities to relate the conversation to the family's culture. However, nothing is forced. Respect is conveyed as a natural part of the Home Session. Even the Toy Demonstrator's growth-enhancing modeling is on a "take it or leave it" basis.

• Program participants are treated with courtesy and respect by all staff members, regardless of the positions the latter hold in the Program.

These precautions have been developed to protect families against socio-ethical abuses in the Mother-Child Home Program. They have been incorporated to give families a reasonable assurance that the Program will be a dream and not a nightmare of the future.

Many home-based programs with a variety of purposes have sprung up in the wake of the Mother-Child Home Program (Morrison, 1978; Bryce & Lloyd, 1980). They are usually staffed by people whose enthusiasm for their program and genuine caring for the families served by the program are evident to any observer. Yet often a staff's compassion is greater than its awareness that good intentions are not enough when delivering programs to the homes of families, especially low-income families. The latter are all too accustomed to accepting without protest well-intentioned but unrequested aid of one kind or another, whatever the families may feel privately about the unwanted help. This time-honored defense (apparent docile compliance) against the intrusive Helping Hand is reinforced by the passivity and depression endemic among low-income single mothers. The result for a program is often covert resistance and quiet sabotage by its intended recipients. The results for the latter are not only the loss of a program's possible benefits but a reinforcement of their feelings of helplessness and low self-worth.

The Mother-Child Home Program's socio-ethical safeguards free both staff and mothers to concentrate on the joys and responsibilities of the Mother-Child Home Program. Perhaps the safeguards may also serve as a model for the delivery of other home-based programs, to prevent any of them from becoming a nightmare of the future.

4

On the
Shoulders of
Giants

*If I have seen further . . . it is by standing
upon the shoulders of Giants.*
—Sir Isaac Newton

All scientific and social innovators who see a little further
down the road of human progress "stand upon the shoulders
of giants." The "giants" are the great theoreticians and researchers who preceded them and whose work is the foundation of
their own. Similarly, the simple method which was the Mother-
Child Home Program owes much to the originators of many
theories and of many research studies from a broad spectrum
of professional disciplines. Their ideas concerned the differing
and yet often interwoven roles, in the child's intellectual development, of language, of early family relationships, of sen-
sory-motor development, of play and of optimum age periods
for intervention.

Language and Intellectual Development

Most fundamental to the Program was a belief in the critical
role of language in a child's intellectual development. According
to this belief, man's most distinctive attribute is the capacity
both for abstract conceptualization and for its symbolization
through language. Edward Sapir, the father of psycholinguistics,
called language a perfect symbol system that is probably a
vocal expression of the human tendency to see reality symbol-
ically (1921). He theorized that language may have originated

from primitive vocalizations of the "abstract attitude" built into humans, sounds that summarized numerous concrete perceptual encounters between early man and the environment. It is conceivable, for instance, that people developed special grunts to summarize and symbolize the many characteristics of stones appropriate for chipping into tools.

The philosopher Ernst Cassirer elaborated on this theory. His essay on symbolism (1944) discussed evidence for the symbolic nature of language, ranging from conceptual differences between Greek and Latin words for "moon" to the comprehension of the word "water" by the blind and deaf Helen Keller when she felt the pump's water spashing on her hand. Cassirer's reflections were expanded by the research of Russian psychologist, L. S. Vygotsky (1962). Vygotsky cited evidence for the efficiency of language, as a verbal symbol system, for abstracting and summarizing common traits among unlike experiences, as opposed to compiling many concrete instances to convey a general concept.

Jerome Bruner, the American psychologist, later devised a valuable step-by-step framework for viewing the development of symbolization in children (1966). He divided our mental representation of the world around us into three steps: the *enactive* (body "charades" used by the infant to indicate wishes—for comfort, for food, for being picked up—prevailing into the middle of the child's second year); the *iconic* (the predominance of mental images, which may persist among poets and primitives into adult life); and finally the *symbolic*.

At the symbolic stage, children who formerly employed words solely as labels for immediate experience (only Fido, the dog they were looking at or petting, was "dog") at last begin to use words to generalize the common attributes of many such experiences. Fidos of all shapes and colors still have many similarities which may be summarized as a concept and symbolized by the word "dog." The children are at last able to use words as verbal symbols of concepts. Bruner theorized that the child's growing skill in the symbolization of concepts by language probably depends on his interaction with other people around him (1964). Roger Brown, a Harvard University social psychologist, called this interaction "The Original Word Game" (1958). Bruner commented that the Original Word Game may end up by becoming the Human Thinking Game, a phrase which neatly encapsulates what may well be the most important underlying function of language: aiding people's ability to think (cf. Sigel, 1964).

A similarly concise explanation was furnished by developmental psychologist Irving Sigel's "distancing hypothesis" (1971). Sigel suggested that young children must interact with others if they are to use language to stand for increasingly distant "referents" (what the word refers to) in order to aid their intellectual development. The referents that are furthest from sight require the most abstract use of language. "Dog" is a dog the child is petting (no distance: a concrete label), or represents dogs in general (dogs everywhere, a thousand miles away or in the next room, but distant from the child: an abstract symbol).

Consequences of Family Verbal Interaction

The implication of the Original Word Game becoming the Human Thinking Game is that "others" are needed to exchange language with a child in order for him to acquire the words—the verbal symbols—for the conceptual thinking basic to intelligence. The acceptance of this necessity introduces the vital importance of family verbal interaction to a young child's language-induced conceptual growth. After all, for the young child, "others" are most likely to be the child's mother, father, brothers and sisters.

The research that perhaps most laid the groundwork for future empirical studies of how family interaction influences children's linguistic and intellectual growth was that of the British sociologist, Basil Bernstein, almost three decades ago. He examined contrasting kinds of language interaction in families of different socioeconomic status. The contrasting cognitive development of middle-class and working-class children in Bernstein's early studies (1961, 1965) suggested that abstraction-limited patterns of language in the families of British working-class children were linked to parallel limitations in the children's intellectual development.

When two University of Chicago professors, Robert Hess and Virginia Shipman, tested this idea a few years later with the families of Black American middle class and poor children, they found enough support in their resulting data for a trenchant conclusion: "The structure of the social system, and the structure of the family, shape communication and language; and language shapes thought and cognitive styles of problem solving" (1965).

According to both the British and the American studies, the language of parents in low-income families, white or Black, tends to be restricted or "telegraphic." The low-income mother says to her young child going out to play on a wintry day: "Your jacket—put it on!" The middle-income mother is more likely to say in an "expanded" way, "You need your jacket to keep warm on such a cold day—go find it and put it on!" If the child protests, the low-income mother may combine her restricted style of language with a reminder of her dominant status as a parent, "Do it because I told you!" This is likely to be her parental attitude into the child's later years, too.

The middle-income mother's reply to rebellion even with a very young child is not only more expanded but more often will start first with a person-to-person approach: "It's cold outside and you'll feel miserable if you don't put on your jacket. That's why you need a warm jacket today!" That will continue to be her style of parenting as the child grows older.

The differing language and interpersonal styles of the two mothers illustrate the way that "the structure of the social system" (the family's economic status) and "the structure of the family" (parents tending to be authoritarian or egalitarian) "shape communication and language" of parents to children. And the extent to which family language is limited or expanded and the parental attitudes authoritarian or egalitarian, "shapes thought and cognitive styles of problem solving" for the child.

The profound influence of the family-mediated social structure on language and thought was demonstrated also in empirical, statistically supported research which burgeoned between the 1950s and the 1980s (Bee et al., 1969; Birns & Golden, 1972; Caldwell et al., 1966; M. Deutsch, 1965; Farran & Ramey, 1980; Findlay & McGuire, 1957; Goldberg, 1963; Golden & Birns, 1968; Kamii & Radin, 1967; McKinley, 1964; Schacter, 1979; and Siller, 1957).

Research and interest in family interaction influences on child outcomes has continued into the 1980s. Jay Belsky is an outstanding example of a family-oriented scholar in this decade. He is directing a major university study of family interaction and has published many articles in professional journals (e.g., Belsky, 1985). Another is Allen Gottfried, whose own work is incorporated in such compilations of family interaction studies as *Home Environment and Early Cognitive Development* (1984) and *Play Interactions* (Gottfried & Brown, 1986).

The spare outlines of family interaction and concentration on group results rather than on individuals necessitated by the quantitative emphases of these studies have been vividly filled in by observational studies of families during the same period. Here investigators used anthropological methods, a combination of interviews and descriptions of actual family language and oral and written interactions recorded by participant-observers. For example, Denny Taylor (1983) was a participant-observer of "family literacy" in six middle-class, two-parent, white families within a 50-mile radius of New York City, all with more than one child in the family. Four of the six families contained children three years old or younger. Her book presents not only extracts from interviews and observations but actual reproductions of the children's early drawings and writing, all conveying a clear and intimate picture of the family interaction which promotes language and literacy in middle-class families.

Shirley Heath (1983) gave a similarly anthropological but greatly expanded account of family language, writing, and other interaction in three quite different social settings, all three in "Gateway," a mill town of 50,000 in the Piedmont region of South Carolina. She described and compared families along similar dimensions in two working-class neighborhoods of Gateway, one of them mainly rural-rooted and Black ("Trackton") and the other mainly mill-employed for generations and white ("Roadville"). She recorded similar observations along the same dimensions among Black and white "Main-streamers" (middle-class families) who were the majority of the population of Gateway. Childrearing for oral and written literacy was highlighted in all three settings. She, thus, included a broad scope of observations in families and then linked the consistent cultural differences she found among the family interactions to their children's widely differing preparation for school experiences, starting with preschool. The differing family-cultural languages, attitudes and values, including those in regard to literacy and education, deeply affected not only the children's future school careers but also the attitudes of teachers whom they encountered. Through her participant-observer experiences, she became sensitive to both family patterns and teachers' reactions to them. Heath was therefore able to identify many components of the teachers' problems in understanding and integrating the ethnolinguistic needs of their students, especially in the first years of school desegregation. Her study underlines the possible value of the Mother-Child Home Program's role as a bridge between family ethnolinguistic customs and the requirements of mainstream schooling.

In any case, all of these studies, stretching over many decades, have either shown the way, or provided further illumination, for many of the educational intervention programs, preventive and remedial, that focus on children from low-income families.

Mother-Child Love and Intellectual Development

Whatever the constrictions on concept-building verbal interaction in low-income families, research into socioeconomic influence on language and thought has detected no significant differences in the amount of warmth and affection between parents and children in the middle-income and low-income families. The tendency of poorer parents to use restricted language and authoritarian attitudes with their young children, rather than "person-to-person" attitudes and expanded language, is a difference in interpersonal style, but not in affection.

Strong mother-child attachment develops through the

mother's everyday care-giving, first to her infant and later to her child. Mother-child love occurs regardless of social class. It is crucially important to mental health according to studies of the mental-emotional impact of family relationships on children and adults. John Bowlby (1952) and Mary Ainsworth (1973) were among the first of the many investigators in this area, and Berry Brazelton (1986) is one of the most recent. However, Bernstein, and Hess & Shipman, and others of their research generation found evidence, in addition, that the use by parents of expanded language, and eventually of a person-to-person approach, is more functional for the young child's intellectual and social-emotional development than restricted language and an authoritarian attitude.

When mothers make conscious attempts to add intellectual stimulation to their relationships with their young children, the children show significant cognitive benefits. Irwin found many years ago that mothers' reading stories to their young children resulted in their toddlers' improved speech development (Irwin, 1960). Many later studies supported Irwin's findings: Freeburg & Payne, 1967; Gordon, 1969; Karnes et al., 1970; Laosa, 1983; Levenstein, 1970; Moore, 1968; Norman-Jackson, 1982; and Schaefer, 1969.

"Ur-Education"

Earl Schaefer, the University of North Carolina psychologist, in fact suggested that early home education be given a name connoting its almost primeval nature—"Ur-Education"—and that it be recognized as a legitimate preliminary to classroom schooling (Schaefer, 1970). Implicit in his idea is his belief, which is also that of the Mother-Child Home Program, in the vital link between the mother and toddler's verbal-cognitive interchange and the mother-child emotional relationship.

In short, intellectual stimulation can best benefit the pre-preschool child when it is embedded in the attachment between the mother and child within the familiar setting of their own home. The close connection between early learning and mother-child attachment was also demonstrated by the developmental psychologist, Urie Bronfenbrenner, in his well documented review of the effects of early deprivation on humans and animals (1968).

One of the most remarkable and valuable features of Ur-Education is that the Teacher (mother) and Student (child) need no extra incentives to engage in it. The interaction and associated activities are deeply satisfying to both, so strong is the motivation provided by what Bronfenbrenner once described as "that irrational affect called love."

Certainly the interaction will be reinforced by "props," Harvard Professor Courtney Cazden's label for objects such as books and toys which can encourage conversation between the child and others (1970, 1972). Developmental psycholinguists now speak of the "props" a little differently. They have broadened their attention not only to children's linguistic development but to the *context* in which that development occurs (Bates, 1976).

Gordon Wells, formerly Director of the University of Bristol's Centre for the Study of Language and Communication and its longitudinal family language study, pointed out the practical necessity for a context obvious and of interest to both parent and child, if the child is to make maximum use of the parent as a teacher. He commented: "It is difficult to overemphasize the importance of strategies that increase the child's motivation to converse. Those whose children were most successful were not concerned to give systematic linguistic instruction but rather to ensure that conversations with their children were mutually rewarding" (1985).

The Mother-Child Home Program thus had the good luck to anticipate by 20 years the necessity of creating a context that is "mutually rewarding" to both parent and child and for "increasing the child's motivation to converse" within a context which has interesting immediacy: play with toys and books. The Program also conjectured that toys which offer problem-solving challenges can exploit children's intrinsic motivation to master the environment through play, resulting in a gain of self-confidence through a feeling of self-competence ("effectance"), as postulated by R. White (1963).

However, the affectionate verbal interaction between mother

and child, within the context of their mutual attachment as well as of their mutual interest in the play materials, was assumed by the Mother-Child Home Program to be the main component of the child's early intellectual stimulation. Strong support for this assumption came many years later from an important replicative study by Clarke-Stewart and her colleagues (1979).

Its major effects probably begin as the infant is emerging into the period of what Cassirer called *reflective intelligence,* signaled and reinforced by rapid language development (Bates, 1976; Clarke-Stewart, 1973; Levenstein, 1983; Nelson, 1973). This occurs at about the age of two years (cf. Bayley, 1965; and Hebb, 1949) and coincides with the child's heightened attachment to the mother; with his greatly increased curiosity about the environment; with his growing skill with using *symbolic representation* (Bruner, 1966); with his developing sophistication in using his arms and legs and hands—in short, with a near explosion of the child's rapidly developing skills and feelings.

It is also the time for optimum development of the parent-child network. By the age of about four years children have incorporated the main effects of this revolution and become eager for experiences away from mother, father, and the family home.

Intervention at an Early Age

Probably, then, if parents have not been able to take full advantage of the period before the child reaches four to develop a strongly and mutually supportive parent-child network, a dip in cognitive development may be expected (cf. Golden & Birns, 1968). Poverty ("the structure of the social system") takes its toll in constraining parents from helping their children to avoid this downward turn which can gravely handicap their future academic achievement.

Many parents (especially low-income single mothers of limited education) need an intervention program to help them to help their children. Educator Benjamin Bloom's large collection of evidence (1964) seemed overwhelmingly to indicate that such intervention to prevent the cognitive dip should occur between the ages of two and four years, as the optimal, and possibly critical, period to prepare children for school learning.

Even before the publication of Bloom's book, tremendous impetus was given to the whole field of early childhood intervention research by a careful review, written by psychologist J. McV. Hunt, containing impressive evidence for the role of environment in the growth of individual intelligence (1961). It promised new hope for the prevention of the personal tragedy and social problems generally posed by the educational disadvantage of the poor.

Partly as a result, federal and private funding were made available in the 1960s and early 1970s (via the usual competitive grants) for studying carefully structured preschool classroom duplications of what developmental psychologist Bettye Caldwell aptly called (1967) the optimal learning environment for young children which should be copied in the classroom: "... the child in his *own home*, within the context of a warm and nurturant relationship *with his mother* or a reasonable facsimile thereof, under conditions of varied sensory and cognitive input." [Emphasis added.]

Curiously, back in the 1930s a duplication of "home" conditions did occur within a serendipitous and remarkably effective "intervention program" in a strange setting—a program which had a strong intellectual impact on the young children it included (Skeels & Dye, 1939). An unplanned impromptu "tryout" of the program took place in an Iowa state residence for the mentally retarded. This pilot version was spontaneously carried on with some very young children by the residence staff and by the toddlers' retarded teenage and adult fellow residents. The children had been diagnosed as retarded and therefore placed in the residence, supposedly for life. The adults, whether staff or residents, were given no training or direction. To the amazement of the professionals, they provided apparently IQ-raising emotional, verbal, and cognitive stimulation by playing and talking with the toddlers (who perhaps supplied some welcome stimulation of their own in a place where little children were seldom seen). Some of the staff even took them on visits to their own homes. In a more systematic experiment with this "method," it was observed that toddlers lost their retardation, became adoptable and grew up to be nonretarded, well-functioning adults (Skeels, 1966).

From the mounting evidence it seemed clear that the ideal preventive intervention program to combat educational disadvantage should be the home itself, rather than a duplicate of it. It seemed equally clear that children's first "interveners" should be not teachers but people who cared deeply and enduringly about them—in fact, their parents. It should take advantage of the attachment-oriented interaction already existing between mother and child and give the low-income mother the option of being her child's primary intervention agent.

Theory Into Practice:
The Mother-Child Home Program

In creating the Mother-Child Home Program, a careful attempt was made to work out a delicate balance between enough structure to turn theory into Program reality, and the preservation of the mother's autonomy as well as her relationship with her child. The theory for the goals and procedures of Schaefer's Ur-Education paralleled by the Mother-Child Home Program was echoed and neatly summarized in a paragraph from Urie Bronfenbrenner's 1974 review of early childhood education research:

> *In the early years of life, the psychological development of the child is enhanced through his involvement in progressively more complex, enduring patterns of reciprocal, contingent interaction with persons with whom he has established a mutual and enduring attachment (Bronfenbrenner, 1974).*

Dr. Bronfenbrenner's succinct paragraph could serve as a synopsis for most of this chapter. It could also be translated into specific features of the Mother-Child Home Program:

- *The early years of life* are from two to four years of age.

- *The psychological development of the child is enhanced* by verbal *interaction* centering around Program toys and books.

- The toys, books and curriculum are *progressively more complex* as the child matures in the Program.

- Mother and child are encouraged toward *patterns of reciprocal, contingent interaction:* responses of mother to child and of child to mother.

- The *persons with whom he or she has established a mutual and enduring relationship* are, of course, the child's parents—and particularly the mother, who is the chief Program team member.

Dr. Schaefer's concept of "Ur-Education" did not focus on the Ur-Educator, usually the mother in the case of the low-income child. Nor did Dr. Bronfenbrenner mention the mother's psychological development. In fact, none of the theoretical or empirical studies had much to say about the feelings and thoughts of the mother, in spite of her crucial involvement as the child's first teacher. There was little speculation or information about the effect on her of the "reciprocal, contingent interaction" with her child.

However, one of the basic assumptions of the Mother-Child Home Program was the validity of psychologist Robert White's theory that "effectance"—the feeling of self-competence that comes from having an effect on the environment and persons in it—leads to self-confidence (1963). The belief was that mothers as well as children could derive feelings of effectance and self-confidence from the Program. The Program could indeed end up by being as important for strengthening a low-income mother's mental health as for the prevention of her child's educational disadvantage.

From the reciprocal interactions, a benign parent-child network could evolve which would be supportive for both mother and child. Bettye Caldwell and her associates at the University of Arkansas have found through HOME ("Home Observation for Measurement of the Environment"), a brief home interview instrument created by Dr. Caldwell, that infant experience with home and parents predicts children's later intellectual status (Caldwell et al., 1966; Bradley & Caldwell, 1984). If, in actual intervention with the Mother-Child Home Program, evidence of such a parent-child network is demonstrated, it might also yield some glimpses of how the links between children's early family experiences and later cognitive development are forged, and of whether there are indeed some benign consequences for mothers.

5

How
High Was
Up?

Individual Results: The Willards and the Carters

Carol Willard and Jo-Jo Carter, and their mothers too, had had a lot of fun in the Mother-Child Home Program. But the Program's basic goal was dead serious: to help children, and hopefully their mothers, to escape from permanent poverty through education. The Willards and the Carters had had a good time and had acquired respectable libraries of toys and books. But had they actually been equipped by the Program to use the public school effectively to climb out of the underclass? If so, how far up?

The Verbal Interaction Project (VIP) traced Jo-Jo, Carol and their mothers for six years, in order to answer these questions with "hard data"—quantitative results—like the number of Home Session appointments kept by mothers, or test scores achieved by the children. The children's progress was evaluated by psychologists "blind" to their treatment status when Carol and Jo-Jo were two years old (just before they entered the Program) and when they were four (just after the Program). The children were then re-evaluated every year until near the end of second grade when they were eight years old. During that six-year period their mothers were observed in Home Sessions, interviewed, and videotaped in play with their children.

Both children had started off at the age of two with almost identical IQs, at the low end of the average range (93 for Carol and 91 for Jo-Jo). If they had retained that level of learning ability into elementary school, they might have been at a disad-

113

vantage in trying to keep up with a classroom curriculum geared, as most are, to at least mid-average learning competence (IQ about 100). And if their learning ability gradually declined as they grew older, the fate of many underclass children, they would have been at even greater disadvantage. The Mother-Child Home Program aimed at preventing that handicap (Levenstein & Levenstein, 1971).

With both Carol and Jo-Jo, it seemed to succeed. At the end of the two-year Program, when they were each almost four years old, Carol had achieved an IQ of 105, and Jo-Jo an IQ of 109, both above mid-average. Their IQs were now about 15 points above those found to be typical for four-year-olds of their socioeconomic status in a huge survey which included 26,000 children and their mothers (Broman, Nichols, & Kennedy, 1975).

In fact, their IQs at age four promised good elementary school progress in future years. If they maintained that level, they should be able to keep up with their more economically favored classmates in such basic subjects as reading and arithmetic.

This indeed happened. Near the end of second grade both Carol and Jo-Jo produced age-normal reading, arithmetic and IQ scores. Thus their achievements after two years of school seemed to demonstrate that the Program had created a solid foundation for their learning in higher grades. They would be able to acquire skills basic to whatever careers they chose for finding their way out of the underclass.

It may say something about the light, nonintrusive touch of the Mother-Child Home Program that the children's personalities as expressed in their behavior during the evaluations seemed essentially unchanged. According to psychologists' observations in evaluation sessions, many of their personal characteristics endured from age two (before the program) to age four (just after the Program) to age eight when Carol and Jo-Jo were in the last months of second grade.

At the end of the Program the evaluating psychologist commented in her notes about four-year-old Carol:

> Carol is extremely shy. Took long time for her to even have eye contact with me, let alone move her

hands or speak or participate in any way. Did finally finish the tests but answered very few questions involving expression of ideas—couldn't get herself to speak whole sentences. But understood instructions, difficult concepts quite easily.

A second psychologist evaluated Carol in second grade, when she was almost eight years old. She wrote:

A quiet, soft-spoken child who showed little emotion throughout the session. The child was cooperative and seemed to be doing her best. She had a good attention span and sat well during the session.

The psychologist's written comment about Jo-Jo right after the end of the Program, when he was four years old, was:

Understands instructions quickly, has rapid grasp of abstract concepts, etc. Is interested, curious about everything, but activities and use of his intellect seem hindered by his fear of the unfamiliar. Probably would have scored higher if more items at 6 year level were pursued by psychologist. However, he became sulky, wanted to leave, so test was terminated.

When Jo-Jo was eight years old and near the end of second grade, he was evaluated by the same psychologist who had seen Carol at this point. She commented about Jo-Jo:

A somewhat shy child who seemed reluctant to respond unless he was sure of any answer. Jo-Jo smiled brightly when he successfully answered a question and seemed very pleased with his success. He appeared afraid to be wrong and rarely said "I don't know" but stared into space until I finally went on to the next question. This prolonged the testing session. The child sat well throughout the long session, however, and had a good attention span.

The Program's purpose was not to change the personalities of the children but to help them to become ready for school learning. For these two children both goals seemed to have been accomplished.

The mothers were not as similar in their Program gains as their children were, except that both showed exceptional co-operation in fulfilling Home Session requirements. Mrs. Carter had kept all but one of her Home Session appointments. She had taken over the Home Sessions almost from the first and seldom relinquished them to her Toy Demonstrator. Given the Guide Sheets, she had quickly learned their use and pro-ceeded to go into action to help her child. The videotapes of her play sessions with Jo-Jo showed that she had learned to be a sensitive, responsive teacher-playmate for her own child. She now encouraged his questions and the verbal give and take between them. By actual count of her videotaped play behaviors with four year old Jo-Jo just after the Program, she had interacted with Jo-Jo a total of 260 times. This was consid-erably higher than the average of 228 for the Program mothers in her "cohort" (those who had entered the research Project in the same year).

Mrs. Carter's ability to mobilize herself to start college at the end of the Program, reflecting an improvement in the mild depression she had started with, may or may not have been the result of her Program participation. The cause of a gain of this sort is hard to identify. However, there seemed to be a link between the confidence she displayed more and more during the Program and her taking this step to climb out of the underclass.

Mrs. Willard also showed excellent cooperation by her high rate of kept appointments: 65 out of a possible 69 Home Sessions. However, her progress in the Program was less spec-tacular than that of Mrs. Carter. From Mrs. Willard's shy and almost silent videotaped play sessions with Carol immediately after the Program, it would seem that she had learned little. The average number of interactions she had with Carol during those sessions was only 104, far below the group average of 228! Yet her Home Session participation increased from 16 percent to 45 percent during Year Two of the Program. Further, the noticeable improvement in her personal and household management suggested important mental health effects of the Program which did not appear in the "hard data."

Group Results, Design I:
Location-Randomized Experiments

The Mother-Child Home Program seemed to be successful with the Willards and the Carters. Yet their individual results were not sufficient proof that the Program had been responsible for their gains. There was no doubt that Carol and Jo-Jo had progressed intellectually since the age of two. By second grade they had even demonstrated their good school learning and thus were well prepared for succeeding in higher grades, a major Program goal. There was also no doubt that their intellectual and academic competence was above that to be expected for their low-income group. But could the Mother-Child Home Program take credit for their good development?

This is a question that every would-be social program must answer about its encouraging results. To pose the question in another way: will hard research data demonstrate that the program can really work for most of its intended population? Staff, or even participant, enthusiasm about the program is not enough. Only systematic, and preferably experimental, evaluation research will give an objective estimate of program effects. It is this kind of evaluation, not glowing testimonials, that policy makers generally prefer to use in deciding whether to invest the sizeable amounts of money which are needed for widespread utilization of a program.

The VIP researchers sought to answer the crucial question of Program effectiveness through experimental evaluation research, by measuring and comparing the progress of whole groups of Program and Non-Program mothers and children, besides that of individuals like the Willards and the Carters. With individual data, too many chance factors might have been the actual cause of a child's success, rather than the program that was taking place at the same time. Experimental research resulting in successful group rather than individual data virtually rules out such chance factors as causes of the effect (Rossi et al., 1979).

Therefore, with six annual cohorts entering the Project between 1967 and 1972, the VIP conducted "Design I" (location-randomized) experimental research to compare the results for Program groups with the results for similar Non-Program groups. To be able to generalize the results to the Program's intended population, all families in the experiments shared certain key low-income features: parents' education no higher than high school and occupations no higher than semi-skilled.

To begin the Design I research in July 1967, three low-income housing projects, eighteen miles apart from each other, were randomly assigned (by tossing a penny) to one of three treatment plans. The enrolled children in one housing project (Tests-Only Group) would receive only a developmental evaluation service. The two-year-olds in the second housing project (Gifts-Only Group) would receive, with all of their young brothers and sisters, weekly gifts not meant to stimulate conversation (scarves, stepstools, flashlights), along with an evaluation. The mother-child pairs in the third housing project (Program Group) would receive evaluations and a one-year version of the Mother-Child Home Program. Thus, regardless of where they lived, all two-year-olds in the three groups would receive multiple developmental evaluations for their mothers' information. They would also receive referrals to community resources for any help with problems revealed by the evaluations.

The Program staff then invited all mothers of two-year-olds in each housing project into the treatment plan randomly assigned to that project. They thus followed the essential feature of the Design I experimental research plan: random assignment of subjects by location rather than by individual.

In each housing project almost all—85 percent—of the mothers accepted the treatment randomly assigned to their site. The treatment plans were then carefully carried out with each mother-child pair.

Each year after 1967, through 1972, new groups of mothers were invited into what had become a two-year Program, and two new control (Non-Program) groups were formed. All were from the Program and Gifts-Only housing projects or from slum dwellings nearby. They lived, as did the first 1967 cohort, in poverty pockets of Nassau County (paradoxically, one of the richest counties in the United States). Acceptance of the assigned treatments continued to be from 85 to 100 percent.

Since in 1967, and also in later years through 1972, no more than fifteen percent of Design I mothers rejected the proffered treatments, the "self-selection" of mothers for the Design I experiments was very low. This made it likely that at least as many Hesitaters as Strivers were in the yearly cohorts. Actually, the impression of staff members who interviewed the mothers was that Hesitaters outnumbered Strivers, an impression supported by their later Home Session interactive behavior.

It seemed probable also that the Design I dyads fairly represented most of the low-income mothers and children throughout the country. They not only had the educational and occupational hallmarks of poverty, but more than a third of the families were female-headed and receiving welfare aid. In addition, the impression of the staff was that many if not most mothers were passive and depressed, Strivers as well as Hesitaters. They were, in sum, a representative sample of the intended recipients of the Mother-Child Home Program.

The families reached by the 84 replications of the Program during the past 15 years had the same characteristics. Further, according to reports from their Program Coordinators, almost every mother accepted the Program when it was offered.

Important as it was to ascertain that the Program was acceptable to its intended population, it was equally important to find out if the Program worked. The Design I research used as its subjects the six 1967–1972 yearly cohorts who represented the country's low-income families and who were in the model Program, or were in Non-Program groups, in order to answer the following five questions:

1. Did the Program work—did it prevent low-income children's educational disadvantage when they reached elementary school?

2. Was a two-year rather than a one-year Program necessary?

3. Could high school educated Toy Demonstrators deliver the Program as effectively as the Masters-Degreed social workers who pioneered the role?

4. Was the Program really as popular with mothers as it seemed?

5. Did mothers' verbal behavior in Home Sessions predict their children's future performance and behavior in school?

Many kinds of data from several kinds of evaluation, and many kinds of assessments (by standardized and VIP-created tests) produced the answers. All results were in an affirmative direction.

Question 1: Did the Program prevent low-income children's educational disadvantage?

Yes, for as far as the Program children and their Non-Program controls were fully followed—129 children into third grade, and 76 into fifth grade, 58 into seventh grade, and 25 into eighth grade in the Pittsfield, Massachusetts replication of the Mother-Child Home Program.

As many children as funding permitted were followed well into their school years, because the ultimate indication of a preventive program's effectiveness must lie in Program graduates' future academic and intellectual performance. Preschool IQs are useful mainly because they predict young children's later school progress. However, the real test of the Mother-Child Home Program was the Program children's ability to cope with the challenges of school, as well as their academic and intellectual superiority to comparable Non-Program children in school years.

The third grade follow-up results for six groups of children in Design I are summarized in Table 5.1 ("Design I: Children's Mean IQ and Academic Scores at Entry [Age 2], at Program's End [Ages 4 & 6], and in 3rd Grade [Age 8]"). Three of the six groups were Program graduates, and three were Non-Program (control) children from closely similar backgrounds. Table 5.1 reports several kinds of test scores at different age levels, beginning at age two for most of the groups (one control group was first tested at age four and one at age six) and ending for all six groups at age eight, in third grade. Third grade is often considered the "fork-in-the-road" school grade for academic success or failure (Kraus, 1973).

As can be seen in Table 5.1, the third grade reading and arithmetic skills, and the IQs were at a normal level for the 78 Pro-

Table 5.1

Design I: Children's Mean IQ and Academic Scores at Entry (Age 2), at Program's End (Ages 4 & 6), and in 3rd Grade (Age 8)

Design I Group	Entry & Posttest IQs			Third Grade Scores (Age 8)			
	Entry IQ Cattell Binet Age 2	Post IQ Binet Age 4	Age 6	IQ WISC	Read. WRAT	Arith. WRAT	Special Class
Program Groups							
1968 N = 24	88.4 91.3	109.0	—	103.9	101.7	99.8	12.5%
1969 N = 25	85.5 —	103.7	—	98.3	97.8	99.9	13.0%
1970 N = 29	88.6 —	107.2	—	100.8	101.7	104.8	7.1%
Non-Program Groups							
1967 N = 14	93.4 88.0	96.3	—	96.1	87.4	90.1	35.7%
1967 N = 10	— —	91.0	—	96.3	91.1	91.4	—
1972 N = 27	— —	—	90.7	93.9	90.5	93.7	7.4%

gram graduates. These not only surpassed those of the control group, but they were well above the scores to be expected, according to other investigators, from children whose fathers had had 9 to 11 years of school (Schaie & Roberts, 1970). Fewer than a third of the Program graduates had severe school problems. Fewer than 12 percent had been placed in special classes for slow learners.

Table 5.1 shows that Program graduates surpassed the Non-Program children both immediately after the Program and in third grade. The Non-Program children's third grade scores lagged so far behind those of Program graduates that they were at or below the levels anticipated for children whose fathers had had 9 to 11 years of school (Schaie & Roberts, 1970). The low scores of the Non-Program children typified the educational disadvantage which had been prevented for the Program children (Broman et al., 1975).

Table 5.2 is a reproduction of Table 14, "Mean IQ Score for Early Education and Control by Project, by Age," in a monograph containing a "meta-analysis" of follow-up data from 11 well-known early childhood program research projects that started before 1968 and became associated as the "Consortium for Longitudinal Studies." The meta-analysis was published as a Monograph of the Society for Research in Child Development (Lazar & Darlington, 1982).

Table 5.2

Mean IQ Score for Early Education and Control by Project, by Age

Project and Age	Mean IQ Program	Mean IQ Control	t	p	Program N	Control N
Beller:						
Pretest	92.16	91.19	.39	.699	57	53
6	98.59	91.19	2.74	.007	56	53
7	98.36	94.40	1.55	.125	53	53
8	97.83	92.78	1.96	.053	52	50
9	97.61	93.07	1.67	.099	51	46
10	98.44	91.74	2.58	.012	50	46
Gordon (no pretest available):						
3	94.86	91.39	1.79	.075	145	51
4	93.89	88.37	2.54	.013	134	52
5	94.04	88.81	2.52	.013	135	52
6	94.01	88.59	3.01	.003	128	51
10 (F1976)[a]	83.13	78.79	1.44	.161	71	19
Gray:						
Pretest	89.43	85.76	.98	.331	44	21
5	96.05	87.38	2.45	.020	43	21
6	94.98	82.78	2.90	.008	42	18
7	97.71	91.33	1.61	.121	41	18
8	93.63	87.89	1.22	.232	38	18
10	88.42	84.94	.89	.384	38	18
17 (F1976)[a]	78.74	76.44	.55	.588	34	18
Levenstein:						
Pretest[a]	83.75	84.26	.22	.829	176	27
3	100.12	95.47	1.90	.066	134	19
4	104.82	95.64	3.88	.000	117	33

Table 5.2, continued

Project and Age	Mean IQ Program	Mean IQ Control	t	p	Program N	Control N
5	107.07	103.17	.90	.401	97	6
6	103.44	87.30	2.41	.037	71	10
7[a]	102.50	99.86	.59	.561	38	14
8[a]	100.82	96.90	1.47	.148	57	30
10 (F1976)[a]	101.86	93.56	3.35	.001	51	25
Miller (no pretest available):						
4	92.87	89.21	1.76	.086	213	34
5	97.33	90.00	3.31	.002	210	34
6	94.06	93.74	.12	.902	200	31
7	92.48	92.48	- .00	(.999)	192	29
8	89.72	94.00	-1.38	(.176)	174	29
13 (F1976)[a]	84.96	91.00	2.19	(.038)	109	18
Palmer:						
Pretest[b]	94.42	85.32	4.71	<.001	120	63
4	97.74	93.31	2.20	.030	221	59
5	96.41	91.13	2.56	.013	207	48
12 (F1976)[a]	92.13	88.86	.99	.327	104	28
Weikart:						
Pretest	79.57	78.54	.89	.373	58	65
3	79.91	79.60	.26	.794	45	50
4	92.69	81.66	5.04	.001	58	65
5	94.05	83.20	5.33	.001	57	64
6	91.25	86.34	2.39	.019	56	64
7	91.72	87.07	2.31	.022	58	61
8	88.11	86.85	.56	.574	55	62
9	87.71	86.77	.44	.664	56	61
10	84.98	84.61	.17	.861	57	57
14 (F1976)[a]	81.02	80.71	.14	.885	54	56

Note.—t and p are based on unequal variance estimate. Scores are Stanford-Binet unless otherwise indicated. F1976 indicates follow-up Wechsler IQ score in 1976. Age of testing is in years. From "Lasting effects of early education: A report from the Consortium for Longitudinal Studies" by I. Lazar and R. Darlington, *Monographs of the Society for Research in Child Development,* 1982, 47, (2–3, Serial No. 195, Table 14, p. 45. Reprinted by permission.

[a]WISC (Weikart, Levenstein) or WISC-R Full Scale IQ.

[b]Pretest IQ available for only one-half of program subjects, see Appendix B.

[c]Levenstein pretest IQ is PPVT.

Table 5.2 makes the same point in regard to the IQ effects of the Program as did Table 5.1, but this time for 51 Program graduates and 25 Control children when they were 10 years old in fifth grade. (Their Ns differed from other Mother-Child Home Program Ns in Table 5.2 because new "waves" of children entered as subjects at age two and were then followed to some grade levels.) The IQs of the 51 first Mother-Child Home Program graduates to reach fifth grade continued to surpass those of the Non-Program Control children and, as in third grade, reached national norms.

The difference of 8.30 IQ points between the fifth grade Program graduates' mid-average IQ of 101.86 and the Control Group's low-average IQ of 93.56 had high statistical significance ($p<.001$). The difference also had an important practical significance. It could mean the distinction between the ability to read easily at grade level or laboring, perhaps unsuccessfully, to do so.

That the Program was responsible for this achievement is also borne out by significant correlations between Program participation and reading ability in third, fourth, and fifth grades, as presented in Table 5.3 ("Effect of Mother-Child Home Program [MCHP] on Reading Scores," adapted from Table 13 of the Lazar & Darlington monograph).

Table 5.3
Effect of Mother-Child Home Program (MCHP)
on Reading Scores[1]

Grade and Program	Program Coefficient	t	p
Grade 3: MCHP (N = 73)	9.42	2.83	.006
Grade 4: MCHP (N = 47)	11.69	2.71	.010
Grade 5: MCHP (N = 39)	11.42	2.52	.017

[1]Adapted from "Lasting effects of early education: A report from the Consortium for Longitudinal Studies" by I. Lazar and R. Darlington, *Monographs of the Society for Research in Child Development,* 1982, 47 (2–3, Serial No. 195), Table 13, p. 42. Reprinted by permission. [Note: "MCHP" is identified as "Levenstein" in the original table.]

Serendipitously, Table 5.2, with its list of IQ results from seven prominent early childhood education programs, afforded an opportunity to compare the Mother-Child Home Program's IQ results with those of six other programs, also begun before 1968, whose longitudinal IQ data were available to be included in the Lazar & Darlington study. All seven showed the promising result of a significant IQ rise immediately post-Program. But only two continued to show a significant superiority over the Controls by age ten years. Indeed, they both were either slightly above ("Levenstein") or only slightly below ("Beller") national IQ norms.

However, many Consortium programs, both individually and in the pooled analysis, demonstrated significantly reduced rates of assignment to special education classes, of grade retention, and of post-high school legal troubles. In addition, the early education program graduates as a whole did better than their controls not only in these important areas but in the expression of satisfaction with their programs by both the graduates (who were old enough to do so) and their parents.

Nonetheless, the IQ benefits of the minimal intervention of the Mother-Child Home Program (no more than 46 half-hour Home Sessions in each of two years) were shown by the Lazar & Darlington meta-analysis to be retained by its graduates for six and a half years, into fifth grade.

A separate "pooled analysis" study of the school progress only of the 1968 cohort to the end of seventh grade found that no child in the Program group had failed any school grade, while 14 percent of the control group had done so (Royce, Darlington, & Murray, 1983).

A Replication's Longitudinal Evaluation of the Mother-Child Home Program's School Effects

Program Effects into Eighth Grade in Pittsfield, Massachusetts

The truest test of an early intervention program designed to prevent school disadvantage in economically disadvantaged pre-preschoolers is not IQ results at the age of four years, or even ten years, but children's ability to cope with actual school tasks. An even better measure of the program's success is the extent to which economically disadvantaged children in a replication of the Program can keep up with their non-disadvantaged classmates in reading and other basic school work.

Program graduates, in contrast with Non-Program graduates from the same disadvantaged backgrounds, should show *little or no educational disadvantage* in elementary school. They should show their readiness by eighth grade to tackle the challenges of high school and thus the probability that they will graduate from high school—that they will win that precious and now almost indispensable diploma.

Lack of continued funding prevented the Verbal Interaction Project's follow-up research of the model Program's effects past seventh grade, when graduates of the Mother-Child Home Program indeed seemed to have escaped the school problems typical of low-income children.

However, one of the Program's oldest replications, operating with Chapter One funding in a school system, continued follow-up studies of the Mother-Child Home Program through eighth grade. As arranged by the Chapter One director, Dr. William J. Cameron, a team of outside evaluators of the Pittsfield, Massachusetts, Public Schools replication of the Mother-Child Home Program (called there the "Parent-Child Home Program") studied, in a version of Design I, the academic performance of Program graduates from kindergarten through eighth grade (DeVito & Karon, 1984). Their report is given here in some detail because it gives a glimpse of the standards followed by Chapter One programs in fulfilling government mandates for program evaluation and accountability, and it also illustrates the understanding by evaluators of the programs they are evaluating. The report begins:

Background

   The Pittsfield Parent-Child Home Program (hereafter called PCHP) is a home-based preschool project funded under Chapter 1 of the Educational Consolidation and Improvement Act (ECIA). PCHP was im-

plemented in 1970–1971 in the Pittsfield, Massachu-
setts school system and was based on the Verbal
Interaction Project/Mother-Child Home Program
(VIP/MCHP) developed by Phyllis Levenstein.

The VIP/MCHP, as developed by Levenstein, is
based on the assumption that cognitive enrichment
for young children should occur with early speech
development and should be an integral part of the
child's relationships with significant family members,
primarily the mother. If this cognitive enrichment
occurs, it is likely to prevent later educational disadvantagement. Developers of the project felt that cognitive enrichment, with family verbal interaction as
its cornerstone, occurs in middle-income families as
a matter of course, but is much less likely to occur
in low-income families.

As a result of this thinking, a program was established to enhance the cognitive development of two
and three year olds from low income families, through
exposure to home-based stimulation centered on increased verbal interaction with their mothers around
toys and books. This program was called the Mother-
Child Home Program.

The report followed its introduction with an accurate description of the VIP/MCHP. It then continued:

Pittsfield's Implementation of VIP/MCHP
The Parent-Child Home Program in Pittsfield began
as a pilot program in 1970–1971 with 16 families. In
the years since, the program has expanded and ma-
tured. In the earliest years of its replication in Pittsfield, continuity of staff was problematic. In recent
years, however, more stability in staffing was
achieved due to better pay and benefits for demonstrators. The project, as currently operating, seems to
be a close replication of the VIP/MCHP on which it
is based.

Need for Evaluation of PCHP

Evaluation of the PCHP program in Pittsfield is necessary for several reasons. First, program evaluation can assess whether the stated objectives of a program are being achieved. In the case of PCHP, the major goal is linked to prevention of disadvantagement instead of remediation, and thus the evaluation should be geared to this point. Second, all Chapter 1, ECIA funded programs must be evaluated on a periodic basis to comply with the federal law. Third, the evaluation activities can point to potential changes or refinements in the project operations that, if implemented, may improve the functioning or overall effectiveness of the project.

Purpose of the Evaluation

The major purpose of the evaluation performed on the Pittsfield PCHP program during 1983–1984 was to examine the sustained effects of program participation for students in grades K–8 who had been in the PCHP for two years. This study expands on an earlier longitudinal evaluation . . . conducted in Pittsfield on PCHP participants through grade four.

The major part of the DeVito & Karon report went on to present the details of their evaluation and its outcomes, starting with Program children's short-term Peabody IQ gains from a pre-Program IQ of 89.6 to a post-Program IQ of 105.7.

Major Findings and Conclusions

The interpretations of longitudinal evaluation data must be seen in a global context. Due to attrition over time, (students moving out of Pittsfield and hence being unavailable for follow-up testing), relatively small numbers of participants (with project groups of 20 or less per year) and many different grades (K–8) included in the study, the interpretations of program effectiveness should be taken with some caution. There are, however, several trends that appear to be clear from the analysis.

1. Any long-term examination of an educational program must first assess whether the initial program treatment was successful. This is elementary since only successful practices and programs can show sustained positive effects. *The data for this study clearly showed that the project has been an overwhelming success in raising cognitive development scores of participants.* Both year one and year two of the program produced substantial and significant positive changes in the PPVT IQ test scores of the PCHP participants.

2. Some of the PCHP participants moved from that program to the Pittsfield nursery school program as four year olds. The PCHP students without the Pittsfield nursery school experience performed as well as those who attended the four-year-old program. This finding, however, does not necessarily reflect negatively on the effect of the nursery school program since it was impossible to determine whether those students not attending Pittsfield's nursery program had another pre-school experience as four year olds (day-care, private nursery school, etc.), and the number of PCHP students not attending Pittsfield's nursery program was quite small.

3. The results indicate that positive effects are sustained into the kindergarten year by participants. When compared to a randomly selected comparison group of Chapter 1 participants, the previous PCHP students clearly outperformed the comparison group.

4. The next two grades (1 + 2) showed a less encouraging trend with no significant differences being evident between PCHP or comparison groups.

5. The intermediate grade grouping (grades 3, and 4–5) showed mixed results. Grade three students significantly outperformed comparison group members on 3 or 4 measures (with the other a non-significant difference), while the fourth graders achieved this in 1 of the 4 measures used.

6. In examining the upper grade grouping (6–8), a

rather dramatic turnaround appeared evident. The
PCHP group significantly outperformed the comparison group of Chapter 1 students on each of the four
measures. In fact, when compared to a randomly
selected group on *non*-Chapter 1 students, the PCHP
was outperfromed in only two of the four measures.
This is particularly impressive when one considers
that a further analysis indicated that the non-Chapter
1 comparison group significantly outperformed the
Chapter 1 comparison group on all measures, but
achieved this result relative to the PCHP group in
only two of the four measures.

7. The CAT [California Achievement Test] scores
as measured in normal curve equivalents (NCE) indicated that the average scores attained by the PCHP
group were very favorable in comparison to the national averages of the CAT norming samples, even
at grades 1 and 2. An NCE of 50 is considered average
for the norming group and is equal to the 50th per-
centile. . . . *The PCHP group, across grades and measures,*
achieved NCE average scores ranging from 48.12 (slightly
below average) to 60.14 (above average).

8. The examination of results relative to subject
matter (reading, language and math) seems to indicate
that achievement of PCHP participants in later years
was somewhat better in reading and language arts
than in math. This would appear to be consistent
with the project's emphasis on verbal interaction as
a treatment.

In summary, the PCHP program appears to be successful in sustaining the effects achieved during participation in the program and in preparing students
to use the increased cognitive development for future
school endeavors. The project selects those students
for participation who appear to be most 'at-risk' at
two years of age and for whom the prognosis of adequate performance throughout their school years is
doubtful. Overall, it appears that program interven-

tion for these students as two and three year olds had lasting effects, since as a group *they met or exceeded national achievement norms and generally outperformed the groups to which they were compared.* (DeVito & Karon, 1984.)

Note that in the Pittsfield adoption, Program graduates not only were superior to Non-Program children of similar background, but they met *national standards for the achievement tests* (reading, language arithmetic, and total scores) into eighth grade. The 1984 Pittsfield follow-up study thus resulted in an impressive demonstration that even away from the original site of its development, the Program was effective in *closing the achievement gap* which usually separates disadvantaged students from their more advantaged classmates, even when the former have had the benefit of center-based preschool programs (Hebbeler, 1985).

Other Evidence of Program Effects on Children at Educational Risk

Other types of data, collected during the Design I years, added to the encouraging assessment of Program effectiveness with children at risk for educational disadvantage. For example, a sibling comparison was made between the IQ scores of seven VIP Program graduates immediately after the Program ended and those of ten older brothers and sisters at the same age of four years (whose group scores can be found in Table 5.1, identified under "Non-Program" as "N = 10"). The Program children achieved IQs that were significantly higher (by 16 points) than those of their older siblings who had reached the same age without any experience with the Mother-Child Home Program.

Another such study was done at the VIP with a much larger group of children, all of whom had been in the Program (Phillips, 1972). This study also showed a very significant difference among siblings, but from a totally different perspective. Fifty-two families having two children in the Program in different years were selected for study. This time the average IQ of 52 two-year-olds just entering the Mother-Child Home Program was compared with the IQ that their older brothers and sisters had achieved earlier, at their own entry into the Program. The average IQ of the older siblings at Program entry proved to have been 87, slightly below low-average. We hypothesized that if the mothers had learned parenting skills helpful to their old children's development, they would probably apply them spontaneously to the younger brothers and sisters. In that case, the younger siblings should *enter* the Program with higher IQs than their older brothers and sisters. This in fact turned out to be so. The average IQ of the younger siblings at Program entry was 95, a difference of eight points from the pretest IQ of their older brothers and sisters. This intellectual superiority of the younger children goes contrary to the findings of most research comparing younger and older siblings, in which the older children are almost invariably superior to the younger ones (Sutton-Smith & Rosenberg, 1970).

That "pretest differential" of eight points was the kind of result one would expect if mothers transfer their Program-learned skills to the baby next in line. The VIP discovery of the pretest differential in the younger children of Program-experienced mothers was not definite proof that this actually does happen, because no Non-Program control groups were used for this comparison (i.e., maybe all the children in that housing project were getting brighter between 1967 and 1969). Still, it was a persuasive sign that the Program truly accomplished a major goal: converting the mother to more effective parenting methods which would carry over to her other children.

Question 2: Was a two-year rather than a one-year Program necessary?

Apparently a second Program year serves for consolidation of the children's gains.

Program children who received fewer than two full years of the Program made good initial gains but, on the average, began to lose them when they reached third grade (Madden, Levenstein, & Levenstein, 1976):

a. The average IQ of children who had received Year One of the Program in 1967 rose from 90 to 106 in one year. However, by third grade, five years after Program entry, the group's IQ was down to 95.

b. The average IQ of children who had received Year One of the Program in 1967, and half of the Year Two toys and books in 1968, rose from 83 to 102. However, by third grade, five years after Program entry, the group was down to an IQ of 96.

c. On the other hand, the average IQ of children who had received Year One of the Program followed by a shortened Year Two (fewer Home Sessions but most of the toys and books) rose from 83 to 104, and it receded only to 100 (mid-average) after five years.

It may be recalled that children who received a full two-year Program maintained their IQ gains so that they stabilized at an IQ of about 100 by fifth grade.

Question 3: Could high school-educated Toy Demonstrators deliver the Program as effectively as the Master-degreed social workers who had been the first Toy Demonstrators?

Yes, by all criteria. With Program training and continuing group and individual supervision, high school educated Toy Demonstrators proved to be as effective (judging by child and mother outcomes), caring, and reliable as the original social workers. Mothers reported their satisfaction with them, and, as for the children, neither their happiness in the Program nor their test scores seemed affected. Most of the Program children whose normal IQ scores at follow-up are contained in Tables 5.1 and 5.3 had had high school educated Toy Demonstrators.

Question 4: Was the Program really as popular with mothers as it seemed?

Yes, all evidence points to genuine enthusiasm. The enjoyment of almost every *child* in the Program was so obvious that it needed no formal measurement. (The VIP produced an informational film, "Learning in Joy," because of the obvious delight of the children it showed playing in Home Sessions.)

The mothers expressed their enthusiasm for the Program by coming into it, by staying with it, and by keeping most of their Home Session appointments. This "voting with their feet" was more impressive than their many spoken and written endorsements:

a. When offered the Program, 85 percent or more in each cohort accepted enrollment in it.

b. Ninety percent of the mothers stayed in the Program for at least one year, and 75 percent stayed in it until the end of Year Two.

c. Eighty-five percent of the Home Session appointments were honored, although sometimes rescheduled by mothers.

The Program's popularity and the mothers' reliability in using it were considerably beyond the usual low cooperation of low-income parents with parent education programs (Chilman, 1973).

Question 5: Did mothers' behavior in Home Sessions predict their children's future performance and behavior in school?

Yes, apparently. The Design I research team tried to pin down what specific kinds of parental behavior toward young children, as observed in Home Sessions, would predict the children's competence and happiness in school years.

Program mothers' verbal interaction behavior (measured by "Parent and Child Together" or "PACT," a VIP-created instrument) was rated in Home Sessions during 1974, when the children were three and a half years old, and then correlated with their children's school skills three years later, when the children were in first grade. Some strong correlations emerged. As can be seen in Table 5.4, when mothers had been verbally responsive to their preschool youngsters, the children showed attitudes and behavior in first grade which have crucial relevance to school success—and to their development as happy human beings:

1. They enjoyed working on new school tasks.

2. They finished their tasks without constant reminders.

3. They were well organized in their school work.

4. They were creative.

5. They seemed to know the difference between the real world and fantasy.

6. They could express ideas in language.

7. They could protect their own rights.

8. They were self-confident but could request help when necessary.

9. They were cheerful and seemed happy.

Table 5.4

Correlations of Mothers' Home Verbal Interaction at Child's Age 4 with Child Competencies in First Grade at Age 6
(Pearson's r, N = 39)

Child Competencies in First Grade at Age 6	Mothers' Verbal Interaction at Child's Age 4			
	Responds verbally to request	Verbalizes expectation of child	Tries to talk with child	Verbalizes reasons to obey
Independence				
Accepts, asks for help	.38*		.38*	
Protects own rights	.33*			
Self-confident	.47*		.49*	
Task Orientation				
Completes tasks			.35*	
Enjoys mastering tasks	.48†		.54†	.36*
Cognitive Orientation				
Well-organized	.39*		.41‡	.35*
Verbalizes ideas	.48†		.48†	
Knows difference between fact & fancy	.61†	.34*	.61†	.52†
Creative, inventive	.40*		.52†	.44†
Emotional Stability				
Cheerful and content	.33*		.39*	.33*
Spontaneous	.42‡		.47†	.34*

*p<.05
†p<.005
‡p<.01

In other 1974 Design I studies (Levenstein & Madden, 1976) mothers' total VIP-created PACT scores for parental behavior observed in Home Sessions correlated significantly with the childrens' IQ scores at the end of the Program. The IQ scores of the children also correlated highly with the childrens' own social-emotional behavior encouraged by mothers in Home Sessions, as measured by the children's scores on the VIP-created "Child's Behavior Traits" or CBT (Levenstein & Staff, 1976).

A supportive mother-child network was made visible in these Design I correlations. Mothers' verbal interaction and other Positive Parenting intertwined with their children's competence at age three and a half years and predicted their first grade classroom skills at age six and a half. According to these data, the network that supported the children's first grade success was already in place by the end of the Mother-Child Home Program's intervention. This was the parent-child network hypothesized to be latent in every family, and built in as the very cornerstone of the Program itself.

Summary of Design I Research Results: The Program, Yes

The Design I research results indicated that Carol's and Jo-Jo's good intellectual and academic progress after they had graduated from the Mother-Child Home Program was not an aberration but a typical Program outcome. The Verbal Interaction Project's location-randomized experiments showed that Program graduates were significantly superior in academic and intellectual attainment, not only to those of Non-Program children with the same underclass background, but to the low levels expected for their socioeconomic status.

The Program elicited commitment from the mothers, and could be carried out effectively by Toy Demonstrators with no more than high school education. This opened up a new kind of job opportunity for women of limited education, including former Program mothers, and thus also the possibility of lowering the cost of Program implementation (salaries take up most of the budget in replications).

Follow-up studies by the Verbal Interaction Project, by the Consortium for Longitudinal Studies, and by Chapter One evaluators for the Pittsfield, Massachusetts schools, all indicated the lasting educational benefits of the Mother-Child Home Program. The three kinds of longitudinal studies demonstrated that Program graduates did indeed escape, into the eighth grade of elementary school, the educational disadvantage that is usually the fate of children from economically disadvantaged families.

Finally, the parenting behavior encouraged by the Program was found to be significantly related to children's preschool and school competence, pointing up the vital presence of the supportive mother-child network hypothesized when the Program began. It seems clear that mothers can have a powerful influence on their children's future school success if they utilize in children's early years the preventive method described in this book.

Group Results, Design II: Subject-Randomized Experiments

Data Puzzles

By June of 1973, encouraging preliminary results of the Design I research were available. However, to assess the Program's affects further, we decided to use another experimental research design, Design II, for gathering data on more mother-child pairs. These new subjects would be those who entered the research as Program or Non-Program subjects from 1973 to 1976.

Design II is thought by many research experts to be a preferred experimental method. This is because in Design II the *subjects* are randomized rather than the locations. Thus every dyad would have an equal chance, by the toss of a coin, to be either in a Program or Non-Program group. However, they would all be required to agree initially to be experimental subjects and to take a chance on being assigned to one of the two groups. Their invitation would have to be, in effect, an invitation to "join a lottery" in which the prize was enrollment in the Program.

This Design II procedure meant that mothers eligible for the cohorts of 1973, 1974, and 1975 were told about the Program but were not invited into it. Instead, they were invited into a 50-50 chance of receiving the Program through random assignment. Their children would receive, in either case, yearly developmental evaluations whose results would be shared with the mothers.

The evaluation outcomes for the 1973, 1974, and 1975 cohorts were puzzling. Table 5.5 ("Design II: Children's Mean IQ Scores and Rates of Mothers' 'Lottery' Acceptance") shows that the IQ scores of both the Program Group and the Non-Program Group rose over the course of two years for those three cohorts. Sometimes the Program Group's scores were superior, sometimes they were not. In any case, the scores for both Program and Non-Program groups were far above those to be expected of children in their low-income circumstances!

Table 5.5
Design II: Children's Mean IQ Scores and Rates of Mothers' "Lottery" Acceptance

Children's Entry Year and Group	N	Entry IQ	Posttest IQ	Rate of Mothers' "Lottery" Acceptance
1973:				68%
Program	18	90.4	102.8	
Non-Program	16	92.4	101.1	
1974:				47%
Program	22	89.6	103.2	
Non-Program	26	93.1	105.3	
1975:				50%
Program	17	—	101.3	
Non-Program	12	—	108.3	
1976:				27%
Program	29	95.9	107.0	
Non-Program	26	95.1	101.0	

At the same time, we observed that an average of only about half (52 percent) of the eligible mothers in these three cohorts had accepted entrance into Design II—that is, had accepted the offer of only the chance to receive the Program. This contrasted sharply with mothers' 85 percent acceptance of the Program itself in Design I.

Foiling the "John Henry Effect"

After consultation with Dr. Donald Campbell, a generally acknowledged expert in the design of social/educational experiments (Campbell & Stanley, 1969), we surmised that the "John Henry Effect" might be confounding our research. John Henry was a mythical American hero famous in folklore for his successful competition with a mechanical steam hammer. His name has been borrowed to describe the observation by researchers that people who don't receive a special treatment often work harder to show that they can do just as well without it (Saretsky, 1972).

Thus, in our own research, Control mothers, interpreting the experiment as a competition, might have been exerting special effort to have their children compare well with Program children on evaluations at the end of the Program.

Consequently, it was decided to enroll the 1976 cohort of mothers differently from other Design II cohorts, while still following the rules for a Design II (subject-randomized) experiment. Early in the summer of 1976 the research staff randomly divided a cohort of 70 low-income mothers into two equal sub-groups. The mothers were those who had taken advantage, for their two-year-olds, of eye-speech-psychological examinations called the "Early Screening Program" run by the Verbal Interaction Project for one of its sponsors (Family Service Association of Nassau County).

The Mother-Child Home Program then invited the 35 mothers in one of the two sub-groups to enroll in the Program, letting the toss of an imaginary penny decide which sub-group that would be. The invited sub-group thus became the Program Group for the 1976 cohort. The difference from previous Design

II randomizations (for the 1973, 1974, and 1975 cohorts) was that the Program mothers were not informed about the controlled study, while the control (Non-Program) mothers were not aware of the existence of the Program.

All of the 1976 mothers who were asked to join the Program did so. However, three families moved out of the Program's service area before the Program started.

The second sub-group of mothers was not invited into the Program and did not know of its existence. Since the Early Screening tests were conducted by the Verbal Interaction Project, and the evaluations of children in both Program and Non-Program sub-groups continued for six years into second grade, the conditions seemed perfect for a long-term Design II experiment. Over a six-year period of time it would be possible to compare Program children and their mothers with their randomly chosen counterparts who had never been in the Program nor had been told about it.

Loopholes

It seemed to be a great idea for conducting a subject-randomized experiment. As is usual with experiments carried on in a real-world, and thus unpredictable, field setting, and like the VIP's other Design II experiments, the idea's execution proved very difficult in practice.

Nevertheless, the VIP researchers and Program staff paid careful attention to the smallest details, to prevent mistakes from ruining the experiment. All had to be exactly as outlined in the research plan for the results to be valid.

After randomization, the Program and Non-Program dyads were almost interchangeable with each other regarding features characteristic of low-income families throughout the country:

- No parent at home had more than a high school education or semi-skilled occupation.
- Eighty-four percent of the families were female-headed and receiving welfare assistance.
- The families were eligible for low-income public housing.

All loopholes in the Design II, anti–John Henry Effect experiment seemed to have been closed.

Nevertheless, one loophole was left. We had too briefly considered, and too quickly discarded, the possibility that the mothers who had entered their children in the Early Screening Program were not truly representative of the whole low-income group. With hindsight, it now seems obvious that for mothers to reach out to the Early Screening Program at all was an unusual act of energy and daring for low-income mothers, especially those who could be identified as members of the underclass.

Certainly, the initiative it took to arrange to be in the Early Screening Program was not typical of Hesitaters. It was the kind of opportunity that attracted Strivers, however. Strivers were able to muster the will to fill out a simple form given by their welfare workers and mail it, in order to enroll their children in the Early Screening Program. It was probably mainly Strivers who actually did so, and thus a self-selected group of mothers. In support of this guess, we noted that out of four hundred who received invitations to enroll in the Early Screening Program, only 25 percent of the welfare mothers responded.

This extremely high percentage (75 percent) of nonenrollment for the Early Screening Program seemed unimportant at the time it occurred, just as the high nonenrollment rate (an average of 48 percent) had seemed in the previous Design II experiments. Also, the outward characteristics of both Program and Non-Program 1976 families were like those of most low-income families.

The VIP researchers had not been aware that another characteristic might be equally important to consider in recruiting a cohort truly representative of the intended population. That characteristic was *motivation*.

Strivers and Hesitaters in Design I and Design II Experiments

The VIP researchers had not considered the possibility of highly motivated Strivers predominating in the 1976 cohort.

Shortly after the 32, 1976 Program dyads started their Home

Sessions in Year One of the Program, the mothers' interaction ratings in Home Sessions were noted to be particularly high, a characteristic whose full significance was not immediately grasped. The ratings were used for purposes of supervision by the Toy Demonstrators to communicate the mothers' progress to the Coordinator, and were not considered pertinent research data. The trait revealed by the ratings was the apparent interest of the 1976 Program mothers in quickly learning the Toy Demonstrator's techniques and in starting to use them immediately, just as Mrs. Carter did. By Home Session Two, 23 out of 32 mothers (72 percent) were rated as interacting more than half of the time, which with a certain amount of hindsight seemed a exceptionally high percentage.

Was such Striver-type behavior also a usual feature in Design I Program mothers? To what degree was such Striver-type behavior common among Program mothers in Design I?

To begin to answer this question, it was necessary to locate Design I case records, which were more than ten years old and had been through a major office move. Fortunately, it was possible to find the case records of almost all of the dyads in the 1969 cohort, the first in which interactive ratings were a feature of Home Session records. Luckily, also, staff anecdotal records endured which made it clear that the 1969 mothers were typical of Design I mothers.

The Home-Session, maternal interaction ratings of the 1969 Program mothers were reviewed. This scrutiny revealed that only nine of the twenty-four 1969 Program mothers achieved "high" (greater than 46 percent) interaction ratings by Home Session Two. Thus 37 percent of the 1969 Program mothers resembled their 1976 counterparts in their Striver-like behavior. They were, it appeared, bona fide Strivers.

However, the remaining fifteen—63 percent—of the 1969 Program mothers showed very little interaction with their children until well into Year One or even into Year Two.

The "very interactive" behavior with their children of most 1976 mothers and of some 1969 mothers by Home Session Two was like Mrs. Carter's Home Session behavior with Jo-Jo. In short, these mothers identified themselves as Strivers by their marked positive interactions with their children by Session

Two. And like Mrs. Carter, 21 of the 23 Striver-mothers in the 1976 cohort made it obvious by the end of Year One that they no longer needed the Toy Demonstrators to model the Program curriculum. Therefore, their Home Sessions were eliminated in Year Two. They received only the toys, books and Guide Sheets in the second year of the Program.

On the other hand, 28 percent of the 1976 Program mothers, and 63 percent of the 1969 mothers clearly indicated in their Home Sessions that they were Hesitaters. Like Mrs. Willard, they interacted very little with their children in early Home Sessions and throughout most of Year One of the Program. The quality of their interaction was also limited. They wanted, and received, Home Sessions in Year Two.

The high proportion of Strivers as compared to Hesitaters among the 1976 Design II mothers reversed the relative numbers of Strivers and Hesitaters found among the 1969 Design I mothers. Table 5.6 ("Striver and Hesitater Program Mothers in Design I [1969 Program] and Design II [1976 Program]") shows this reversal. The table presents statistical evidence that the reversal was real: there was a significantly greater proportion of Hesitater-mothers in the 1969 group than in the 1976 group.

Table 5.6
Striver and Hesitater Program Mothers
in Design I (1969 Program) and Design II (1976 Program)

Research Design	Striver Mothers	Hesitater Mothers	Totals
Design I (1969 Program)	9	15	24
Design II (1976 Program)	23	9	32
Totals	32	24	56

X^2 significant, $p < .05$

The 1969 Design I mothers' low amount of self-selection in joining the research project, by readily coming into the *Program* to begin with, seemed to have yielded a high proportion of 1969 Hesitater Program mothers. On the other hand, it appears that the high self-selection of the 1976 mothers as *research* subjects resulted in the predominance of Strivers in the 1976 Program Group.

Further, because of the 1976 mothers' initial randomization by subject (the Design II requirement which virtually equalized the characteristics of Program and Non-Program groups) Strivers would probably predominate among the Non-Program mothers as well. Yet how could this be investigated without observing the Non-Program mothers in Home Sessions, which were, by definition, nonexistent?

High School Graduation: Hallmark of Strivers

The proportions of Strivers and Hesitaters among the Design II (1976) and Design I (1969) Program mothers were paralleled by the mothers' educational attainments. Strivers were far more likely than Hesitaters to have actually graduated from high school rather than to have dropped out as soon their school attendance was no longer compulsory (age 16 in New York State).

Of the 23 Strivers among the 1976 Program mothers, 18 had completed high school. Only three of the 1976 Program Hesitaters had done so. That this was a statistically significant difference between the Strivers and the Hesitaters is shown in Table 5.7 ("Design II: High School Graduation of Strivers and Hesitaters Among 1976 Program Mothers"). There was a less than two percent probability that this distinction between Strivers and Hesitaters would have occurred by chance.

Table 5.7

Design II: High School Graduation of Strivers and Hesitaters Among 1976 Program Mothers

High School Graduation	Striver Mothers	Hesitater Mothers	Totals
High School Graduation	18	3	21
No High School Graduation	5	6	11
Totals	23	9	32

X^2 significant, $p < .02$

High School graduation distinguished even more sharply the Striver from the Hesitater mothers in the 1969 Program Group. Table 5.8 ("Design I: High School Graduation of Strivers and Hesitaters Among 1969 Program Mothers") shows the numbers of high school graduates among Strivers and Hesitater mothers in the 1969 Program Group. Seven of the nine Strivers had graduated from high school, but only three of the 15 Hesitaters had done so. As indicated in Table 5.8, there is a statistical probability of less than one percent that this was only a chance difference between the Striver and Hesitater Program mothers.

Table 5.8
Design I: High School Graduation of Strivers and Hesitaters Among 1969 Program Mothers

High School Graduation	Striver Mothers	Hesitater Mothers	Totals
High School Graduation	7	3	10
No High School Graduation	2	12	14
Totals	9	15	24

X^2 significant, $p<.01$

1976 Non-Program Mothers: Strivers the Majority

The 1976 Non-Program mothers had been chosen when the "subject pool" (that is, the Early Screening Program mothers) had been randomly divided in half. Any mother had an equal chance of being assigned either to the Program or to the Non-Program Group. Because of the randomization, the two groups of mothers should have been almost identical with each other on the low-income criteria which made them eligible for the subject pool in the first place. This turned out to be so: no parent had an occupation higher than semi-skilled or an education higher than high school; and both parents were eligible for low-income housing. The average school grade level for the Program mothers was 11.2. The average grade level for Non-Program mothers was 11.3

However, were the two groups of mothers also equal in motivation—in other words, in their proportions of Hesitaters and Strivers? The question was answered for the Program group through Home Session observations. But it could not be answered in that way for the Non-Program Group, which had no Home Sessions.

Nonetheless, the significant link between Striver status and a mother's graduation from high school made it possible to estimate rather accurately the proportions of Strivers and Hesitaters within the 1976 Non-Program Group of mothers. Of the 33 mothers randomized into the Non-Program Group and remaining for two years, 23 (70 percent) were high school graduates, and 10 (30 percent) were not.

The proportion of high school graduates in the Non-Program Group of mothers was even higher than the proportion of high school graduates in the Program Group.

Therefore, there was a strong probability that the 1976 Non-Program Group of mothers at least equaled, and very likely surpassed, the Program Group in its high proportion of Strivers as compared to Hesitaters. Strivers could be said, with considerable assurance, to be in the majority within the Non-Program Group of mothers.

Children's Outcomes in Design II Research
1976 COHORT

We have seen that a large majority of the 1976 mothers, both Program and Non-Program, were Strivers. It is not surprising that they reached out for the Early Screening Program and consequently became involved in the Program's research. They were similar to most volunteer research subjects (described in an exhaustive 1975 review by Harvard psychologists Rosenthal and Rosnow) in their high motivation, in their drive to help their children and in their expectation of their children's doing well on evaluations. In spite of their low-income status, they did not quite exemplify the mothers for whom the Mother-Child Home Program was created.

In fact, whether they and their children actually needed the Mother-Child Home Program is questionable. The Program help of most use to them, in preparing their children for school, were the toys and books, and the addition of Program techniques to their own. Yet regardless of whether they received even those elements of the Program, the likelihood was that their children would do well intellectually and in school. The preponderance of Strivers among the 1976 mothers, therefore, would have weighted their children's scores toward the high end of the IQ continuum, even if their children had not been in the Program.

This surmise was supported by the longitudinal IQ results for the 1976 children in both Program and Non-Program groups, as summarized in Table 5.9 ("Design II: 1976 Children's Mean IQ and Academic Scores at Entry [Age 2], at Program's End [Age 4], and at End of Second Grade [Age 8]"). By the end of the Program, the IQs for both groups were (like those of Carol and Jo-Jo) at or above mid-average: Program Group IQ, 107; Non-Program Group IQ, 101.

Table 5.9

Design II: 1976 Children's Mean IQ and Academic Scores at Entry (Age 2), at Program's End (Age 4), and at End of Second Grade (Age 8)

Design II 1976 Group	Entry IQ	Post-Program IQ	Scores at End of Second Grade		
			WISC IQ	WRAT Reading	WRAT Arithmetic
Program Children	95.9	107.0	100.9	102.5	105.3
	N = 29	N = 29	N = 21	N = 21	N = 21
Non-Program Children	95.1	101.0	101.7	104.5	104.1
	N = 26	N = 26	N = 19	N = 19	N = 19

The Program Group's IQ superiority was statistically significant; but the Non-Program Group's IQ was mid-average, predicting normal school progress! Sure enough, the Non-Program children demonstrated normal school progress when they reached school—as did the Program graduates.

When all of the 1976 children (the majority from Striver families) were re-evaluated in subsequent follow-ups into second grade, the Program graduates' statistical superiority washed out. The Program graduates lost a few IQ points, and the Non-Program children gained a few. By second grade, both had settled into an IQ of about 100. Both IQs were not only mid-average by national norms but many IQ points above those to be expected for children at their low-income level.

As a matter of fact, both groups of children from the 1976 "Striver" cohort, whether or not they had been in the Mother-Child Home Program as little children, were by second grade quite similar in school achievement to their more economically advantaged classmates. Neither of the two 1976 groups of children could be called educationally disadvantaged, although they were economically disadvantaged (Madden, O'Hara, & Levenstein, 1984).

1973, 1974, AND 1975 COHORTS

Similar short-term IQ results had emerged, immediately after the two-year Program, from the evaluations of the children in the other three Design II cohorts. As can be seen in Table 5.5, whatever the rate of acceptance by mothers for being volunteer experimental subjects, the IQ outcomes for both Program and Non-Program children met national norms.

The 1974 cohort demonstrated a low acceptance rate among the mothers—48 percent—and yielded high IQs for both Program and Non-Program children: 103.2 for the Program children, and 105.3 for the Non-Program children. However, the 1974 "Non-Program" children had actually received a watered down version of the Program: all the Program toys and books on the same schedule as the Program children and for the same two years. The 1974 "Non-Program" children's high IQ outcomes indicate the benefits of giving the Program curriculum materials (toys and books), without the Home Sessions, to the children of Striver-mothers.

As another difference among Design II cohorts, the 1973 mothers were referred by public health nurses and social workers whose names were then used as an introduction by VIP staff. This probably accounted for the 1973 mothers' somewhat higher rate of acceptance (63 percent) than that of other cohorts.

These differences among the Design II cohorts' recruitment or treatment inevitably cloud the interpretation of the results. Nonetheless, the low acceptance of subject status in all three cohorts contrasts sharply with the almost unanimous acceptance of particular treatments in the Design I cohorts. The low acceptance rates indicate that mothers who accepted membership in the subject pool were highly self-selected. They were thus likely to have the self-starter qualities that characterize human research volunteers (as shown by Rosenthal and Rosnow) as well as identify Striver-mothers in our own research.

A Footnote on Effects of "Striver-Bias" in Human Research

As part of their monumental review of "volunteerism"-caused sample bias, the psychologists Rosenthal and Rosnow (1975) grouped studies according to the characteristics of volunteer subjects. Some of their main conclusions were that volunteers for human research, as opposed to nonvolunteers, tend to be better educated, better motivated, more intellectually alert, and more willing to risk the unusual. Also, they are more likely to expect to be favorably evaluated than nonvolunteers.

Parents who volunteer themselves and/or their young children as subjects for research are just as likely as any other volunteers to have these characteristics. This seemed to be so in the Verbal Interaction Project's Design II, subject-randomized, research. The low acceptance rate for participation in the research (52 percent overall) virtually assured that the self-selected volunteers would turn out to be mainly Strivers. (The Design I mothers agreed to participate in *programs,* not in a subject pool for experimental research. Their very high acceptance rate of 85 percent indicates mothers' far greater willingness to accept being in a program rather than to accept subject-status.)

The self-selection by Striver-mothers for the Design II experiments yielded results possibly illuminating for research methodologists but not for Program effects. That kind of self-selection can create especially far reaching problems when it interferes with standardizing the very tests upon which researchers rely to find out "how high is up."

A dramatic though little known example of volunteer effects on the norms (score standards) of a famous IQ test occurred in the 1972 renorming of the Stanford-Binet Intelligence Scale. The two- to five-year-old preschoolers tested for this updating of the Binet standards (either brought to the testing center by their parents or in private nursery schools) produced a much higher average IQ than the school-age children who were also tested in public school as part of the school day for the same norming. For example, the average 1972 IQ of the school children at age nine was 102 by the previous 1963 norms. The preschoolers' average IQ by those norms was 110!

In the world of testers and researchers, this difference of eight points is not a trivial amount. The average IQ of the preschoolers should have been about the same as that of the school children. Further, the difference was no accident peculiar to preschool years. According to a retest three years later, most of the discrepancy persisted into the preschoolers' school years.

The author of an article which appeared in the *Journal of Educational Measurements* suggested an explanation for the preschoolers' IQ superiority:

> There may be a tendency for parents of young children not in school to be less willing to permit a child to be tested if the child has not appeared to be an advanced or competent youngster, and for this reason there may be a tendency to get somewhat upgraded samples of preschool children. No clear evidence of this is available, but we do have some impression that in the initial sampling there was more loss of very young children from the designed sample than was the case of children of school age (Thorndike, 1977, p. 201).

In other words, parents proud of their children may have been more willing than others to allow their children to be tested, or to bring them to the testing center (cf. Rosenthal & Rosnow, 1975). The author of the article quoted above was in a good position to speculate about this, since he had directed the 1972 norming himself. He then noted that about half of the cross-sectional IQ decrement disappeared in retesting three years later. He added that one other possible explanation for the continuing decrement was that the younger children watched educational television "not available to their elder brothers and sisters" (Thorndike, 1977, p. 201). Although research has not otherwise shown the influence of TV programs on IQ, the theory should not be disregarded as a possibility.

However, in much research of programs for preschool children, the Stanford-Binet Intelligence Scale is a major measuring tool. If the norms are actually "super-norms," based (because of mothers' self-selection) on the scores of children brighter than most preschoolers, young children's preschool Stanford-Binet IQs may seem to be low when they are really close to normal. (Throughout its research of the Mother-Child Home Program the Verbal Interaction Project used the 1963 Binet norms, the most recent available when the research started.)

The problems of self-selection leading to sample bias in a relatively straightforward procedure like test norming are multiplied when parents choose to involve or not to involve themselves and their children in longitudinal research to study the effects of a pre-preschool program.

Videotaped Interactive Behavior of 1976 Program Mothers

The Home Session interactive behavior of the 1976 mothers was convincing evidence that most of them were Strivers with little need for the Mother-Child Home Program. Did this mean, though, that they derived no benefit from the Program? Was their demonstration of interactive behavior by Home Session Two simply the emergence of their previous usual conversational habits with their children? Or did the 1976 mothers instead learn quickly, remember, and continue to practice the Program's verbal interaction techniques?

To answer this question, it was necessary to find some way of comparing Program with Non-Program mothers in their habitual ways of talking with their children. We could not compare Home Session behavior because Non-Program mothers, of course, had no Home Sessions. We solved the dilemma by videotaping individual mothers from both groups in play with their children at the VIP office. The procedure will be described in some detail since it was different from the standardized testing which was otherwise used to measure Program effects.

VIDEOTAPING PROCEDURE

The videotaping was planned to give both groups exactly the same experience in a situation which was equally strange to all the mothers and children.

Each Program and Non-Program mother was requested, as part of the arrangements for post-Program testing, to allow us to videotape her and her child playing with some toys, as well as being offered the opportunity to view the film later herself. Most agreed.

The person (a staff member unfamiliar to both Program and Non-Program mothers) who drove the mothers and children to the after-Program evaluations showed them to the "video playroom." It was actually a stripped-down office furnished mainly with a child's table and two chairs for mother and child. Two attractive toys expected to be new to all of the dyads were arranged on the table, and a video camera was on a tripod in one corner. A cable connected it with a video recorder and monitor screen in the next room.

The two toys were prearranged on the table in the same way for each mother-child pair: 1) two cars and a locomotive that could be linked by hook-eye connections to form a stylized, colorful freight train; and 2) an unassembled form board puzzle with multicolored niches, surrounded by the eight forms, of differing shapes (circle, square, oblong, triangle) and of contrasting colors, which were designed to fit into the niches.

The driver explained: "This is the play room and toys we talked about. Here's a chair for (Child) and one for you. (Child) may play with the toys after I leave you and, of course, you may help in any way you like. That video camera will take the pictures. I'll turn it on just before I leave you and (Child), and I'll turn it off when I come back. I'll be back in ten minutes." She answered the mother's questions, if any, by saying pleasantly, "That's up to you."

The car driver then turned on the cameras and left, shutting the door behind her. After ten minutes, she retuned to shut off the camera and to escort the mother and child to the next testing station.

Some time later the videotape was viewed and scored by a trained rater who did not know whether or not the mother and child on the videotape had been in the Program. She watched the tape four times in order to be able to count the exact number of times a mother showed ten kinds of interactive behaviors that had been selected as likely to be shown during a ten-minute play session. Nine were types of interactions encouraged by the Program (Items 1–9) and one was discouraged by the Program (Item 10).

Item 1. Gives label information: "This is a circle."

Item 2. Gives color information: "Blue circle."

Item 3. Verbalizes actions: "We make the train go."

Item 4. Gives number or shape information: "Four wheels."

Item 5. Solicits information, not "yes" or "no": "What is this shape?"

Item 6. Vocalizes praise: "Good!" "Uh-huh!"

Item 7. Stimulates divergence, fantasy: "Roll the round puzzle piece."

Item 8. Smiles or other positive gesture: Hugs or pats child.

Item 9. Replies to child's vocalization within three seconds.

Item 10. No reply to child's vocalization within three seconds.

The Rater tallied the count for each item on a VIP-created instrument called "Maternal Interactive Behavior" or "MIB." The MIB contained the ten interactive behavior items and space to record how often they occurred. The total count for all the MIB items except for Item 10 became the "Total Positive Score." The score for Item 10 was subtracted from that score to get the final "Total MIB Score." The Total Positive Score and the Total MIB Score for the 1976 mothers are reported in the last two rows of Table 5.10 ("Design II: MIB Scores of 1976 Program and Non-Program Mothers in 1980 Follow-up Study").

MIB RESULTS

The MIB scores returned an emphatic "Yes!" to the question of whether Program mothers had learned, practiced and remembered the Program's verbal interaction techniques. In the 1978 after-Program rating of all 1976 mothers in videotaped play with their children, the Program mothers scored very significantly above Non-Program mothers in their interactive behavior with their children, an average of 50 percent higher. Moreover, as can be seen in Table 5.10, the Program mothers maintained their superiority when videotaped again in play with their children in 1980 when the youngsters were five-and-a-half years old and in kindergarten.

Table 5.10
Design II: MIB[a] Scores of 1976 Program and Non-Program Mothers in 1980 Follow-up Study

MIB Item	Program Group N = 19	Non-Program Group N = 18	Difference
1. Gives labels	36.90	14.78	22.12[†]
2. Gives colors	13.53	4.72	8.81[*]
3. Describes actions	88.47	58.83	29.64[*]
4. Gives numbers, shapes	12.74	5.22	7.52[*]
5. Asks information	21.63	9.50	12.13[*]
6. Praises child	7.00	3.28	2.32
7. Aids divergence	9.37	3.83	5.54
8. Smiles at child	2.74	2.56	0.18
9. Replies to child	48.74	32.11	16.63[*]
10. No reply to child	12.32	17.89	5.57[*]
Total Positive Score[b]	241.11	134.83	106.28[†]
Total MIB Score[c]	228.79	116.94	111.85[†]

[a]Maternal Interactive Behavior
[b]Sum of Items 1 to 9
[c]Sum of Items 1 to 9, minus score for Item 10.
[*]$p<.05$
[†]$p<.01$

The Program mothers had learned from their Home Sessions, and had retained at least through their children's kindergarten year, the specific, Program-related interactive behavior which they showed before the video camera. The Non-Program mothers had had no opportunity to learn these specific techniques and therefore could not demonstrate them in the MIB situation.

RELATION OF MOTHERS' MIB SCORES TO CHILDREN'S SCHOOL-AGE COMPETENCE

In spite of the differing proportions of Strivers and Hesitaters among the mothers in the Design I and the Design II research, there were some dramatic similarities between Design I and Design II mothers. These similarities were in the influence that their interactive behavior had on their children's school-age competence.

As with the influence of the Design I 1972 mothers' verbal interactive behavior in preschool years on their children's first grade competence, the Design II 1976 mothers' verbal responsiveness on the MIB correlated significantly with their children's kindergarten and second grade competence. Specifically, MIB Item 9 ("Replies to child's vocalization") correlated with the children's:

- intellectual ability;
- reading ability;
- social-emotional competence;
- social responsibility;
- self-confidence.

Moreover, the mothers' warmth toward their children as expressed in MIB Item 8 ("Smiles or makes other positive gesture") also correlated significantly with the children's:

- intellectual ability;
- reading ability;
- social-emotional competence;
- social responsibility;
- self-confidence.

On the other hand, the data analysis of the MIB scores indicated that mothers' bombardment of their children with a relentless barrage of information was dysfunctional for the children. The correlations between such MIB items as "Gives label information," "Gives color information," and children's school age competence were usually negative.

Thus the Design II "MIB versus child competence" not only revealed in a different way and with different subjects the suportive network built by mothers' verbal responsiveness. It also issued a sharp warning that the early childhood learning that plays its part in weaving the supportive parent-child network can function best in a family climate of nondidactic spontaneity and joy.

Downward Extension of the Mother-Child Home Program to Age One

In an attempt to test whether the Mother-Child Home Program might be especially effective if it were extended downward to begin at one year of age, the 1977 cohort of mothers was enrolled for Design II research of the Program's Downward Extension.

Fifty mothers of children between 10 and 14 months old agreed to be research subjects to explore this variation. All met the low-income criteria of being at or below high school graduation and having a semi-skilled or lower occupation. The proportion of those who accepted the invitation to become research subjects to those who were invited was 68 percent, much higher than acceptance rates in the other Design II cohorts—probably because the mothers were assured that all 50 would eventually receive the Program.

The fifty mothers were randomly assigned either to receiving a Program variation suitable for babies immediately ("Program A"); or to receiving the standard Program a year later when the child would be about two ("Delayed Treatment Group"). The two groups would then be compared on child and mother outcomes at various evaluation points.

Unfortunately, both groups turned out to be unusually mobile geographically. By the end of the two Programs, in fact, almost half of the subject families had moved away from the area, leaving too few dyads for reliable evaluation (O'Hara & Levenstein, 1979).

Still, Program staff members made two general observations which may be useful to anyone contemplating similar infant programs. One was that Program A was welcomed as warmly by mothers as the Program for two-year-olds had always been. The other observation was that Program A delivery was difficult both in planning and execution because Home Sessions were so frequently disrupted by the babies' physical needs (napping, feeding, diapering). These reasons, as well as the lack of reliable outcome data, prevent the Verbal Interaction Project from advocating application of the Mother-Child Home Program to children under the age of two years.

A Design II Study of a Program Replication's Short-Term Effects: Hamilton, Bermuda

Scarr & McCartney, reporting (1987) on their Design II study of the Program's short-term effects on Bermudian mothers and their children, ages two to four years, arrived independently at a conclusion like the VIP's in regard to the Program's lack of effect on children not at risk for educational disadvantage. They described their sample as "not on average socioeconomically disadvantaged" (p. 20) and commented: "Children in Bermuda were not found, as a group, to be at educational risk" (p. 21). This was apparent in their own sample of Bermudian children. The pretest Stanford-Binet IQs of the two-year-olds in both Program and Non-Program groups were normal and almost identical (99.8 and 99.3).

Almost all of the mothers accepted the initial "lottery" condition and stayed in the study until the end of the Program, whether assigned to Program or Non-Program treatment. (Since the sample's educational and occupational data are described only generally in the report and with few other demographic or sociocultural details furnished, no explanation can be ventured for the marked differences from New York mothers' low acceptance of the VIP's Design II "lottery" offers.)

The children's post-Program IQs were numerically higher for the Program group (106.6) than for the Non-Program group (103.1), but the difference was not statistically significant. Both IQs were slightly above mid-average and augured well for the children's future school progress. The authors' conclusion (p. 20) was that "the program is not effective in a group of children with 2-year-old IQ scores that averaged 100," i.e. does not predict school disadvantage.

Summary of Design II Research: Sample Bias Masks Effects

Design II research outcomes in the VIP samples were equivocal. Instead of producing definitive evidence for or against the effectiveness of the Program in preventing the educational disadvantage of low-income children, as intended, the Design II research unexpectedly yielded information of a different sort, valuable especially to research methodologists.

Selection bias in the samples of VIP mothers who volunteered for the subject-randomized research casts doubt on the appropriateness of Design II experimental research methods for the evaluation of the Mother-Child Home Program or for any similar intervention. The low acceptance rate for the "lottery" condition inherent in such research reflected strong self-selection by the mothers resulting in a Striver predominance in the sample. Trying to control for the "John Henry Effect" in the 1976 Design II cohort only intensified the problem. The low overall participation acceptance rate in Design II contrasted dramatically with the high acceptance rate in Design I, in which Hesitaters were in the majority. The 1976 cohort represented Design II experimental research at its most rigorous.

The 1976 Design II mothers had seemed by their average low educational and occupational levels to represent the Program's target population. Yet the high rates of 1976 Program mothers' Home Session activity and the unusually high proportion who had graduated from high school identified the majority in the 1976 Design II cohort as Strivers, in contrast to the majority of Hesitaters in Design I. As might be expected, the 1976 control children's normal academic achievement and school-age IQs were like those of the Program graduates in both Design I and Design II. It suggested that neither the Program Group nor the Non-Program Group in the 1976 Design II cohort had really needed a preventive intervention Program.

It was a striking consequence of the motivational heterogeneity of the underclass, made up as it is of both Strivers and Hesitaters. The Program for the 1976 dyads in Design II had reached mainly Striver-mothers rather than the Hesitater-mothers who were the Program's intended population and who had demonstrated marked Program effects in Design I.

However, like the Design I findings, the Design II data identified a mother-child network supportive of the child's development. Design II mothers' verbal responsiveness was discovered, as in Design I, to be positively related to important aspects of their children's school-age competence. Further, mothers' nonverbal warmth toward their children was also linked to that competence. But mothers who bombarded their children with didactic information had a negative effect. This underlines the importance of the preschool child's learning in joy if that learning is to have a favorable effect on later academic achievement.

Mental Health Gains of Program Mothers

There was another important similarity between the Program Hesitaters in Design I (the 1969 mothers) and the Program Strivers in Design II (the 1976 mothers). By the end of Program Year Two, almost all of the 1969 Program Hesitater-mothers (thirteen out of fifteen) and more than half of the 1976 Program Hesitater-mothers (five out of nine) had become Strivers in their Home Session behavior.

Eyewitness stories by Coordinators both in the model Program and in Program replications suggested that this transformation carried over into other areas. The Hesitaters' increased interaction in Home Sessions was the weather vane for a quiet change in the mothers' mental health. Thumbnail sketches like the following two are typical of a flood of observations by Coordinators about Hesitater-mothers:

The mother of two young children expressed, at her entry into the Program, a feeling of hopelessness and inability to cope with the behavior of her two young children. They refused to wear any clothing, and feces were in evidence on the apartment floor. Social work reports were that the mother had grown increasingly withdrawn, depressed, and passive. For example, she did not complain to her landlord when, as frequently happened, there was no heat in winter.

By the end of the Program, the children were clothed, the apartment was cleaned up, and the mother had informed the landlord that she would withhold rent payments until services and heat were provided.

*   *   *   *

A 17-year-old unwed mother who lived with her own mother was on the verge of dropping out of high school when she entered the Program with her two-year-old. In Home Sessions she tended to be passive and to let her own mother carry on the interaction with the child. But the Toy Demonstrator directed all of her modeling techniques to the mother.

At the end of the Program, the mother informed the Toy Demonstrator, "You've taught me that I have so much to give to Joe that I want to learn more. I'm going to graduate and go on to junior college!"

*   *   *   *

These anecdotes, and many more like them, cannot easily be turned into hard or quantitative data, so they must be regarded as "soft," qualitative data. However, the profusion and consistency of similar observations from the model Program and from replications indicate that the Program effected a highly visible improvement in the mental health of Hesitater-mothers.

The Program's mental health benefits to Strivers were less dramatic but surprisingly evident. Just as Mrs. Carter apparently moved from mild depression to college enrollment by the end of the Program, other Striver mothers utilized their Program experience in a positive direction. Some excerpts from actual interview notes recorded by Coordinators highlight what was sometimes a subtle process:

Nicole and her mother were observed playing and talking together around the toys and books. . . . This young mother gave some evidence of using her Program techniques with her older children as well.

* * * *

Heather's mother says she find the Guide Sheets helpful in aiding her to organize play sessions not only with our toys and books but with Heather's other toys as well.

* * * *

Ms. B is an 11th grade student at Cleveland High School, seems determined, and has some practical goals for herself as well as her child. Also, Elissa's physical activity is now seen as meaningful rather than just misbehavior.

* * * *

Mrs. H. speaks very quietly but the depressed tone was no longer evident as it had been in her initial interview. She feels that her four year old son is getting something out of it, too, so she arranges for him to sit in on sessions.

* * * *

Since I had recruited the D. family initially, it was great to see Raphael now in relation to how I saw him three months ago. He is calmer and his physical aggression is channeled more constructively. Mother talks about 'do's' more than 'don'ts.'

* * * *

Mrs. J. reiterated her happiness with the Program. She is very 'school and learning' oriented. She did talk about the fun they had with the dishes and telephones. She said she has been able to relax more since the beginning of the Program and see the fun side of the Program, with the help of the Toy Demonstrator.

* * * *

I visited Mrs. L. and Tina for Mid-Year Evaluation in their home. We had a 'Royal Tour' of the new apartment, which she had mobilized herself to find after first Program year. It is spacious and uncluttered. Mrs. L. pointed out everything. Mrs. L. is so invested in her home. So much effort and energy has been put into it, and it means many things to her re her place in society. It reflects the order she so needs.

*   *   *   *

It is clear that both Hesitaters and Strivers gained personally from the Program, in ways sometimes intangible, sometimes concrete and practical. Participant mothers, variously, used the Program imaginatively, increased their child rearing skills, were better able to cope with everyday problems, had less tension and depression, were more inclined to take charge of their lives and shared a common tendency to display a greater sense of their own worth.

In the main, the changes come under the heading of the improved mental health which was a major goal of the Mother-Child Home Program.

Note: The Verbal Interaction Project's raw research data are still stored, exactly as originally formatted, at the offices of The Verbal Interaction Project, Inc., Wantagh, New York, in approximately 800 individual folders, one for every child who has ever been included in the VIP's research of the model Mother-Child Home Program.

6

From Laboratory to Real World

Haste Maketh Waste—and Sometimes Tragedy

Even sophisticated observers may think that the essential tasks for producing a new social program occur during its development: the creation and refinement of an idea; the carrying out of a model program; and research of the model's effectiveness. Once these steps have been accomplished, the program developer simply hands over the program to its new administrators in the "real world," and moves on to other projects—or at least so it seems.

Alas, it's not so simple. What was successful in the research setting may turn out to be a failure in the real world. Model programs are usually meticulously organized and implemented; their staff members are highly skilled and/or closely supervised; their physical settings are close to ideal; and funding is adequate to maintain those standards. If model program standards are not maintained away from the research setting, and the social program, so carefully developed in the laboratory, is diluted in its "real world" replications, the glowing preliminary results will be socially meaningless.

Two contemporary examples of such diluted application have recently been brought to public attention by the mass media. One of them creates a predicament for working mothers, especially for the 52 percent with children under six (Sidel, 1986). It is the failure of daycare centers to live up to the standards set by model daycare programs that had been carefuly researched and found to have good effects on children. The media have focused on horrifying disclosures of sexual child abuse at a miniscule number of daycare facilities. These sad discoveries have tended to obscure the more general—and serious—problem among the daycare centers. This is that many, perhaps most, are of poor quality, thus threatening the psychological and even physical health of the children.

Daycare centers' excellence, however, must be limited as long as they follow neither federal nor consistent state standards (Young & Zigler, 1986) and are staffed, as they often are, by a bare minimum number of teachers and aides who are, furthermore, paid at or slightly above minimum wage. Daycare services must be, after all, "labor intensive." Their quality depends on the number and skills of the staff members. If the latter are few and poorly paid, model daycare standards cannot be followed. Yet, excellent daycare centers are an acute social need.

The other example is embedded in the now acute social problem of the urban homeless. At least 40 percent of them (Lamb & Talbott, 1986) are handicapped by such severe mental illness that they should have intensive services or even hospitalization. Instead, they drift from shelter to shelter and sometimes cannot be persuaded to enter any at all, especially public shelters, which are often inadequate, sometimes unsafe, and not always even available. The severely mentally ill are prominent among the bag-ladies and derelicts of our cities. Their presence on the streets is the tragic though unanticipated consequence of a social program applied too soon, without enough trial of its implementation in the real world.

This program consisted of the release from mental hospitals of seriously disturbed patients who had been rendered harmless by "wonder drugs," the tranquillizers which began to be generally used in the fifties and sixties. The move was supported for humane and mental health reasons by hospital staffs, on the assumption that ample community supports would be permanently provided for the released patients through "Community Mental Health Centers," supervised group homes and the like. Congress passed federal legislation in the mid-sixties to support some of these backups but made no provision for long-term funding.

By 1980, three specialists, in a book about the de-institutionalization experience of Worcester State Hospital, were noting bluntly: "The rapid depopulation of state hospitals was undertaken without careful planning with community agencies to develop the support services needed for the maintenance of large numbers of disabled patients outside of institutional settings" (Morrissey, Goldman, & Klerman, 1980, p. 5).

There had been no prolonged trial period nor follow-up study of what would happen to the released patients if—or when—federal funds for local care dried up, which was precisely what occurred after the first few years. Yet patients without family resources, who cannot live on their own and for whom there are no adequate community facilities, continue to exist outside of mental hospitals.

Compared to their patient loads before 1955, psychiatric hospitals are now almost empty, but the original idealistic plans to help patients regain their independence seem to have resulted mainly in cost saving for the states. Patients had been transferred from the "back wards to the back alleys" (Borus, 1978). The social consequences of their deinstitutionalization had not been adequately tested in the rush to implement what had sounded like a good idea for helping patients without burdening communities.

Outside Judgments of the Mother-Child Home Program

The Mother-Child Home Program's dissemination sounded like a good idea too, but we guessed that the Program should be tested not only in its original model but also for its practicability in real world settings. This did not depend on opinions of the Program by experts outside of the Verbal Interaction Project (VIP), but their favorable judgments encouraged the effort.

Evaluation experts with a mission of finding effective programs to prevent or remediate educational disadvantage became interested in the Mother-Child Home Program (MCHP) within a few years after it began.

- In 1971, The American Institutes of Research reported to the U.S. Office of Education on the results of a nationwide search for exemplary "compensatory education" programs. The Mother-Child Home Program was one of two preschool programs among the ten which were finally selected (Wargo, Campeau, & Tallmadge, 1971).

- In 1972, the U.S. Office of Education (now Department of Education) selected the Mother-Child Home Program as one of two preschool programs among 15 programs in compensatory education chosen as models for the country. The U.S. Office of Education then published a booklet describing each Program, with one of them entitled: "Model Programs, Compensatory Education, Mother-Child Home Program, Freeport, New York" (DHEW publication No. OE, pp. 72–84).

- In 1974, a U.S. Office of Child Development review of early intervention programs described the Mother Child Home Program in some detail, pointing out many distinctive characteristics of the Program ("The mother not only trains the child, but the child also trains the mother" and "The strategy addresses processes not in the child but in the two-person system which sustains and fosters his development") and naming it as among the most promising of those reviewed (Bronfenbrenner, 1974, p. 27).

- In 1975, another review of early intervention programs devoted five pages to the Mother-Child Home Program, preceded by the author's comments: "Most thoroughly tested of the programs for preventing retardation through parent education is Phyllis Levenstein's. Since the course of her investigations approaches the ideal for the development of a program of intervention more closely than any other I know of, it seems worthwhile to summarize the process in some detail" (McV. Hunt, 1975, p. 19).

- Also in 1975, a conclusion in a review of early intervention programs which involved parents was: "The Mother-Child Home Program was shown to be highly effective" (Goodson & Hess, 1975, p. 24).

- In 1978, the U.S. National Institute of Mental Health selected the Program as one of five "visible successful models of programs which enable families to play an important role in improving child mental health" in the preface to a pamphlet called "Parent-Child Program Series, Report No. 1, Mother-Child Home Program" (DHEW Publication No. ADM 78–659).

- Late in 1978, the Program's research results were scrutinized by a federal panel of research experts, the Joint Dissemination Review Panel, drawn from the National Institute of Education and the U.S. Office of Education. The Panel pronounced the Mother-Child Home Program "a program that works," which made it a member of the National Diffusion Network of the U.S. Department of Education. Information about the Mother-Child Home Program and about other "programs that work" is disseminated in an annually updated catalogue of successful educational programs (e.g., *Educational Programs That Work*, 1987).

- The Program's 1982 evaluation was the indirect consequence of a study of the combined follow-up results from eleven systematically researched preschool programs, in which the graduates of the Mother-Child Home Program were found to be significantly superior to controls in their freedom from special class placement and in their IQs, with their IQs not only superior to those of Controls but also *meeting national IQ norms* (Lazar & Darlington, 1982).

Maine to Alaska to Bermuda

While these outside evaluations were taking place, and while the Verbal Interaction Project's own research was continuing, a slow process of developing the Program's "exportability" was also being carried on by the VIP. The big question was whether the original Program, pioneered as part of laboratory research in Long Island communities, could be duplicated in the "real world." The question of practicability was paramount. It included the awareness that any effectiveness the Program had demonstrated in a protected setting would be transmitted to other locations only if the Program's method could be replicated exactly elsewhere.

The Mother-Child Home Program had been intended for adoption, if it worked, by schools, by public and private social agencies, by churches, by Native American Indian tribes, by any organizations concerned about the future of disadvantaged children and families. After the demonstration of its effectiveness in the laboratory, it was meant to be a social program with a potential for applicability in any setting of the country.

By the end of 1978, after 12 years of the Program's operation and the research of its effects involving the cooperation of 800 Freeport Program and Non-Program mother-child dyads, the first part of the Verbal Interaction Project's mission was accomplished. That was the year that the Mother-Child Home Program was validated as effective, as a "program that works," by the federal Joint Dissemination Review Panel.

To complete the rest of its mission, the Verbal Interaction Project continued to field-test its own system for guiding the Program's countrywide implementation, a system whose development had paralleled the research of the Program. The system gradually became an efficient and highly regarded way of "exporting" the Program intact, preserving its human values while furnishing the guidance and technical materials need to reproduce it. By 1972 it was possible to report on the early results of the Program's first outside replications (Levenstein, 1972) and by the next year to describe techniques already found effective in guiding them (Levenstein, Kochman, & Roth, 1973). Two years later the IQ effects in several replications and the possibility of the Program's application to prevent mild mental retardation were the subjects of another report (Levenstein, 1975).

Between 1969 and 1984 the Verbal Interaction Project trained the Coordinators for 84 replications of the Mother-Child Home Program in 16 states from Maine to Alaska, and in Canada and Bermuda. The replications (or "adoptions," as they were sometimes called) reached 4000 dyads in a variety of populations vulnerable to educational disadvantage, mainly low-income. They were sponsored by schools, by churches, by private and public social agencies, by mental health clinics, and by

Native American Indian tribes—by an amazing variety of auspices giving a variety of primary services.

- The Family Counseling Service (Region West) in Newton, Massachusetts, provided services designed to strengthen and enrich family life. Counseling, family life education, vocational training and testing were offered. The main focus was on high-risk families (abused children, very low income, mental retardation, etc.). Special preference was given to non-English speaking families. Began replication of the Program in January 1970. *Still in operation.*

- The Pittsfield, Massachusetts, Public Schools started a Mother-Child Home Program in September 1970 for a low-income, ethnically mixed, mainly white population in a small industrial city in the Berkshire hills. The Program was considered to be a bridge to the school. Later a preschool classroom provided extra enrichment for Program graduates. *The Program is still in operation and serves as a model for Massachusetts school systems.*

- Great Neck/Manhasset Public Schools in Long Island, New York, have replicated the Program since 1971 to service children from poverty areas in their otherwise affluent communities. The school districts feel that the Program has served to enhance the value of schooling in the eyes of the mainly Black, low-income population, and that children in the Program are better equipped for school entry than those in pre-Program years. *Still in operation.*

- Talbot Perkins Children's Service in New York City services foster children, who receive, in addition to other services, the Mother-Child Home Program, begun in 1972. For some children returning to their birth-mothers, the Program has provided a bridge between foster home and natural home, as a stable factor in the child's life. For almost all children, it enhances their relationships with their foster mothers. *Still in operation.*

- Westchester Jewish Community Services, originally in cooperation with the White Plains, New York, Public Schools, began a Mother-Child Home Program in November 1972, in Westchester County, one of the wealthiest in the country. There are now two Programs in the county, under the same sponsorship, and serving low-income families who provide a cross-section of the ethnic minorities in the county. They live in low-income housing projects and other poverty areas. *Still in operation.*

- The Tri-County Community Action Committee of Caldwell, Ohio, began the Program in 1973 to serve Appalachian families, who were mainly white and rural, with an average of tenth grade education for the adults. Families were scattered in a 50 mile radius of the home office, some in isolated hollows. For many of the children and mothers the Mother-Child Home Program was one of a very limited number of contacts with the outside world. *Terminated in 1977 because federal Appalachian Commission funding stopped.*

- Bethesda United Presbyterian Church in Pittsburgh began the Program in 1973, as one of its many social services. Its area was a depressed inner city section, the largest Black ghetto in Pittsburgh. *Terminated in 1978 when funding stopped.*

- Dulac Community Center was located at the tip of a bayou in southwestern Louisiana. Surrounded on three sides by the Gulf of Mexico, the Center offered the Mother-Child Home Program in 1975 to Indian, Black, and White families in the communities of Dulac and Houma. Oil rigs and shrimp boats dominated the life of the region. *Program terminated for lack of funding.*

- PROP (People's Regional Opportunity Program) of Portland, Maine, began a Mother-Child Home Program in 1973, to serve low-income, younger siblings of Head Start children. *When Head Start funds were cut in 1975, the Program had to be terminated.*

- Acoma Parent-Child Development Program of San Fidel, New Mexico, began a Mother-Child Home Program in 1975 in the Indian pueblo of Acoma, high atop a mesa, 65 miles southwest of Albuquerque. Three small settlements, situated at some distance from each other, housed the bulk of Acoma's population of 3,000. The Program was designed to include local cultural values. *Funding stopped in 1977 in spite of petitions and protests by mothers.*

- Bermuda's Department of Social Services began a Mother-Child Home Program in 1976, for low-income families in some areas within its Commonwealth, an island better known for its attractive climate and beauty than for its educational needs. In April of 1982, the Program was established as an islandwide service. *It is still in operation.*

- Rural CAP/Upper Tanana Development Corporation in Tok, Alaska, started a Mother-Child Home Program which was divided among Athabaskan Indian villages in a remote section of Alaska. In this setting, "training the trainers" and Program delivery were put to its most severe test. Toy Demonstrators had to fly monthly to Fairbanks for supervision and to pick up the toys and books. *The Program started in 1976 but ended in 1977 because of logistic and funding difficulties.*

- Child and Family Services of Western Manitoba in Brandon, Manitoba, Canada, began a Mother-Child Home Program in September 1984 to serve mainly Native Canadian Indian families receiving Income Security (welfare support). Parents are almost all single mothers with an unusually limited amount of education. The replicator offers voluntary and mandatory services to families over an area covering 1300 square miles. Brandon itself is a small city 120 miles north of Winnipeg. Agriculture is its main industry. *The agency plans to continue the Program.*

These instances of Program replication give some hint of the diversity of sociolinguistic subcultures reached by the Mother-Child Home Program. For each of them the Program served as a two-way bridge to the mainstream culture. At one end of the bridge—a dyad's home—the Program adapted itself in every way possible, without violating its basic principles, to the subculture of that home. Books often contained translations into the family's language; the mother was encouraged to use her own cultural associations in conversing with her child; the Toy Demonstrator was helped to understand (and sometimes helped her Coordinator and the Verbal Interaction Project to understand) the customs of the subculture. The other end of the bridge was fixed in the "mainstream" culture dominant both throughout the United States and in a dyad's particular geographical locality. The Mother-Child Home Program's goals and curriculum represented mainstream culture. The method of the Program formed a gentle link between the literacy and customs of that dominant culture and the subculture of the home.

The Verbal Interaction Project devised a training system for local implementation of the Mother-Child Home Program which individualized the guidance of each Program replication and the subculture in which it was embedded. It may be that this humanization of the training process, along with firm emphasis on basic Program standards, were the factors that prevented the erosion that is the usual fate of social programs when they are duplicated away from the model program's site. The more faithful the Program copies were to the original Program, the better their chances for benefitting Program participants in the same ways. Therefore, most Replicators (sponsors) and Coordinators of adoptions were more than willing to be helped toward becoming true Program replications.

Basic Program Standards: KEEP (Key Elements for Establishing Program)

The Program's basic standards were made explicit in a *Manual for Operating a Mother-Child Home Program* and in the 35 items of a check-off list called KEEP (the acronym for "Key Elements for Establishing Program"), abstracted from the Manual:

- Before replication of the Mother-Child Home Program (MCHP)
  1. "Initiator" receives MCHP information.
  2. Replicator employs Coordinator (at least B.A. or equivalent).
  3. Coordinator is trained by Verbal Interaction Project (VIP).

- During first two years of MCHP Replication
  4. Coordinator has frequent mail/telephone contacts with VIP.
  5. VIP monitors replication by end of Year 2, for certification.

- Toy Demonstrator (TD) Qualifications and Initial Training
  6. TD's participation is voluntary.

7. Initial TD training equals six to eight 2-hour sessions.
8. TD has appropriately accepting attitude toward dyads.
- Toy Demonstrator (TD) In-Service Training and Supervision
  9. Mothers are introduced to TD by Coordinator.
  10. TD writes Home Session record for each Home Session.
  11. Weekly TD Conference (group supervision by Coordinator).
  12. Emergency Home Session coverage ("buddy system").
  13. TD records two Home Sessions yearly (audio or video).
  14. TD and Coordinator have individual conferences twice a year.
  15. TD writes end-of-year evaluation of MCHP toys and books.
  16. TD writes end-of-year evaluation of MCHP.
- Mothers and Children in the MCHP
  17. Parents' participation is voluntary and without fees.
  18. At least half of the families must meet underclass criteria.
  19. Children are about age two at entry and have two MCHP years.
  20. Coordinator conducts Initial Interview with mother.
  21. Coordinator conducts Mid-Year Interview with mother.
  22. Coordinator conducts Final Interview with mother.
  23. Explicit confidentiality/intrusiveness safeguards for families.
- Home Sessions
  24. Two Home Sessions weekly in Year 1; two, one or none in Year 2.
  25. At least one parent (or surrogate, if needed) at Home Session.
  26. Home Session techniques: TD models interactions.
  27. Home Session's ultimate aim: mother leads, TD follows.
- Toys, Books, and Curriculum
  28. First "toy" is a toy chest.
  29. Gifts of 11 toys and 12 books yearly to mother and child.
  30. Toys and books presented weekly in age-appropriate sequence.
  31. Creation of Guide Sheets from VIP's model (VIP Form #23).

- Coordinator's Administration of MCHP
  32. Follows Manual and uses VIP Forms appropriately.
  33. Files on families are well organized, up-to-date, confidential.
  34. "Work Flow Sheets" (or effective substitute) are kept current.
  35. Effective system for storing and keeping track of toys and books.

Current Replications of the Mother-Child Home Program

As of 1987, 19 Replicators were conducting 20 replications of the Mother-Child Home Program in four states (Massachusetts, New York, Pennsylvania and South Carolina) and in Bermuda and Canada. (Appendix 2 contains a list of the 1986–1987 Replicators, including the current names and telephone numbers of their Program Coordinators.)

Seven of these replications have been in operation for 10 years or longer: four in school systems in Massachusetts (Cambridge, Pittsfield, and Lawrence) and in New York State (Great Neck/Manhasset) and three in family and child social service agencies in the same two states. All seven are still faithfully following the model Program's guidelines as outlined in KEEP.

Another eight replications have been conducted continuously from five to eight years: five are in Massachusetts school systems, and the other three are family service agencies in Massachusetts and New York, and the Department of Health and Social Services in Bermuda. These eight, like the seven which are even older, continue to include the model Program's essential elements.

Two more Program adoptions—sponsored by a New York State family service agency and a Canadian family and children's service agency—began in 1984, have gone through their in-service training periods, have passed their two-year Evaluations and are now certified replications of the Verbal Interaction Project's Mother-Child Home Program.

Three more—two in school systems in Pennsylvania and one in a South Carolina school system—began training in 1987.

So far all have enthusiastically incorporated the model Program's standards.

The steady adherence to VIP/MCHP standards by Program replications over many years of Program operation is more familiar in fast-food franchises like McDonald's than in the adoption of social/educational programs. An "adoption" of such a program is more likely to become an *adaptation* when sponsors innocently change its essential features for what seem like sensible reasons. Unfortunately, the adapters may not sufficiently realize that every change may dilute and even destroy the program's original effectiveness.

The persistence of Mother-Child Home Program replications in maintaining the standards of the model Program is an indication of the Replicators' commitment to the welfare of their Program's participants—caring that the mothers and children have the best chance of receiving what the Program promises. Perhaps their persistence also testifies to the efficacy of the VIP's replication techniques. It tends to indicate the success of dissemination methods developed over 18 years, and continuously reviewed for updating and refinement, to equip Replicators with the Program supports they need for true replications of the Mother-Child Home Program.

A State-Wide Dissemination Model

The replications in the Massachusetts school systems are coordinated by the State Director of "Parent Assist," the statewide network of all the Massachusetts school replications. Judy Stolzberg, Parent Assist's State Director, acts, in effect, as the Verbal Interaction Project's Field Consultant to these replications. One of her unique qualifications for the role is that she is also the Coordinator of the Pittsfield Schools' replication of the Mother-Child Home Program, and has been so since its inception in 1970.

Mrs. Stolzberg's success as Massachusetts State Director breaks ground for experienced Coordinators to perform the same service in other states of the country, with the support and technical aid of the Verbal Interaction Project.

Cost and Sample Budget

When the model Program first began in 1967, following the pilot program, the average annual cost for each mother-child pair was $400. It is now (in 1987) from $1000 to $1500, depending mainly on the size of the Coordinator's salary and those of the Toy Demonstrators (if paid Toy Demonstrators are used instead of volunteers). Salaries make up most of the Program costs. Surprisingly, the Program supplies (gifts of toys and books) are the smallest part of the expenses; even when combined with office supplies, they comprise less than 15 percent of a Program budget.

The annual budget for a replication of the Mother-Child Home Program serving 25 mother-child dyads might look something like this:

Paid Staff Members	% of Time	At Salary	Actual Cost
Coordinator	100	$16,450	$16,450
Paid Toy Demonstrator	100	$4/hour 35 hours/week, 35 weeks/year)	$4,900
Paid Toy Demonstrator	50		$2,450
3 Vol. Toy Demonstrators	60	—	—
Secretary	20	$10,000	$2,000
Non-Salary Items			
Program Supplies (toys and books)	25 dyads	$150/dyad	$3,750
Office supplies	—	—	450
Rent, telephone, cleaning (Replicator's "in-kind" contribution)			0
		Total	$30,000

The total for a budget naturally depends on its individual items, which may differ markedly among replications. As one example, the items for Toy Demonstrator salaries may disappear completely because a replication may decide to lower costs by accepting only volunteers as Toy Demonstrators. On the other hand, the same item may greatly increase if the

Replicator decides to hire all paid Toy Demonstrators, perhaps as an entry-level job training program. If all salary items do stay in the budget, differences may come from the fact that salaries vary greatly in different parts of the country. What is far too low a salary in one place, may be high in another. The example above assumes, for example, that the Coordinator is an inexperienced professional hired by a Replicator whose paid Toy Demonstrators (inexperienced and of less than high school education) are supplemented by three unpaid volunteer Toy Demonstrators. Clearly, each replication budget must be adapted to local conditions, although the sample budget above appears to represent a fair approximation of many replication budgets in 1987.

It is also the Verbal Interaction Project's experience that every replicator is able to provide the minimal space and equipment which are needed to implement the Mother-Child Home Program: an office large enough to hold two desks, a telephone, a folding conference table, some chairs and storage space for the books and toys. Anything beyond that, such as a separate office for Toy Demonstrators, adds to the morale of Program staffs but has not been considered essential for operating a replication of the Mother-Child Home Program.

Funding for Replications of the Mother-Child Home Progam

All replications are supported through a replicator's own financial resources, unfortunately meager nowadays. But often a Replicator is able to supplement its slender means by grants from local foundations or by government aid. The latter (also scanty these days) can be from the immediate community, or from the state, or from federal sources.

Although there may be less of it now than in previous years, federal aid is still usually available through Chapter One of the Educational Consolidation and Improvement Act to schools. The Act (as ESEA Title One did before it) provides support for compensatory programs that reach out to children at risk for educational disadvantage. Federal funding of this kind has been utilized by most schools which have replicated the Mother-Child Home Program.

Program Evaluation in Replications

Many of the early replications conducted in-house evaluations of the Program's effect on children by having the children's cognitive development assessed before and after the Program. By 1974, the 1970 to 1972 IQ data from eight replications had been sent to the Verbal Interaction Project for statistical analysis. On analysis, the average pre-post IQ gain for children in these replications was about 15 IQ points (Levenstein, 1975). This large gain, encouraging as it seemed to be, was of dubious reliability because of flaws in the research design. For example, comparison of posttest results with those obtained at pretest is considered a weak research design in preschool research because of the many factors which might have caused the difference, such as the maturation factor—the natural improvement in little children's IQs simply because they have grown older and can deal better with the test material. On the other hand, an excellent research design may produce valid short-term IQ results—but from a nondisadvantaged sample.

In contrast, as previously described, a reliable positive evaluation has come from the Pittsfield Public Schools, the only replicator to have conducted long-range evaluations of its Program through follow-up studies of the Program graduates after they reached school. Chapter Five ("How High Was Up?") reported the favorable follow-up findings from this replication, called the Parent-Child Home Program (which celebrated its 15th anniversary in May, 1985). As was noted in Chapter Five, the Pittsfield replication was given its latest evaluation, for the 1983–84 school year by experts from outside of the school system. The evaluators measured the reading, language, and math progress of Program graduates from kindergarten through eighth grade and compared it both to the progress of Non-Program children of similar background and to the national norms of the achievement test which was used, the California Achievement Test (CAT). The results made it obvious that the graduates of the Pittsfield Parent-Child Home Program, across grades and measures of this follow-up study, had achieved scores which took them out of the group eligible for Chapter One aid. *They could no longer be considered educationally disadvantaged.*

Five Steps to Program Replication

All Replicators go through the same five major steps to achieve authentic replications of the Mother-Child Home Program with the help of the Verbal Interaction Project:

1. The Replicator requests detailed information about the Program.
2. The Replicator's director signs a Program plan which includes following model Program standards.
3. The Coordinator is trained by the Verbal Interaction Project.
4. The Verbal Interaction Project stays in close touch with the Coordinator for the first two years of Program replication.
5. The Verbal Interaction Project awards a Certificate of Approval to the Replicator for two years of successful Program replication.

Each of these steps, however, requires a little more explanation.

Information to the Replicator About the Mother-Child Home Program

Potential Replicators sometimes learn of the Program's existence by hearsay, but usually through seeing mention of it in professional journal articles, in the columns of newspapers, or in the catalogue of federally approved *Educational Programs That Work,* published by Sopris West, Longmont, Colorado. A staff member ("initiator") writes for details to Dr. Phyllis Levenstein, Verbal Interaction Project, Center for Mother-Child Home Program, 3268 Island Road, Wantagh, New York 11793. The Verbal Interaction Project responds with information on the Program and its research results (most of which is now summarized in this book), and replication procedures, including the availability of a videocassette version of the Program's 26-minute informational film, "Learning in Joy."

Typically, a future Replicator takes a while to absorb the information before deciding to embark upon a Program replication, sometimes as long as three years, often three months or less. A dialogue begins with the Verbal Interaction Project by telephone and/or by letter about what responsibilities a replication entails for the Replicator. If a Replicator holds to the decision, the Verbal Interaction Project goes into action to help.

Signed Promise to Follow Program Plan and Standards

However, the Verbal Interaction Project's resources are too limited to share teaching time and technical materials with groups which do not plan to use them to achieve a true replication and thus a real chance for Program participants to benefit in the same ways as those in the model Program. Therefore, the Replicator's Director is asked to sign a "Proposed Plan for Replicating the Mother-Child Home Program," which includes an agreement to follow the Program's basic standards. This, of course, has no legal force but is simply a declaration of "honorable intention" as a condition for getting materials and guidance from the Verbal Interaction Project.

Those standards are detailed in the 35 items of KEEP which were listed earlier in this chapter. The items were carefully selected from the Program Manual to be in truth the essential features of the model Program.

KEEP delineates concretely the dimensions of a Replicator's commitment to a genuine duplication of the model Mother-Child Home Program. A true replication should fulfill 30 out of the 35 KEEP items.

The Verbal Interaction Project, on the other hand, may agree to minor departures from KEEP, so long as they don't violate the philosophy or basic method of the Program. A minor modification might be a change from semi-weekly to weekly Home Sessions in order to accommodate an Alaskan schedule of airlifts to Eskimo villages. Another, and more usually requested change, might be the addition to the model Program of mothers' group meetings around some topic of common interest. Still another is a "two-tier" program in which 50 percent of the dyads may be, for special reasons, of middle or high income.

Replicators may also choose their own titles for their replications. Any is acceptable so long as it stays within the spirit of the model Program. For example, "Tots and Toys" (never yet chosen!) might be a little too cute for some tastes but is still philosophically acceptable. "Tot Teachers," on the other hand, is not acceptable because the word "teach" is *verbum non gratum* in the Mother-Child Home Program. (Sometimes it must appear unavoidably in a sponsor's administrative documents, perhaps in the sponsor's title for the Toy Demonstrators [e.g., "Teacher Demonstrators"] because of the administrative requirements of an agency or school system.)

Coordinator is Trained by the Verbal Interaction Project

The Coordinator receives the same Program information that was sent to the Replicator's "initiator," and much more. The Coordinator begins the new Mother-Child Home Program equipped with a huge set of "technical materials," in fact everything needed to run a Program except for the toys and books. The materials include Manuals, practical information, and many pre-printed forms with permission to reproduce them for use in running the Program. (For a list of these materials, please see "Index to Technical Materials for Operating a Mother-Child Home Program" in Appendix 1). The Verbal Interaction Project has trained the Coordinator in their use, as well as in the philosophy and background of the Program, and in approaches to families, community agencies, and Toy Demonstrators.

The training can be through one of two options: three days' training of the Coordinator at the Verbal Interaction Project/ Center for Mother-Child Home Program in Wantagh, Long Island, New York; or a three to three-and-a-half day Training Institute at the Replicator's offices, which can be attended by any of Replicator's staff along with the future Coordinator. In either option, the Verbal Interaction Project provides copies of the technical materials listed in Appendix 1 and continues to provide telephone or written consultation as needed.

The Verbal Interaction Project keeps in close touch with the new Coordinator for the first two Program years, telephones at least every six weeks, lends an understanding ear, acts as a trouble shooter, and reinforces the original training. The VIP issues new technical materials whenever they are available (new videocassettes of mother-child interaction and/or model Home Sessions, or suggestions for new toys and books). Each Coordinator may become a "Verbal Interaction Project Associate" (and receives a newsletter and may attend an Annual Associates' Workshop to share experiences with other Associates).

Certificate of Approval

When a replication has maintained Program standards for two years, the Verbal Interaction Project recognizes the achievement by awarding a Certificate of Approval to the Replicator for its successful implementation of the Mother-Child Home Program. "Successful replication" is defined by the Program's adherence to 30 of the 35 standards in KEEP. However, some KEEP items are more essential than others, depending on the replication's setting or on other individual circumstances.

In any Program, for instance, the KEEP item "Parents' participation is voluntary" is more important than the KEEP item "TD records two Home Sessions yearly (audio or video)," desirable as the latter is for Toy Demonstrator training. A good reason for perhaps eliminating the recording requirement might be found in a Mother-Child Home Program conducted in a remote corner of the Appalachian Mountains. The logistics for setting up recording equipment in a house in a mountain hollow may make it impracticable to obtain an audio or video record of a Home Session.

A replication which fulfills 90 percent of the KEEP items is considered to be a true replication, but this is on condition that none of the most essential of the 35 essential items are omitted! It seems clear that in the last analysis the Verbal Interaction Project must make a subjective judgment about some aspects of the readiness of a replication to earn the Certificate of Approval. Nevertheless, a surprisingly small proportion of the decision is thus based on subjective criteria. The Certificate of Approval is awarded on the basis of the following criteria, most of which, like some of the KEEP items, necessarily require judgment calls by the Verbal Interaction Project:

1. Recording of adherence to 30 out of 35 items on a copy of KEEP which has been filled in and signed by the Coordinator and countersigned by the Replicator-administrator.

2. Coordinator's satisfactory group supervision (one Toy Demonstrator Conference observed either directly or through an audio or video tape recording).

3. One satisfactory Home Session (observed either directly or

through video/audio tape recording).

4. Program records found to meet VIP standards, as seen in:
   a. six Home Session reports written by Toy Demonstrators;
   b. one two-year dyad file folder recorded by Coordinator;
   c. VISM list and VISM Guide Sheets for one Program year; and
   d. Coordinator's Work Flow Sheet (or equivalent) for a year.

5. Adequate insight shown by Coordinator in talks with VIP staff about relations with own and Replicator staff; about community attitudes toward the Program; and about past or anticipated problems and solutions.

Seed to Blossom: The Replication System in Practice

In September of 1984 a private social agency called "Family Keystone" (not its real name) started a replication of the Mother-Child Home Program (MCHP) which won its Approval Certificate two years later, in 1986.

The training and guidance of Family Keystone's replication by the Verbal Interaction Project (VIP) is unusually well documented, not only through VIP's logs but through detailed letters from the replicator's staff. This is because Family Keystone's location is 2500 miles from the VIP office, in the southern reaches of the North American continent, and telephone calls to and from the VIP in Wantagh, New York, are expensive. To save telephone time, preliminary letters from (and to) Family Keystone's staff members preceded telephone conferences and thus prepared the conference participants for the issues to be raised on the telephone. The result was a sizable documentation of Replicator-VIP interaction, enhanced by the well selected detail and the clarity of Family Keystone's letters to the VIP. Therefore, the Program's implementation within "Family Keystone" was chosen as an otherwise typical example of how the VIP's replication system works in actual practice. Names and other identifying features are disguised, but aside from these necessary alterations, the content of this chronological account is exactly as it was originally written.

June 1982

Family Keystone's Director of Preventive Services, Mrs. Frances White, sent for and received information on the Mother-Child Home Program from the Verbal Interaction Project. Part of Mrs. White's letter was typical of such letters of inquiry:

> I have been most interested in the description of the Mother-Child Home Program in the National Institute of Mental Health Monographs.
>
> The description of your Mother-Child Home Program sounds like one from which we could gain enormous assistance in establishing our Home Management-Parent Aid Program which is designed to work with our most vulnerable families. The training program used with the Toy Demonstrators and the curriculum and suggestions with respect to toys and books would be most helpful.

June 1984

Telephone from Frances White and Louise Bromley, Keystone staff members, to the Verbal Interaction Project. They wished an update of information about the Mother-Child Home Program, especially new research results since Mrs. White's inquiry two years ago. But on the basis of the information they had, Family Keystone had already decided to replicate the Mother-Child Home Program, mainly with low-income Native American Indian families.

Two days later, Mrs. White sent a letter to the Verbal Interaction Project which enclosed brochures about her agency and read in part:

> I am enclosing a copy of our 1984 Annual Report and several of the Preventive Program brochures we had developed for a child welfare conference.
>
> I hope that we will develop a solid family resource bank of books, toys and teaching elements for parents as well as programs into which they can move as they are ready.

As you will see from our brochures, we already have a fair degree of involvement in their homes both from our statutory programs staff, our Family Aides and also from the Preschool Program.

A possibility I'd like to explore is whether some of the Toy Demonstrators might be drawn from our client group. Our experience with the Family Aides has been a very positive one as we have seen their growth over the last two years. It is much more dramatic than that of clients with whom they themselves have worked.

July 1984

Telephone call from the Verbal Interaction Project to Mrs. White, agreeing to aid her agency's replication and to start arrangements for an experienced Field Consultant to train replication staff at the agency in an on-site Training Institute, the training option chosen by Family Keystone. The Verbal Interaction Project would provide the Field Consultant with films, videotapes, and two sets of technical materials for Mrs. White and the future Coordinator, Louise Bromley (with permission to copy them for any other staff members attending the Training Institute). Family Keystone would pay the Field Consultant directly for her travel and other expenses and the VIP fee for conducting the Training Institute and other training contacts. Mrs. White agreed to work this out directly with the Field Consultant by letter and telephone, with the knowledge that the Field Consultant would keep the Verbal Interaction Project informed of each step.

The following day Mrs. White sent the VIP a "letter of intent" to replicate the Mother-Child Home Program. Her letter crossed with one from the VIP Director to Mrs. White, enclosing updated research information and reading in part:

It's also occurred to me that you might like to get some telephone evaluations of our work with replications, so I've included a list of our current replicators, as super-imposed on an old list (soon to be put in tidier form, when some expected additions come in). I believe a call from you would be welcomed by any of the Coordinators (or their administrators) but I especially suggest Mrs. Judy Stolzberg, the Coordinator for the Pittsfield, Massachusetts, Public Schools' Mother-Child Home Program. Mrs. Stolzberg is also the State Coordinator for "Parent Assist" (i.e., Mother-Child Home Program) replications in 8 or 9 other Massachusetts school districts.

A week later the Verbal Interaction Project equipped the Field Consultant (Naomi Feldheim) with all the technical materials she would need to lead a Training Institute at the offices of Family Keystone, August 21 to August 24, 1984. At the end of July the Field Consultant wrote to Frances White to confirm the travel arrangements for her trip.

August 1984

The Director of the Verbal Interaction Project and the Field Consultant conferred August 1 and agreed on the syllabus (adapted from previous Institutes) for the 8/21–8/24 Training Institute at Family Keystone:

MOTHER-CHILD HOME PROGRAM
TRAINING INSTITUTE, AUGUST 21–24, 1984

Tuesday, August 21
9:30–12 noon   Session 1
   Description of the Mother-Child Home Program (MCHP).
   Informational film about MCHP, "Learning in Joy."
   Overview of Home Sessions. MCHP film, "Three Families."
1:00–4:30 PM   Session 2
   Main components of Mother-Child Home Program.
   Research of MCHP by Verbal Interaction Project.

Wednesday, August 22
9:30–12 noon   Session 3
   Language as it relates to cognitive-affective development.
1:00–4:30 PM   Session 4
   Poverty: The low-income family.
   Related film (to be announced).

Thursday, August 23
9:30–12 noon   Session 5
  Audio-visual materials. "Marshak" film.
  Two and three year olds: Their growth and development.
1:00–4:30 PM   Session 6
  The process of mother-child interaction.
  Home Session curricula and techniques.
  MCHP films: "Danielle" and "Michelle."
  Recruitment and training of Toy Demonstrators.
  Recruitment of Mother-Child Home Program families.

Friday, August 24
9:30–11:30 AM   Session 7
  VISM (books and toys) ordering.
  Curriculum Guide Sheets for VISM.
  Questions and answers.

Two weeks after the Director/Field Consultant conference on August 1, and a week before the Family Keystone Training Institute, VIP's Director sent a "welcome letter" to Frances White which also confirmed VIP's July telephone commitments:

> I was glad to receive your July 19 letter expressing the intention of Family Keystone to replicate the Mother-Child Home Program according to the standards of the Verbal Interaction Project. On my part, I will do all I can to assist you.
>
> As a first step, I have asked Naomi Feldheim to present you with two sets of VIP/MCHP technical materials for running an authentic Mother-Child Home Program, which you have my permission to replicate for your own use, by photocopying or other means. Explaining these materials will be an important focus of Naomi's August 21–24 Training Institute which she will conduct at your agency.

The VIP Field Consultant's 8/21–8/24/84 Training Institute at Family Keystone's offices took place as planned. It was attended by several agency staff members besides Frances White and Louise Bromley, in order to prepare their agency colleagues for the coming Mother-Child Home Program replication. All commented favorably on the Institute in their written post-Institute assessments to the VIP of its value to them. Louise Bromley's comment, as future Coordinator of the replication, was typical: "I felt the Training Institute was comprehensive in covering [knowledge of] the many aspects of the Program that will be needed to implement it. I thought it was great."

September 1984

After a post-Institute conference with the Field Consultant, the Verbal Interaction Project Director sent some further requested information and technical material to Louise Bromley, with a letter which read in part:

> Naomi relayed your request for the enclosed papers and reprints and also for some videotapes. The videotape for 'Language and Cognition' is no longer available, so I have substituted a copy of my personal script for the videotaped lecture. Hope you don't mind my scribbled inserts, etc.

> Naomi reports that the Training Institute was highly successful from her point of view, that you were a raptly attentive group throughout and that you were all extremely kind and thoughtful—even to lending her an agency car! I don't know if all Replicators will go that far, but your agency has certainly opened a door to a new way of providing our services to establish Mother-Child Home Programs where they are needed.

December 1984

Letter from Louise Bromley, Coordinator of Family Keystone's Mother-Child Home Program, to the Verbal Interaction Project, in preparation for a telephone conference 1/9/85:

> Thank you so much for the script for Language and Cognition. I found it very helpful.

> We are now into our tenth week of Mother-Child Home Program and feel that it is going well so far. We have a few questions to ask and will telephone

you on Wednesday January 9th at 8:30 a.m. our time (10:30 your time I believe) to discuss the following:

1. In completing PACT, Item 1: Parent tries to enforce directive, how is it rated when the parent enforces the directive in a very negative manner such as yelling or becoming very angry with the child? The same could apply to #13, when parent persists in enforcing directives by yelling or threatening child.
2. In PACT Item #5, how does one rate the family when the scolding is done in a non-verbal manner?
3. How does one rate a family when there is great fluctuation in behavior?
4. When the children were pretested at age two, were they testing within normal limits?
5. How did you find the program worked with extremely disorganized, chaotic households? We have one family in particular. We are wondering if there is enough happening with mother and child interaction to keep involved with the family.

We have 12 families and 8 Toy Demonstrators participating. We had our first family withdraw when the mother, with her four children, left her husband and moved away.

We found the toys and books more costly than we estimated and have used almost all of our two year budget for toys and books in the first year. We are hoping to receive funding for the second year. [They did.]

Fran White and I are excited about the Program thus far, feel that it has great potential in both learning and relationship areas and look forward to talking with you.

A week later VIP's Director sent a reply to confirm the telephone appointment and to request that certain information be available qt the conference:

I will be happy to talk with you and Fran White, as you suggest in your 12/18/84 letter. I'll be looking forward to a telelphone conference at 10:30 AM (New York time) next Wednesday, January 9th, so that I can discuss with both of you the excellent questions you raise. I will also be interested in how the Program is going generally, perhaps touch on how I can be of further help.

In line with the latter, would you please try to fill out the *Proposed Plan* (Form #83) and KEEP (Form #D–88) so that we can talk about them a bit in our 1/9 telephone conference? I believe you have them both in your Training Institute Kit. I should have them eventually in your file here, so that the outline of your replication is at my fingertips as well as yours.

January 1985

The 1/9/85 telephone meeting between Family Keystone and the Verbal Interaction Project Director took place, as arranged. It covered all issues mentioned in Louise Bromley's 12/18 letter and the reply from the Verbal Interaction Project, plus a few others, including those of special relevance to cultural customs and language, and lasted an hour. Three key Family Keystone staff members participated in the conference: the Coordinator of the Mother-Child Home Program (Louise Bromley); the Director of Preventive Services (Frances White); and the Director of Family Keystone, Inc. (Brian Palmer).

Near the end of January the Verbal Interaction Project called Frances White (Louise Bromley was not available) to tell her that the Proposed Plan (Form #83) and KEEP (Form #D–88) were now in a simplified version and would be sent to Louise Bromley, as MCHP Coordinator. One completed copy of each should be returned to the VIP.

On 1/31 the forms were sent to Louise Bromley, as promised by the VIP.

March 1985

Letter from Louise Bromley (Family Keystone's MCHP Coordinator), enclosing completed copies of the Proposed Plan and

KEEP sent to her 1/31, and setting up a telephone conference for April 17:

> Please find enclosed Forms D–88 and 83. I found them fairly easy to complete. I wasn't sure if "No. mothers" referred to number of mothers in the program or number of single mothers.
>
> The Toy Demonstrators have three weeks of visiting left. Then I will visit each of the families again and the children will be tested on the Psycho-Cattell and Peabody Picture Vocabulary Tests. I don't know what results of these tests will be but the results we have seen have been very rewarding and exciting.
>
> Mothers who have not kept appointments and have not spent time playing with their children are now there for Home Sessions and interacting with their children.
>
> Do you have information on the validity and reliability of the PACT?
>
> In the second year of the program do the Toy Demonstrators meet weekly? Is the visiting with the families carried on in the same manner?
>
> Fran is away on holiday until April 15, 1985. We will call on Wednesday, April 17, 1985 at 10:00 your time to talk further.

April 1985

Letter from Verbal Interaction Project's Director, confirming the 4/17 telephone conference and enclosing the requested research data:

> Thank you for your 3/22 letter and the carefully filled out Forms 83 and D–88.
>
> Enclosed is a copy of a presentation on which a chapter in *Parent-Child Interaction* is based. The tables in it give the correlations of PACT verbal interaction items with children's school competencies, as well as

concurrent correlations. The high coefficients are evidence of the validity of linking the competence of children to their early verbal interaction with their mothers.

I look forward to talking with you (and Fran?) at 10 AM New York time on Wednesday, April 17, 1985.

The telephone conference between the VIP Director and Family Keystone staff (Bromley, Palmer, and White) occurred on 4/17 as agreed. The meeting lasted almost an hour and included discussions of measures to evaluate the Program's effects on mothers and children, and of issues raised by Louise Bromley in her 3/22 letter. Louise also requested a review by the VIP of her list of VISM (toys and books) and of some Guide Sheets, all to be sent with an expanded description of the community and families reached by Family Keystone, and by its Mother-Child Home Program.

May 1985

Long letter from Louise Bromley, Family Keystone's Mother-Child Home Program's Coordinator, enclosing for VIP review her VISM list, a few Guide Sheets, and a table of Program dyads' demographic characteristics. Her letter described in some detail the community and population served by Family Keystone, Inc., and by its MCHP; and it set up a 6/19 telephone conference with the VIP:

> Please find enclosed a list of VISM that we used this year and the Guide Sheets for the three substitutions. The substitutions "All Fall Down" and "Pat the Cat" were made when the books we ordered that were on the suggested list did not come in. The puppet had Goldilocks at one end and a bear at the other, with a skirt that could be flipped either way. It was popular with the older children. There was a colorful inexpensive book telling the story to accompany it.

> Here is more information on the type of people the agency serves. The agency serves about 1300 square

miles in South Western [location]. The area is largely rural with increasingly large farm operations requiring limited labor and dying villages as a result of the migration of the young people to the larger urban centres.

Granmount [fictitious name] is the largest city in the county and is the service centre for most of the rural area. Its population is around 40,000. There is still a core of descendants of pioneer families, but their names are disappearing from local business. There is a sizable degree of movement because of the number of transfers of junior people in national companies. It is also the first stop for many of the Natives from six small [Native American] reservations in the area. They are very transient, moving back and forth from the Reserve, with consequent problems in finding adequate housing and employment. Their children move schools frequently in a school year.

Our family service caseloads are highest in Granmount. About fifty percent are concerns about adolescents. This crosses all income levels. The demise of private schools has closed one alternative formerly open for many upper middle income families. The other fifty percent are families with infants, toddlers, and school aged children. The referrals range from physical and sexual abuse to neglect, inadequate parenting or "cries for help" from overwhelmed single parents. In the core area where the majority of our second fifty percent of families live, only one out of ten households includes children under 18. The bulk of housing is older homes converted into suites, or low cost housing. There is not a clearly recognized slum area.

While Native Indian families make up less than 15% of the caseloads, a disproportionately higher number of their children are [discovered to be in need of help], usually because of inadequate care, leaving the

Demographic Characteristics of "Family Keystone" Families in Mother-Child Home Program (N = 13)

Highest School Grade Achieved by Mothers:
None: 1   Gr. 8: 4   Gr. 9: 3   Gr. 10: 4   Gr. 11: 1
Mean Grade 8.5

Age of Mothers in Years at Beginning of MCHP:
20: 2   22: 2   24: 2   25: 3   26: 1   32: 1   33: 2
Mean Age: 25.5 yrs.

Source of Family Income:
Welfare: 10   Partial Assistance: 1   Self-Supporting: 2

Ethnic Background:
Native American: 7   Part-Native American: 1   Caucasian: 5

Marital Status:
Married: 2   Single: 10   Common-law: 1

Language at Home:
English: 11   English and Sioux: 1   English and German: 1

Mean N of Children Living at Home:
2.4 children

Age of Fathers in Years (N = 13):
22: 2   23: 1   26: 1   27: 2   29: 2   37: 1   38: 1   Unknown: 3

Highest School Grade Achieved by Fathers (N = 13):
3: 1   4: 1   7: 2   8: 2   10: 1   11: 1   12: 4   Unknown: 1
Mean School Grade: 8.8

children alone or abuse. A very high proportion of the families are abusing alcohol but not ready to seek or accept help.

The population involved in the program this year were thirteen families, all were referred by social workers of Children's Aid Society. This meant there was concern related to the care of the children. This could range from a parent's request for information about the care of their children to parents who are neglecting and abusing their children. All were of low income and all mothers' education was below the Grade 12 level. One family withdrew after twelve sessions when she left her husband and left the area with her children.

Please find enclosed a chart listing the characteristics of the families involved in the program. There was an error in Form #83. Average education of all mothers involved in the program should be 8.5, while the average education of all fathers was 8.8.

The visiting and the assessment of the children are now completed. The data are not yet all in.

Fran and I will telephone you on June 19, 1985, at 10:00 AM your time to talk further.

In order to make sure the replication is satisfactory, I am wondering in what areas we need to make changes next year.

I would like to discuss KEEP #4 and #13 with you. Would your suggestion of a telephone call every six weeks be suitable for #4?

June 1985

As had become usual, the Director of the Verbal Interaction Project met by telephone 6/19/85 with three Family Keystone staff members: Louise Bromley, Frances White, and Brian Palmer. And, as usual, the conference lasted about an hour.

Most of it was devoted to the VIP's review and critique of the Coordinator's well-chosen VISM list and generally excellent Guide Sheets, as well as comments on her Program dyads' demographic and subcultural characteristics in relation to their special needs from the MCHP. Questions were asked about a recent *Child Development* article written by the Director and two VIP colleagues.

The VIP Director also announced some VIP plans for the future: the coming Fall 1985 issues of *VIP Update,* a newsletter to be mailed regularly to Coordinators; the informal organization of Coordinators into "VIP Associates," with an Associates Conference planned for June 1986; the updating of the 1985 list of Replicators; and the coming publication of *Messages from*

Home, a book about the MCHP and its effects, written by Dr. Phyllis Levenstein.

July 1985

In response to a telephone message from the Verbal Interaction Project's Field Consultant, Frances White telephoned the Consultant to verify information about Family Keystone, for the 1985 Replicator list. The Mother-Child Home Program replication had gone well in the first year; it had met all of the agency's expectations.

October 1985

The Verbal Interaction Project sent three items to Louise Bromley (and to all other Coordinators): a list of current Replicators, as of 1985; a blank Form #200, "Replication of Mother-Child Home Program," to be completed with basic information and returned to the VIP so that it could be entered into the VIP's computer as a "data base;" and the Fall 1985 issue of the newsletter, *VIP Update.* The latter included more details about "VIP Associates"; a welcome to three new Replicators; and the important follow-up news that low-income graduates of a MCHP replication in Pittsfield, Massachusetts schools were not only outperforming non-MCHP comparison children but were performing up to national norms, in 8th grade. (Eighth grade is the highest grade for which there has been a formal follow-up study of MCHP effects.)

November 1985

Letter from Louise Bromley, enclosing Form #200, relating her MCHP's progress, and arranging a telephone conference for 11/27/85:

> Thank you so much for the VIP Update. The VIP Associates offer many possibilities and we welcome any information etc.
>
> We are just beginning our second year of the Mother-Child Home Program, with eleven families returning

for Program II and four new families beginning the first year. Of our original thirteen families in the first year, one family moved away shortly after the program began, and the second family moved out of town this summer after completing the first year. We are fortunate in having the other eleven return. We began with four new families for Program I instead of the expected five because one mother entered an alcoholic rehabilitation program; we hope to include her later.

All of the Toy Demonstrators returned except one who obtained full time employment. We have five new Toy Demonstrators.

Last year's experience was a very positive and rewarding one for all of us, and we look forward to this year. I believe I indicated in our last telephone call there was not a statistically significant increase in the children's cognitive development. However, all the children remained at the same level of development or showed an increase, and we regarded this as positive, as often children from [this local sociological] background show a decline from age two on.

There was a statistically significant increase in the mother's interactive behavior with her child as rated in the PACT, and in the child's socio-emotional development as rated on the CBT. The relationship between CBT and PACT scores was also statistically significant.

The individual gains in the families reported by the mothers and the Toy Demonstrators added to our feelings that the program was a worthwhile and exciting one. I hope the second year goes as well.

I will telephone you on Wednesday, November 27, 1985 at 10:00 AM EST to ask some questions re: Form 200 and discuss things more fully.

The Verbal Interaction Project replied by telephone, to reschedule the telephone conference for 12/4/85.

December 1985

The Verbal Interaction Project Director and Louise Bromley, Coordinator of Family Keystone's Mother-Child Home Program, were the only two participants in the 12/4 telephone conference, which lasted about half an hour. Louise's questions about her database Form #200 were discussed, as were the contents of her November letter. In addition, she had some questions about the supervision of her Toy Demonstrators (she now had a large number, some experienced and some not); about criteria for reducing Home Sessions for Striver-mothers in Program Year Two; and about the use of videotapes and "MIB" ratings to measure changes in mothers' interactive behavior with their children.

As with all other VIP interactions with Mrs. Bromley and her colleagues, this conference demonstrated her sensitivity to the nuances and myriad aspects of the MCHP, as well as her knowledge of the Program, her intelligence, and her respect for human beings in coping with Program problems.

January through April 1986

A VIP Field Consultant, Marcia Yeates, had several telephone conferences with Louise Bromley, initiated by Mrs. Yeates, partly general inquiries and partly to begin arrangements for Mrs. Bromley's attendance at the Annual Associates' Workshop in June, 1986. Louise Bromley telephoned at the end of April to ask the cultural advisability of various end-of-Program activities: presentation of certificates to the mothers, having a party at the end of Program II, recommending use of public library.

May 1986

Louise Bromley notified Marcia Yeates by telephone that she would be attending the June Associates' Workshop, and that she had requested a letter from the VIP Director allowing her to combine attendance at the Workshop with a VIP evaluation of her two years of work preliminary to receiving the VIP Certificate of Approval.

June 1986

The VIP Director did write to Louise Bromley, as follows:

> I'm delighted to hear that you will attend the Associates workshop, that you'll be staying for your Program's certification evaluation—and that your family will be with you to do some sight seeing—a great idea!
>
> I've enclosed a copy of our Criteria for Certification and of KEEP, partly so that you will know what our standards are and partly so that you can gather together the necessary AV tapes and documents. As you can see, you will need to bring video or audio recording of a Home Session and of a Toy Demonstrator Conference and five kinds of documents: a filled-in and signed KEEP; six Home Session Reports; one dyad file folder; your VISM list and VISM Guide Sheets for one Program year; and your Work Flow Sheet, or its equivalent, for one Program year.
>
> Naomi will conduct the certification evaluation at our office here in Wantagh. I'm pretty sure you will find it an interesting and non-threatening experience, like a continuation of your training by Naomi. It will last from about 10 AM to about 4 PM on July 1 or 2. Naomi plans to pick you up at the Holiday Inn and bring you back there at the end of the day.

June and July 1986

Louise Bromley did attend the Associates' Workshop at the end of June, received a Certificate of Attendance for the Workshop, and then qualified for her agency's receiving a Certificate of Approval on July 1. Naomi Feldheim, the Field Consultant who conducted the Evaluation, ended her accompanying notes with the comment: "It was deeply gratifying to see LB's excellence in adhering to VIP's standards. With no site visits, LB has conscientiously contacted PL or me with questions concerning

ing the quality of her Program replication, and a Certificate is most assuredly recommended."

On July 21, 1986, the VIP Director sent a Certificate of Approval to Brian Palmer, Family Keystone's Director. She also sent, as a surprise, a Certificate to Louise Bromley, to recognize and honor her leadership in upholding Verbal Interaction Project standards as Coordinator of her replication of the Mother-Child Home Program.

"Do-It-Yourself" Program Use by Parents

Unlike the parents reached by the Mother-Child Home Program of "Family Keystone," many parents of pre-preschoolers can afford to buy toys and books which fulfill most of the Program's standards as described in Chapter Three ("Getting Up from Under"). And because of their Striver status, most middle-income mothers and/or fathers would be able, by reading and heeding Chapter Three in this book, to dispense with a Toy Demonstrator's modeling. Following the Program's curriculum and method as they interact with their own small children in a "do-it-yourself" Program would come easily to them.

However, the Mother-Child Home Program and its "curriculum materials"—the toys and books which encompass the criteria recommended in Chapter Three—only provide the means of strengthening the hidden curriculum latent in every family. Middle-income parents may discover, through this book, that they have already brought the hidden curriculum to the fore, as is the norm for most parents with higher incomes and education than the Program's primary intended population. Thus the Program may add little to the intellectually supportive aspects of their usual parent-toddler conversation. Nevertheless, even for such parents the Program's standards for parenting behavior and children's social-emotional development may provide some valuable guidelines for giving their pre-preschoolers a good start toward fulfilling the youngsters' unique potentialities.

Although other families can thus find their way to the Program on their own by using this book as a "do-it-yourself" instruction manual, families in poverty usually need society's help to gain access to the Mother-Child Home Program. Low-income, low-educated parents of preschoolers generally need to have the Program offered by a school or a social agency like "Family Keystone." Their best help is to learn to use the Mother-Child Home Program by demonstration, by hands-on practice with a friendly Toy Demonstrator, and most of all by receiving the gifts of books and toys for their children, which are too difficult to acquire with their own meager resources. It is not hard to identify the low-income parents who most need help in using the Mother-Child Home Program: they are often single-parent heads of families, are supported either by welfare aid or by unskilled jobs, and usually have not finished high school.

These parents must have the assistance of a formal Mother-Child Home Program before they are ready for a "do-it-yourself" version. Yet their continuing the verbal interaction with their children around the curriculum materials after the Program is over, as they usually do, is indeed a "do-it-yourself" replication of the Program. Thus the Program gives low-income families, however handicapped by low education and poverty, a chance almost equal to that of less deprived families to incorporate "do-it-yourself" MCHPs into their interaction with their children long after the formal Program is over.

7

Messages
From
Home

What I have taught my two year old, he remembers very well!
—One mother's written comment
on the Mother-Child Home Program

Almost twenty years went into the Verbal Interaction Project's development and research of the Mother-Child Home Program. In addition, the Verbal Interaction Project built a reliable method of replicating the Program so that it could be exported outside of the research setting. It guided the Program's replication in many geographical settings—inner city, rural, suburban, Alaskan Eskimo villages, New Mexican Indian reservations, northern Canada, the entire Commonwealth of Bermuda—and under the auspices of every sort of nonprofit organization.

Wherever the Program has been adopted, every attempt has been made to keep it an exact copy of the original, in order to give participants the full benefit of the model Program's effects. This also means that the Verbal Interaction Project has had feedback from each replication's experience with what is, in effect, the original Program.

By now the impact of our own experiences combined with those of 84 replications have produced some compelling messages. They come, literally, from the homes of the participating low-income mothers and their children in 16 states and three countries.

First Message: Hope

Every so often in this country the pendulum of public interest in education swings to disquiet about the problems of high school students, particularly those who come from low-income, often underclass, families and who are not planning to go to college. Currently the concern is with the poor academic achievement of many such high school students. Their resulting inadequate preparation for all but entry level jobs is further diminished if a student doesn't remain in school long enough to receive a high school diploma.

During the past few years annual reports from the New York City Board of Education, representative of those from most urban areas, repeat the same dismal story: the number of high school dropouts each year reaches about 11 percent. A 1985 *New York Times* article on one such all-too-typical Board of Education study is headlined: "Study Finds City Schools Made No Progress in Reducing Dropouts" (Rohter, 1985). An opening paragraph reads: "The report found that 11.4 percent of the students in public high schools dropped out during the 1983–84 school year. The study estimated that 38.4 percent of all entering freshmen would leave school before they graduated."

High school is boring and embarrassing for students who are unable to cope with it. Dropping out may seem to be a logical solution to all the problems it poses. This is obvious to most observers. But few people see a connection between the weaknesses in young people's academic performance in high school and the academic problems of children in first grade.

In fact, however, they are so closely related as to be virtually one and the same. Children's disadvantage in acquiring skills as early as first grade, stemming from insufficient preparation before entering school, continues and compounds throughout their school careers, into high school.

As long ago as 1966, the sociologist James Coleman made what could well be a contemporary observation in his famous report, *Equality of Educational Opportunity:* "The educational disadvantage with which a group begins school remains the disadvantage with which it finishes."

Children from Hesitater families of the underclass compose

the largest group which begins school with an educational disadvantage. They often start kindergarten without adequate access to the "hidden family-curriculum" in their preschool years. The gap between them and the children who have had in their own homes this casual, informal preparation for school becomes all too evident in first grade. Such underclass pupils tend to lag in acquiring the reading and arithmetic skills which are the foundation for most of their learning in higher grades. The closer they get to high school, the wider the gap grows.

The first message from home is a message of hope for Program families and for society. The Mother-Child Home Program provides a feasible option to prevent the early elementary school disadvantage which is the precursor of high school failure. It fosters the development in low-income children's homes of the hidden curriculum latent in all families.

In children's very early years, even before they reach center-based preschools, and long before they reach elementary school, much of their academic disadvantage at the high school level can be headed off, and so can some of the cost, to society and the taxpaper, of expenditures for special education, welfare support, and criminal-justice proceedings. A Michigan research group headed by educator David Weikart published a study in 1984 which concretely documented the economic profit to society of effective preschool education (Berrueta-Clement et al., 1984).

The hope embodied in the first message from home is grounded in objective evidence, the short-term and long range data from 16 years of systematically investigating the effects of the VIP's model Mother-Child Home Program on pre-pre-school children and mothers. The research results of in-house and outside evaluations indicated that, on the average, the model Program significantly aided low-income children's intellectual growth and later school performance. Their third grade reading, arithmetic, and intelligence scores were at the level of national norms. Their fifth grade reading and intelligence scores also met national norms and significantly surpassed those of Non-Program children of similar background, as had all their previous scores.

The model Program graduates' performance in high school is unknown since at the last full follow-up study Program children had reached only fifth grade, and funding for continuing follow-up studies did not stretch further. However, most educators would agree that success in elementary school lays the foundation for high school achievement.

The positive results of the follow-up study of Program graduates through eighth grade in the Pittsfield Schools (one of the Mother-Child Home Program's first replicators) supports this view (DeVito & Karon, 1984). It is clear that the Program, both in the original model and in replication, helped to provide low-income children with the home enrichment they needed to achieve success in higher grades by enabling them to achieve academically in the early grades.

The model Program was popular and effective with the mothers as well as with their children. The Program's popularity with the low-income mothers invited to participate was indicated by the high percentage of their accepting Program enrollment and Home Session appointments and of their lasting out two years in the Program. The Program's effectiveness with mothers was seen in the mothers' greatly increased verbal interaction with their children and in the gradual ability of most Hesitaters to display Striver-like behavior—perhaps actually to become Strivers—by the end of the Program.

Second Message:
The Existence of a Mother-Child Network

The second message from home is that a supportive mother-child network, only surmised when the Program began, actually does seem to exist. Correlational statistical techniques revealed that the Program evoked from mother-participants the kinds of interaction with their preschool children that fostered the children's ability to cope with elementary school challenges. Mother and child together—responding positively to each other in play and conversation—wove a strong mutually supportive network from their interaction and its link to their emotional relationship. Like many invisible supports between parents and children, it was hard to tell which strands came from the mother and which from the child.

When the mothers showed verbal and other kinds of positive interactive behavior during the child's preschool years at home, the children were rated as having specific competencies in first and second grade. That is, if the mothers actively conversed with their preschool children, and also showed them warmth and affection, the children were likely in elementary school to be self-confident, task-oriented, intellectually competent, creative, and to have good reading and arithmetic skills. At the same time, the data indicated the importance of keeping the mother-child interaction casual and nonpressuring. Laughter and joy seemed to play important roles in weaving the network. Didacticism had a negative effect on children's school age learning.

The development of the network from reciprocal mother-child responsiveness was a probable explanation for the power of Dr. Bettye Caldwell's HOME instrument to predict children's cognitive development from their home environments and their mothers' activity in infancy. In the Mother-Child Home Program the mother usually was the one to start the conversational ball rolling between herself and her young child, and to bestow occasional hugs or their equivalents. But the child's responses kept the ball rolling. It was apparent over and over in Program Home Sessions and in videotaped mother-child play that when a child smiled, or replied, or pointed to the right book illustration, or put a puzzle piece in the right place, the mother was delighted. With such positive feedback, she was encouraged to continue the interaction. Together they wove a network that supported the child's school-age competencies, the mother's self-esteem, and the sense of well-being in both of them that comes under the heading of "mental health."

Third Message: Strivers and Hesitaters

Among persistent American social myths is the one that single parents on welfare are apathetic, incompetent mothers whose main ambition is to have more children in order to stay contentedly supported by welfare checks. Evidence against this monolithic and distorted view of the underclass was the third message that came from the Home Sessions of the Mother-Child Home Program. Most social agency staff people whose work is among "The Poor" have seen flaws in the myth but have had few systematically gathered facts to substantiate their perceptions. The third message is of such evidence, from the Home Sessions of the Program. The Toy Demonstrators' regularly recorded ratings of underclass mothers' interactive behavior in Home Sessions with their children provided empirical data to explode the myth of the monolithic poor.

Many mothers, when they enrolled in the Program, were indeed apathetic and unable to deal with everyday crises. It soon began to be clear that they were Hesitaters, immobilized by depression and hopelessness. Their inertia was manifested in their lack of interaction with their children in the first dozen or so Home Sessions of the Program and sometimes throughout the first year of the two-year Program. Superficially, they presented a picture close to the stereotype. But most of the Hesitaters slowly changed—toward more interaction with their children, toward increased initiative in dealing with daily problems, and toward self-respect. Because of their capacity to change, most Hesitaters in the Mother-Child Home Program eventually revealed themselves to be latent Strivers, once the Program offered them the hope of something better for themselves and their children.

Striver-mothers entered the Program with the same external low-income characteristics as Hesitaters but became active in Home Sessions almost at once, at the latest by Session Two. They either already knew, or at once learned from the Toy Demonstrators, the Program's interaction techniques. It was quickly apparent from the Home Session activity of these mothers that their basic difference from the Hesitaters was in *motivation* beyond the universal of mother-love which had drawn them to participate in the first place. They seemed to want to take charge of their lives, to be free of the demeaning welfare morass, to escape from the underclass. They clearly could be called Strivers. They needed little help from the Program except for the gifts of toys and books and perhaps some Toy Demonstrator modeling to guide them away from pushing their children too hard.

Graduation from high school was the only overt background feature that distinguished Strivers from Hesitaters before the Home Sessions began. The high school diploma may well indicate a trait of persistence—the ability to "hang in there"— which is of greater importance than having more education than the Hesitaters. All of the mothers had met the Program's entry requirements of having no more than a high school education. The higher rate of actual twelfth grade *completion* among the Strivers is consistent with staff observations of Strivers as being more psychologically intact than Hesitaters.

Yet many observations suggested that Strivers also had to deal with problems like mild depression and somewhat lowered self-esteem although not to the degree that these problems impeded Hesitaters. Hesitaters improved in their self-confidence and self-competence more dramatically than Strivers as they perceived their own progress in the Program, but the mental health of many Strivers likewise displayed improvement as the Program advanced.

The Program's discovery of both Hesitater and Strivers within its own research samples greatly alters the "lazy welfare mother" stereotype. It leads to the recognition that many mothers on welfare are Strivers. They are so strongly motivated to improve their own and their children's lives that relatively small boosts from a Mother-Child Home Program reduced to a minimum (by deleting Year-Two Home Sessions) can enable them to utilize a valuable method to help their children and perhaps to climb out of the underclass. The Program's experience suggests, too, that if Hesitaters are given a more intensive Mother-Child Home Program (by continuing Home Session in Year Two), they can eventually become Strivers, with the same ultimate goal of achieving independence from welfare support.

Fourth Message: Social Feasibility of the Program

Over the years of developing and studying the Mother-Child Home Program, its practicability for nationwide use was explored and refined. The fourth message from home is that the method is feasible as a social program almost anywhere in this country and probably in many parts of the world. It is exportable, inexpensive, popular at all levels from Program participants to Toy Demonstrators to agency executives, and can generate entry-level jobs through the role of the Toy Demonstrator.

Exportability

The crucial question for any potential social program is whether the model program will be reproducible and therefore effective outside of its original laboratory setting. Ten years went into developing the "exportability" of the Mother-Child Home Program.

The Verbal Interaction Project generated flexible but standard procedures for disseminating information about the Program and for assisting "adopter" organizations to implement accurate replications of the original model Program. The "user friendliness" and efficiency of its procedures is perhaps best measured by the continued existence of 15 very early Program replications with most of their key elements intact. All of the 15 had started before 1980 and some as early as 1970.

It seems clear that the Mother-Child Home Program is exportable with most of its key elements in place. Thus it can be expected to have much the same impact as the model Program with other low-income groups wherever it is replicated.

Entry-Level Jobs in the Program

Program mothers learn the Mother-Child Home Program well from their own experience. When they "graduate," most are ready to be trained by the Program to become paid Toy Demonstrators themselves.

Toy Demonstrators do not have to be former mother-participants. They may have any education or work experience. A Ph.D. psychologist can function as well in the role as a high school educated welfare recipient—but the salary she would command will probably be much larger than the budget can afford. So far, almost all replications have hired Toy Demonstrators of limited educational and work experience, perhaps because it is cheaper to do so but, more important, to give the more limited person experience in an entry-level job.

In that job experience they learn the basic skills necessary for any job. They learn to keep Home Session appointments punctually and consistently, to write legible Home Session Records and keep them up to date, and to show up promptly for weekly Toy Demonstrator Conferences (group supervision). By the time a paid Toy Demonstrator has spent two years in the Program (less time for some), she is ready to go on to outside and perhaps better paid employment.

Popularity

Many observers are won over by the Mother-Child Home Program, possibly because, aside from its outright charm, it has a certain face validity ("Of course—that's it—give them what I had [what I missed] when I was a kid!"). Also, because of its light touch and explicit ethical safeguards, it keeps the Hippocratic oath to "abstain from all intentional wrongdoing and harm . . . and whatsoever I shall see or hear . . . I will never divulge."

Such preservation of family privacy is of crucial importance. Of equal importance is the Program's respect for a family's way of life. The Program tries to incorporate wherever possible the family's cultural/sociolinguistic differences from mainstream culture. At the same time, the curriculum and most of the toys and books are links to that mainstream culture.

Most mothers and children are quickly drawn to the Program and remain committed to it as participants. Toy Demonstrators like the Program because it is enjoyable to learn and deliver, because of being trusted to do a meaningful job in it whose effects are clearly and quickly visible, and because of the job's semi-autonomy within a firm supervisory structure. Program Coordinators and replicator executives become committed to it because it makes sense ("face validity") and because it aids low-income groups with a minimum outlay of resources and maximum approval by the community.

Cost

The annual cost of the Program in 1985 was roughly $1200 for each mother-child pair—lower, if volunteers were used rather than paid Toy Demonstrators. Program budgets are enlarged, not by the cost of the toys and books, but by the amounts going for salaries, which fluctuate in accordance with local standards.

Fifth Message: They Aren't Laboratory Rats

A basic problem in the United States for those who conduct research with young children is that preschoolers, unlike laboratory rats, cannot be commandeered. Nor can they volunteer themselves to be research subjects. Even when an intervention program for young children does not involve research, it requires, in our society, at least the parents' consent and usually their cooperation.

A two-year-old can't join even a nursery school on his own, let alone the Mother-Child Home Program. Certainly a two-year-old child could not agree to be in a "subject pool" and await later randomization into a Program or Non-Program Group, as a preliminary to Design II's subject-randomized research of the Mother-Child Home Program.

Parents who don't cooperate on their children's behalf with an early childhood program, or research of it, have self-selected themselves and their children out of it. Parents who give their cooperation have selected themselves and their children in. They and their children are volunteers for the program or for the research.

Why does this create a problem for research? A parent's lack of cooperation with a program beneficial to child and parent can be considered distressing. But why is this uncooperativeness a problem for research?

The problem, as became clear in the VIP's Design II research of the Mother-Child Home Program's effectiveness, lies in the "sample bias" which can be created by the self-selection of the research subjects. In Design II (randomization by subject) program evaluation research this is likely to result in a subject pool which is not truly representative of whatever population a program is meant to reach outside of the research laboratory.

A high degree of self-selection by subjects to be evaluated for measuring the effectiveness of a potential intervention program becomes a social problem when the program to be evaluated is a potential social remedy. If the children and/or parents enter an intervention program intended to prevent school problems, and there is no difference in child outcomes between Program and Non-Program Groups because most of the parents are Strivers with well-functioning children, the Program's rejection (based on Design II experimental evaluation research) can be a serious loss to society.

The probability is that as long as preschool children are dependent on their mothers or fathers for real cooperation with programs for them, and with the evaluation of those programs, the true effects of the programs will always have to be measured by using Design I experimental research designs (randomization by location or group). Even then the parents' initial willingness to come into a program and their continuing cooperation should be carefully estimated. The ideal Design II experiment, in any case, is probably unattainable with very young children under ordinary conditions, which of course includes parents' informed consent, whenever the self-selection of parents is a factor in research with preschoolers.

Sixth Message: Closing the Gap

The historic goal of preschool and remedial programs for students from low-income families has been to close the achievement gap separating them from children of higher income families.

This was the first paragraph of G. L. Maeroff's news article in the Science section of the *New York Times* for June 11, 1985. It voiced succinctly the goal of the Mother-Child Home Program. His headline read "Despite Head Start, 'Achievement Gap' Persists for the Poor."

It is unfortunately true, as Maeroff goes on to relate, that a 1985 study in one very large school system has found that although the school performance of students who had graduated from Head Start was "better than they would have done without it," the academic achievement of most lagged behind national norms and behind that of the non-Head Start eligible school population (Hebbeler, 1985).

The experience of this school system with Head Start graduates contrasts with the Pittsfield Public Schools follow-up through eighth grade of Mother-Child Home Program graduates. Not only did the Program graduates outperform comparable Non-Program students in their achievement, but *they met or exceeded national norms,* (DeVito & Karon, 1984), like the graduates of VIP's original model Mother-Child Home Program.

The sixth message from home is succinct. For graduates of the Mother-Child Home Program, the achievement gap had been closed.

Seventh Message: Print Literacy in the Electronic Age

We have entered the Electronic Age of Learning. Exciting video and computer possibilities are opening new ways for extending children's cognitive and creative abilities. Just as Gutenberg's 15th Century invention of movable type and the printing press opened the way to literacy for ordinary people, the learning possibilities of the Electronic Age seem to represent another giant step forward.

Yet like other gifts from the gods—like fire which makes a good servant when properly controlled but a bad master when it is not, like nuclear power which still hovers between serving and destroying the human race—electronic learning poses potential problems.

These problems may some day (though probably not soon) be like those forecast by E. M. Forster's fable, "The Machine Stops" (1928). First published in 1909, in the *Oxford and Cambridge Review,* the story envisaged, with eerie technological accuracy, the support of a rather dreary civilization by a vast, world-wide Machine. It served people's every need as they lived their underground lives in cell-like apartments and conducted their contacts with each other by videophone. When the machine faltered, the lights dimmed and the air became foul. At last the Machine stopped, and "civilized" humanity died out (now published as Forster, 1928).

Similar problems already seem to be inherent in the Electronic Age of Learning, although less dramatically as yet. They center around the threat to what some already call "Print Literacy," in contrast to "Electronic Literacy"; and perhaps also around the threat to people's capacity to identify with and feel for others that can grow through acquaintance with books. A few years ago one commentator hailed the "post-literate society" and pointed out that nowadays "the need to read and write is not so urgent as it was" (Schwartz, 1981). Conversely, the need for Electronic Literacy has grown, as predicted. It is also true that reading takes more effort than passively watching a television or even computer screen. However, reading a well-written book can stretch the mind, imagination, and empathy more than the finest video program or film. The very ambiguity of a book calls forth thinking and feeling beyond what the screen can evoke.

Print literacy is necessary to enter the world of books. It is possible that this realm of imagination may soon be closed to all but a print-literate elite to which electronic literacy is more a practical means to an end than a sole source of information and pleasure. Others may acquire enough print literacy to study and carry around the manuals for learning a trade. The rest may swell the numbers of the underclass at the bottom of the social pyramid, an underclass even more illiterate and emotionally alienated than it is today. Without print literacy the climb from the underclass can be hopeless.

The seventh message from home is that the Mother-Child Home Program lays the groundwork for later print literacy and love of books very early in children's experience. Its method for doing so increases children's accessibility to feelings, their own and those of others as well. The increased bonding between mothers and children, the deepened social-emotional development of children are what make possible the growth of human empathy and of humanness itself. The Program has the power to offset some of the nonhuman, even antihuman, aspects of the Electronic Age of Learning.

Eighth Message: Gift from the Underclass?

The eighth (and last) message from home begins with a question. What will be the future utilization of the Mother-Child Home Program?

Will it be used more and more as a resource for the underclass, as was intended at its creation? Will it also be used to add to the resources of middle-income parents and children? Indeed, will it become eventually a gift entirely to the middle class from the underclass mothers who helped to develop it?

The Mother-Child Home Program is only one instance of several well-researched exemplary preschool and elementary school educational programs of the sixties and seventies, which were developed with government or private foundation funds won by competitive grant proposals. Most of these programs have either disappeared or are struggling to stay alive so that they can continue the mission of serving disadvantaged children. They had achieved funding for the development and research of their programs. Alas, as soon as they completed the laboratory work, the funding stopped (and sometimes before then). Few of the thousands of educational programs created in the sixties and seventies with federal funding still survive, although many had demonstrated their effectiveness by careful evaluation research.

Similarly, after a sixteen-year, three-million-dollar investment in the Program's research and development, the Verbal Interaction Project is prepared to train sponsoring organizations anywhere to implement the Mother-Child Home Program with underclass mothers. However, funding of the model Program and its replication training has ended. It had been intended only for support of their development and research—not to have them continue for the purpose of training new replications.

Fortunately, the Verbal Interaction Project is able to maintain its guidance of new Program replications because of the continuing activity of some staff members on a volunteer basis and because of in-kind contributions of space, telephone, and secretarial service. But this is a rare exception. Most programs, to continue and spread their good word, require the nourishment of financial support to prevent their death by malnutrition.

Apart from the Program's readiness to be used for help *to* low-income mothers, it can also be seen as a gift *from* the underclass to any parents who wish to use it, whatever their socioeconomic status. Thousands of underclass families have helped to refine a Program which can be used to aid young children of any income level in almost any part of the English speaking world—and perhaps elsewhere too. All parents are thus indebted to the underclass mothers and their children who pioneered this effective and joyous method of enhancing the skills of young children while adding to the strengths of their parents.

However, the low-income parents for whom the Mother-Child Home Program was intended do not have the resources to utilize it on their own. They must have the assistance of such Program-replicating organizations as schools and social agencies. Yet the funding that makes it possible for organizations to implement the Program has dwindled, and it continues to dwindle.

Therefore the last "message from home" remains a question, and a bittersweet one at that. Will the Mother-Child Home Program turn out to be a gift to all parents and children *except* the very ones for whom it was created? Will the Program develop into a "do-it-yourself" method which may add to the hidden curriculum of the middle class family and eventually further widen the gap between the school performance of middle-income and low-income children?

Will the Program become at last beyond the reach of the depressed, undereducated, single parents and their children who are the chief members of the underclass in this country?

The answer cannot be found in this book. It lies in the hands of policy makers, legislators, executives, and purse-string holders at all levels. Only they can decide whether the Mother-Child Home Program will be a gift *to* the underclass as well as *from* it.

Afterword:
In
Appreciation

The model Mother-Child Home Program owed its existence, research, and replication from 1967 to 1982 to the encouragement and financial support of a large number of federal agencies and private foundations.

The federal agencies were: Children's Bureau and the National Institute of Mental Health, both of the U.S. Department of Health and Human Services; the Center for Educational Communication, the National Diffusion Network, and the National Institute of Education—all from the U.S. Department of Education. Grants from these agencies, based on competitive proposals, totaled one and a half million dollars over 16 years.

The list of private foundations which supported the Mother-Child Home Program and its evaluation research during those years is headed by the Carnegie Corporation of New York and by the Rockefeller Brothers Fund, because of the magnitude and lasting nature of their support. However, the importance to a developing program of a foundation's aid is often determined as much by the strategic timing of that support as by its amount and duration. A relatively small grant for a short period of time was often enough to tide the Mother-Child Home Program over a life threatening fiscal crisis. It was for this kind of rescue that the Program is indebted to two individuals, Irving Brooks Harris and John Tuchler; to Adelphi University (for computer use and office space at the School of Social Work); and to 17 private foundations:

Marion R. Ascoli Fund
Citibank Fund
Frank E. Clark Charitable
    Trust
Foundation for Child
    Development
General Mills Foundation
William T. Grant
Harris Foundation
International Paper Company
    Foundation
Penny Kirschenfeld Memorial
    Fund
Lavanberg-Corner House
Joe and Emily Lowe
    Foundation
Newsday Fund
North Shore Unitarian
    Universalist Society Veatch
    Program
Pittway Foundation
Edward and Emily Roche
    Relief Foundation
Surdna Foundation
Laura B. Vogler Foundation

The total for grants from all private foundations over 16 years was close to a million and a half dollars, almost equal to the federal grants. From 1982 to the present the Verbal Interaction Project has been supported by many modest cash and in-kind gifts, with no cash gifts of more than $10,000 in any year.

The nonprofit Verbal Interaction Project, Inc., is the originator and sponsor of the Mother-Child Home Program, responsible for its research and for its replication outside of the research project. It started under the auspices of Family Service Association of Nassau County; "spun off" to become a not-for-profit corporation with its own Board of Directors for disseminating the Program; and is now affiliated with the State University of New York at Stony Brook through my position there as Adjunct Associate Professor. The Verbal Interaction Project was also responsible for obtaining the grants which supported the model Program as well as its research and replication.

The Project appreciated not only the financial but also the moral support of the officials of the federal agencies and private foundations that awarded the grants. They are too numerous to name individually except for one extraordinarily steadfast foundation officer whose objective though kind interest and encouragement was a mainstay during most of the Program's development. She is Barbara D. Finberg, Vice-President of the Carnegie Corporation of New York.

"Objective" is a key descriptor for the attitude of all Program funders. No funding source, whether federal or private, ever tried to influence the work of the Verbal Interaction Project. Once our proposal (work plan) was accepted, and an award granted for its execution, funders monitored but did not meddle. (Some might argue that there was a kind of meddling in a White House decision to rescind, as part of a sweeping deletion of grant awards, a 1981 grant won by the Project; it ended the model Program and curtailed Project service to Program replications.)

The enthusiasm of the mother-child participants in the original and in replications of the Mother-Child Home Program, and the exceptional dedication of Program Coordinators and the Toy Demonstrators they supervised, were and are constant sources of inspiration.

The Verbal Interaction Project's still active Board of Directors; the scores of volunteers who worked throughout the years as Toy Demonstrators in the model Program; the staff members of the Program and of the Project—all gave unstintingly and cheerfully of their energy and commitment. They are all owed special recognition for their contributions.

Three persons must be exempted from the otherwise unavoidable anonymity of the many staff members to whom I am indebted. The first two are Dr. John Madden and Dr. John O'Hara, Research Associates at the Verbal Interaction Project. Their skills were vital to most of the Project's research methodology and statistical analyses of Program results. The third person who must be named is Dr. Sidney Levenstein, Policy Consultant to the Verbal Interaction Project, and Professor and Chairman of the Research Sequence at the Adelphi University School of Social Work, at the time of his sudden death in 1974. His wise and supportive counsel from the beginning of the Program's development and for much of its research was integral to all aspects of the Verbal Interaction Project and of the Mother-Child Home Program.

Whatever fluency this book has is due mainly to the critical comments of colleagues who consented to review it at various stages. I am deeply grateful to Drs. Beverly Birns, Derk Bodde, Katherine Flegal, Susan Levenstein, John O'Hara, Derek Phillips,

John Spitzer and Eleanor Wolf; and to Myrtle Crawford, Naomi Feldheim, Judy Garodnick, Daniel Levenstein, Cyril Miles, Myron Roochvarg and Isadora Rosenberg.

Phyllis Levenstein

Wantagh, New York
1987

APPENDIX

Index to Technical
Materials for Operating
a Mother-Child Home Program

VIP Form No.	Description or Name
109	Index to Technical Materials
	Program Participation by Mother-Child Dyads
139	Monthly Program Calendar
79A	Dyad Recruiting Letter
42A	Initial Interview (Schedule 1)
46	Dyad's Reference Card
KK	Letter to Introduce Toy Demonstrator (TD)
F	Points for TD to Cover During Meeting with Mother
D	Home Session Confirmation Letter
21	Home Session Record
22R	Record of Toys and Books Assigned
34A	Special Family Problems
33	Dyad's Mid-Year Evaluation of Program
65	Child's Behavior Traits (CBT)
65B	Child's Behavior Traits (CBT) Item Guides
96B	Parent and Child Together (PACT) Item Guides
96A	Parent and Child Together (PACT)
31	Evaluation of Home Session Behavior
Y	Mother's Anonymous Evaluation of Program
	Toy Demonstrators (TDs)
43	Toy Demonstrator's Application Interview
47	Toy Demonstrator's Reference Card
87	Scheduling for TD Training Workshop

VIP Form No.	Description or Name
77P	Training Outline for TD Training Workshop
77	Training Syllabus for TD Training Workshop
K	Toy Demonstrator's VISIT Handbook (Introduction)
23B	Explanation to Parent of Guide Sheet
23(T)	Guide Sheet Outline (Toy)
23(B)	Guide Sheet Outline (Book)
20	TD's Session Evaluation for TD Training Workshop
51	TD's Final Evaluation of Training Workshop
82	Work Assignment Sheet
85	Work Week Schedule
168	Toy Demonstrator's Weekly Time Schedule
34	Toy Demonstrator's Supervisory Notes
95A	Record of Audio-Tape Content (Home Session)
30	Supervisory Evaluation of Toy Demonstrator
	Coordinators' Manual for Supervision of TDs

Verbal Interaction Stimulus Materials (VISM)

L	Criteria for Selection of VISM (Toys and Books)
56	VISM (and Home Session) Schedule—Program I
56	VISM (and Home Session) Schedule—Program II
D118	Suppliers of VISM
13	VISM Order Card
126	VISM Inventory Sheet
25	Supervisor's Record of VISM Disbursed
135	Toy Demonstrator's Evaluation of VISM—Program I
135	Toy Demonstrator's Evaluation of VISM—Program II
162	Evaluation of Possible New VISM

Guidance of Coordinator by Verbal Interaction Project

	Manual for Replication of Mother-Child Home Program
83	Proposed Plan for Replicating Mother-Child Home Program
151A	Basic Standards for Replicating Mother-Chid Home Program
131	Basic Services to Replicators
D88	Key Elements for Establishing Program ("KEEP")
(Book)	Preventing a Dream from Becoming a Nightmare
170A	Criteria for Certification
170B	Certificate of Approval

2

Replicators of the Mother-Child Home Program, 1986–87

United States

Massachusetts

CAMBRIDGE
Cambridge School Department
158 Spring Street
Cambridge, MA 02141
　Senior Coordinator: Ellen Grant
　Telephone: 617–498–9200,
　　Ext. 9625
Year began MCHP: 1972

DEDHAM
Family Service of Dedham
18 Norfolk Street
Dedham, MA 02026
　Coordinator: Franny Frankel
　Telephone: 617–326–0400
Year began MCHP: 1978

FALL RIVER
Fall River Public Schools
1207 Globe Street
Fall River, MA 02721
　Coordinator: Peg Burrows
　Telephone: 617–675–8420
Year began MCHP: 1979

LAWRENCE
Lawrence Public Schools
58 Lawrence Street, Floor 5
Lawrence, MA 01842
　Coordinator: Gail Rosengard
　Telephone: 617–686–7701,
　　Ext. 180
Year began MCHP: 1974

LOWELL
Lowell Public Schools
89 Appleton Street
Lowell, MA 01852
　Coordinator: Elinor Rafferty
　Telephone: 617–937–7622
Year began MCHP: 1979

NEWTON
Family Counseling Service (Region
　West) Inc.
74 Walnut Park
Newton, MA 02158
　Coordinator: Ronni McMillan
　Telephone: 617–965–6200
Year began MCHP: 1970

PITTSFIELD
Pittsfield Public Schools, Plunkett
    School
First and Penn Street
Pittsfield, MA 01201
    Regional (Massachusetts) and
    Senior Coordinator: Judy Stolzberg
    Telephone: 413–443–4572
Year began MCHP: 1970

New York

GREAT NECK AND MANHASSET
Great Neck/Manhasset Public Schools
Child Development Center
10 Campbell Street
New Hyde Park, New York 11040
    Coordinator: Doris Kertzner
    Telephone: 516–482–8650
Year began MCHP: 1973

HARTSDALE
Westchester Jewish Community
    Services
141 North Central Avenue
Hartsdale, New York 10530
    Senior Coordinator: Carol Hallinger
    Telephone: 914–949–6761
Year began MCHP: 1971

HEMPSTEAD
Family Service Association of
    Nassau County
129 Jackson Street
Hempstead, New York 11550
    Senior Coordinator:
    Edith Wasserman
    Telephone: 516–485–4600, Ext. 57
Year began MCHP: 1984

NEW YORK CITY
Talbot Perkins Childrens Services
116 West 32nd Street
New York City, New York 10001
    Coordinator: Denise Freiman
    Telephone: 212–736–2510
Year began MCHP: 1972

OYSTER BAY
Youth and Family Counseling
    Agency of Oyster Bay/
    E. Norwich
119A South Street
Oyster Bay, New York 11771
    Coordinator: Mary Agosta
    Telephone: 516–922–6867
Year began MCHP: 1973

ROSLYN
Roslyn Public Schools
Heights School, Willow Street
Roslyn Heights, New York 11577
    Coordinator: Terry Wolff
    Telephone: 516–621–4900,
    Ext. 248
Year began MCHP: 1978

Pennsylvania

HOLLIDAYSBURG
Hollidaysburg Area School District
201 Jackson Street
Hollidaysburg, Pennsylvania 16648
    Coordinator: Elna Hanly
    Telephone: 814–695–5584
Year began MCHP: 1987

WEST CHESTER
West Chester Area School District
829 Paoli Pike
West Chester, Pennsylvania 19380
    Coordinator: Janice Houser
    Telephone: 215–436–7021 or
    7032
Year began MCHP: 1987

South Carolina

UNION
Union County Schools
P.O. Box 907
Union, South Carolina 29379
    Coordinator: Connie Springs
    Telephone: 803–427–3651
Year began MCHP: 1987

Bermuda

HAMILTON
Bermuda Ministries of Health,
    Social Services and Education
P.O. Box HM 1195
Hamilton 5–24, Bermuda
    Senior Coordinator:
    Conchita King
    Telephone: 809–295–0746
Year began MCHP: 1976

Canada

Manitoba

BRANDON
Child and Family Services of
    Western Manitoba
340 Ninth Street
Brandon, Manitoba, Canada
    R7A 6C2
    Coordinator: Lorraine McLaren
    Telephone: 204–728–7000
    or 1–800–852–2700
Year began MCHP: 1984

APPENDIX

3

Criteria for VISM Books and Toys

A3.1 Books for Two- and Three-Year-Olds (with examples from one year's VISM list)

Criteria	Titles and Authors of Books by Age Groups (in order of presentation)
1. Content geared to children's age and interest; interesting to mothers; leads to verbalized associations; widens experience.	*Two- and Three-Year-Olds* Kunhardts, D., *Pat the Bunny* Brown, M. W., *Good Night Moon* Rojankovsky F. (Illus.), *The Tall Book of Mother Goose*
2. High literary standards.	Keats, E. J., *The Snowy Day* Zion, G., *All Falling Down*
3. Language simple, rhythmic, with some repetition.	Krauss, R., *The Carrot Seed* Keats, E. J., *Peter's Chair* Eastman, P. D., *Are You My Mother?*
4. Reading level within ability of all mothers.	Keats, E. J., *Whistle for Willie*
5. Content, illustrations, and general format attractive to both sexes and any ethnic group.	*Two-Year-Olds* Tresselt, A., *Rain Drops Splash* Tresselt, A., *Wake Up Farm*
6. Illustrations profuse, large, colorful, detailed, rich source of labeling and classification.	*Three-Year-Olds* Brown, M. W., *Runaway Bunny* Seuss, Dr., *The Cat in the Hat*
7. Low anxiety potential.	MacGregor, E., *Theodore Turtle*
8. Durability.	

A3.2. Toys for Two-Year-Olds
(with examples from one year's VISM list)

Criteria	Names and Descriptions of Toys	Criteria Met by Toys
Verbal	*Block Cart*	All but 6, 15
1. Induces language	Wooden wagon, colored blocks	
2. Permits language	with holes, rods that fit into holes	
Perceptual		
3. Strong colors	*Hammer and pegs*	All but 5, 6, 11,
4. Geometric forms	Pegs fixed into wooden bench	13
5. Space organization	can be pounded through to	
6. Size differences	under side; bench can	
7. Sound differences	then be reversed	
8. Tactile differences		
9. Form matching	*Mail Box*	All but 15
	Copy of corner mail box;	
Motor	colored wood beads are	
10. Specific skills	dropped through top holes	
11. Fitting parts	into bin	
12. Hitting		
13. Pulling	*Transportation Puzzle*	All but 7, 12,
14. Lifting	Jigsaw puzzle, each piece	13, 15
15. Diffuse motor	a different vehicle	
discharge		
	Two Plush Hand Puppets	All but 5, 6, 9,
Conceptual	Animals, movable mouths	12, 15
16. Problem solving		
17. Intelligible goal	*Circus Puzzle*	All but 7, 12,
18. Intrinsic reward	Jigsaw puzzle of circus tent	13, 15
19. Imaginative uses	with circus scene beneath	
20. Social concepts		
	Cash Register	All
21. Sex neutrality	Simple copy with cash	
22. Ethnic neutrality	drawer and bell activated by crank	
Other		
23. Low anxiety	*House Puzzle*	All but 7, 12,
24. Safety	Jigsaw puzzle of street and	13, 15
25. Durability	outside of house; inside of	
26. Easy care	house and buried utilities	
for mother	shown under pieces (fewer pieces than same puzzle used with three-year-olds)	

References

Ainsworth, M. D. The Development of infant-mother attachment. In B. M. Caldwell & H. N. Ricciuti (Eds.), *Review of child development research* (Vol. 3). *Child development and social policy.* Chicago: University of Chicago Press, 1973.

Applebome, P. Juvenile crime: the offenders are younger and offenses more serious. *New York Times,* February 3, 1987.

Auletta, K. *The Underclass.* New York: Vintage Books, Random House, 1982.

Bates, E. *Language and context.* New York: Academic Press, 1976.

Baumrind, D. Child care practices anteceding three patterns of pre-school behavior. *Genetic Psychology Monograph,* 1967, *75,* 43–88.

Bayley, N. Comparisons of mental and motor test scores for ages 1–15 months by sex, birth order, race, geographic location and education of parents. *Child Development,* 1965, *36,* 379–411.

Bee, H. L., Van Egeren, F., Streissguth, A. P., Numan, B. A., & Leckie, M. S. Social class differences in maternal teaching strategies and speech patterns. *Developmental Psychology,* 1969, *6,* 726–734.

Bee, H. L., Barnard, K. E., Eyres, S. J., Gray, C. A., Hammond, M. A., Spietz, A. L., Snyder, C., & Clark, B. Prediction of IQ and language skill from perinatal status, child performance, family characteristics and mother-infant interaction. *Child Development,* 1982, *53,* 1134–1156.

Belsky, J. Experimenting with the family in the newborn period. *Child Development,* 1985, *56,* 406–414.

Bernstein, B. A socio-linguistic approach to social learning. In J. Gould (Ed.) *Penguin survey of the social sciences, 1965.* Baltimore, Md.: Penguin, 1965.

———. Social class and lingustic developments: A theory of social learning. In A. H. Halsey, J. Floud, & C. A. Anderson (Eds.), *Education, economy, and society.* Glencoe, Ill.: The Free Press, 1961.

Berrueta-Clement, J. R. B., Schweinhart, L. J., Barnett, W. S., Epstein, A. S., & Weikart, D. P. Changed lives: Effects of the Perry Preschool Program on youth through age 19. *Monographs of the High/Scope Educational Research Foundation,* No. 8. Ypsilanti, Mich.: High/Scope Press, 1984.

Birns, B., & Golden, M. Prediction of intellectual performance at three years from infant tests and personality measures. *Merrill-Palmer Quarterly,* 1972, *18,* 53–58.

Bloom, B. B. *Stability and change in human characteristics.* New York: John Wiley & Sons, 1964.

Bolton, F. G., Laner, R. H., & Kane, S. P. Child maltreatment risk among adolescent mothers: A study of reported cases. *American Journal of Orthopsychiatry,* 1980, *50,* 489–504.

Borus, J. Issues critical to the survival of community mental health. *American Journal of Psychiatry,* 1978, *135,* 1029–1035.

Bower, E. Primary prevention of mental and emotional disorders: A conceptual framework and actional possibilities. *American Journal of Orthopsychiatry,* 1963, *33,* 832–848.

Bowlby, J. *Maternal care and mental health.* Geneva: World Health Organization, 1952.

Bradley, R., & Caldwell, B. The relation of infants' home environment to achievement test performance in first grade: A follow-up study. *Child Development,* 1984, *55,* 803–809.

Brazelton, T. B. Issues for working parents. *American Journal of Orthopsychiatry,* 1986, *56,* 14–25.

Broman, S. H., Nichols, P. L., & Kennedy, W. A. *Preschool IQ: Prenatal and early developmental correlates.* Somerset, N.J.: John Wiley & Sons, 1975.

Bronfenbrenner, U. Early deprivation: A cross-species analysis. In G. Newton & S. Levine (Eds.), *Early experience and behavior.* Springfield, Ill.: C. Thomas, 1968.

————. *Is early intervention effective: A report on longitudinal evaluations of preschool programs.* (Vol. 2). U.S. DHEW, OHD 74–25. Washington, D.C.: Government Printing Office, 1974.

Brown, R. *Words and things.* Glencoe, Ill.: The Free Press, 1958.

Brown, M. W. *Goodnight moon.* New York: Harper & Row Junior Books, 1947.

————. *Runaway bunny.* New York: Harper & Row Junior Books, 1972.

Bruner, J. S. The course of cognitive growth. *American Psychologist,* 1964, *19,* 1–15.

Bruner, J. S., Olver, R., & Greenfield, P. *Studies in cognitive growth.* New York: John Wiley & Sons, 1966.

Bryce, M., & Lloyd, J. C. (Eds.) *Treating families in the home.* Springfield, Ill.: C. Thomas, 1980.

Burgess, R. L., & Conger, R. D. Family interaction in abusive, neglectful and normal families. *Child Development,* 1978, *49,* 1163–1173.

Caldwell, B. M. What is the optimal learning environment for the young child? *American Journal of Orthopsychiatry,* 1967, *37,* 8–21.

Caldwell, B. M., Heider, J., & Kaplan, B. The inventory of home stimulation. Paper presented at the annual meeting of the American Psychological Association, Washington, D.C., 1966.

Campbell, D. T., & Stanley, J. C. *Experimental and quasi-experimental designs for research.* Chicago: Rand McNally & Co., 1969.

Cassirer, E. *An essay on man.* New Haven: Yale University Press, 1944.

Cattell, P. *The measurement of intelligence in infants and young children.* New York: Psychological Corporation, 1940.

Cazden, C. B. The situation: A neglected source of social class differences in language use. *Journal of Social Issues,* 1970, *26,* 35–60

————. Child language and education. New York: Holt, Rinehart and Winston, Inc., 1972.

Chilman, C. S. *Growing up poor.* U.S. Department of HEW, Division of Research, Welfare Administration Publication No. 13. Washington, D.C.: Government Printing Office, 1966.

————. Programs for disadvantaged parents. In B. M. Caldwell & H. N. Ricciuti (Eds.), *Review of Child Development Research,* Vol. 3. *Child development and social policy.* Chicago: University of Chicago Press, 1973.

Clark-Stewart, K. A. Interactions between mothers and their young children: Characteristics and consequences. *Monographs of the Society of Research in Child Development,* 1973, *38,* Nos. 6 & 7.

Clarke-Stewart, K. A., Vanderstoep, L., & Killim, G. Analysis and replication of mother-child relations at two years of age. *Child Development,* 1979, *50,* 777–793.

Coleman, J. S., & Campbell, E. Q. Equality of educational opportunity. Washington, D. C.: U.S. Department of HEW, 1966.

Consortium for Longitudinal Studies. *As the twig is bent.* Hillsdale, N.J.: Lawrence Eribaum Associates, 1983.

Darlington, R. B., Royce, J. M., Snipper, A. S., Murray, H. W., & Lazar, I. Preschool programs and later school competence of children from low-income families. *Science,* 1980, *208,* 202–204.

Day, M. C., & Parker, R. K. (Eds.) *The preschool in action.* 2nd ed. Boston: Allyn and Bacon, Inc., 1977.

DeVito, P. J., & Karon, J. P. *Final report, Parent-Child Home Program,* Chapter 1, ECIA, Pittsfield Public Schools, September 1, 1984.

Deutsch, M. The role of social class in language development and cognition. *American Journal of Orthopsychiatry,* 1965, *35,* 78–88.

Eastman, P. D. *Are you my mother?* New York: Beginner Books, 1960.

Educational programs that work. 13th ed. Longmont, Colo.: Sopris West, 1987.

Farran, D., & Ramey, C. Social class differences in dyadic involvement during infancy. *Child Development,* 1980, *51,* 254–257.

Findlay, D. C., & McGuire, C. Social status and abstract behavior. *Journal of Abnormal and Social Psychology,* 1957, *54,* 135–137.

Flack, M. *Ask Mr. Bear.* New York: Macmillan Co., 1932.

Forster, E. M. *The eternal moment and other stories.* New York: Harcourt, 1928.

Freeberg, N. E., & Payne, D. T. Parental influence on cognitive development in early childhood: A review. *Child Development,* 1967, *38,* 66–87.

Goldberg, Miriam L. Factors affecting educational attainment in depressed urban areas. In A. H. Passow (Ed.), *Education in depressed areas.* New York: Teachers College, Columbia University, 1963.

Golden, M., & Birns, B. Social class and cognitive development in infancy. *Merrill-Palmer Quarterly,* 1968, *14,* 139–149.

Goodson, B. D., & Hess, R. D. *Parents as teachers of young children: An evaluative review of some contemporary concepts and programs.* Rev. ed. Stanford: Stanford University, 1975.

Gordon, I. J. Stimulation via parent education. *Children,* 1969, *16,* 57–59.

Gottfried, A. W. (Ed.) *Home environment and early cognitive development* Orlando, Fl.: Academic Press, 1984.

Gootfried, A. W., & Brown, C. C. (Eds.) *Play interactions.* Lexington, Mass.: Lexington Books, 1986.

Heath, S. B. *Ways with words.* Cambridge, England: Cambridge University Press, 1983.

Hebb, D. O. *The organization of behavior.* New York: John Wiley and Sons, 1949.

Hebbler, K. *An analysis of the effectiveness of Head Start and of the performance of a low-income population in MCPS.* Rockville, Md.: Montgomery County Public Schools, 1985.

Herbers, J. New jobs in cities little aid to poor. *New York Times,* October 20, 1986.

Herzog, E. Social and economic characteristics of high-risk mothers. In F. Hazelkorn (Ed.), *Mothers-at-risk.* Garden City, NY: Adelphi University School of Social Work, 1966.

Hess, R. D., & Shipman, V. C. Early experience and the socialization of cognitive modes in children. *Child Development,* 1965, *36,* 869–886.

Hess, R. D., Holloway, S., Price, G. G., & Dickson, W. P. Family environment and the acquisition of reading skills. In L. M. Laosa & I. E. Sigel (Eds.), *Family learning environments for children.* New York: Plenum Press, 1982.

Hunt, J. McV. *Intelligence and experience.* New York: Ronald Press, 1961.

————. Reflections on a decade of early education. In D. A. Wilkerson (Ed.), *Educating children of the poor—1975–1985.* Westport, Conn.: Mediax, Inc., 1975.

Irwin, O. C. Infant speech: Effect of systematic reading of stories. *Journal of Speech and Hearing Research,* 1960, *3,* 187–190.

Kamii, C. K. & Radin, N. L. Class differences in the socialization practices of Negro mothers. *Journal of Marriage and the Family,* 1967, *29,* 302–310.

Karnes, M. B., Teska, J. A., Hodgins, A. S., & Badger, E. D. Educational intervention at home by mothers of disadvantaged infants. *Child Development,* 1970, *41,* 925–935.

Keats, E. J. *Peter's chair.* New York: Harper & Row Junior Books, 1967.

————. *Whistle for Willie.* New York: Viking-Penguin, Inc., 1964.

————. *Snowy day.* New York: Viking-Penguin, Inc., 1962.

Kerr, P. Crack addiction: The tragic impact on women and children. *New York Times,* February 9, 1987.

Kohn, M. *Social competence, symptoms and underachievement in childhood: a longitudinal perspective.* Washington, D. C.: V. H. Winston & Sons, 1977.

Kraus, P. E. *Yesterday's children.* New York: Wiley-Interscience, 1973.

Krauss, R. *The carrot seed.* New York: Harper & Row Junior Books, 1945.

Kunhardt, D. *Pat the bunny.* New York: Western Publishing Co., Inc., 1942.

Laosa, L. Families as facilitators of children's intellectual development at three years of age: A causal analysis. In L. Laosa & I. E. Sigel (Eds.), *Families as learning environments for children.* New York: Plenum Press, 1983.

Lamb, H. R., & Talbott, J. A. The homeless mentally ill. *Journal of the American Medical Association,* 1986, *256,* 498–561.

Lazar, I., & Darlington, R. Lasting effects of early educaton: A report from the Consortium for Longitudinal Studies. *Monographs of the Society for Research in Child Development,* 1982, *47* (2–3, Serial No. 195).

Levenstein, P. Cognitive growth in preschoolers through verbal interaction with mothers. *American Journal of Orthopsychiatry,* 1970, *40,* 426–432.

———. But does it work in homes away from home? *Theory into Practice,* 1972, *11,* 157–162.

———. *Manual for replication of the Mother-Child Home Program.* Freeport, N.Y.: Verbal Interaction Project, 1973. (Mimeographed)

———. A message from home. In M. J. Begab & S. S. Richardson (Eds.), *The mentally retarded and society: A social science perspective.* Baltimore: University Park Press, 1975.

———. Cognitive development through verbalized play. In J. S. Bruner, A. Jolly, & K. Sylva (Eds.), *Play—its role in development and evolution.* New York: Basic Books, 1976.

———. The Mother-Child Home Program. In M. C. Day & R. K. Parker (Eds.), *The preschool in action.* Second edition. Boston: Allyn & Bacon, 1977.

———. The parent-child network. In A. Simmons-Martin & D. R. Calvert (Eds.), *Parent-child intervention.* New York: Grune & Stratton, Inc., 1979.

———. Ethical considerations in home-based programs. In M. Bryce & J. C. Lloyd (Eds.), *Treating families in the home.* Springfield, Ill.: C. C. Thomas, 1980.

———. Implications of the transition period for early intervention. In R. M. Golinkoff (Ed.), *The transition from prelinguistic to linguistic communication.* Hillsdale, N. J.: Lawrence Erlbaum Associates, 1983.

Levenstein, P., & Levenstein, S. Fostering learning potential in pre-schoolers. *Social Casework,* 1971, *52,* 74–78.

Levenstein, P., Kochman, A., & Roth, H. A. From laboratory to real world: Service delivery of the Mother-Child Home Program. *American Journal of Orthopsychiatry,* 1973, *43,* 72–78.

Levenstein, P., & Madden, J. Progress Report to the Carnegie Corporation of New York, 1973–1976. Freeport, N. Y.: Verbal Interaction Project, 1976. (Mimeographed)

Levenstein, P., & O'Hara, J. M. *Submission to the Joint Dissemination Review Panel of National Institute of Education and U. S. Office of Education.* Freeport, N.Y.: Verbal Interaction Project, 1978. (Photocopied)

————. *Tracing the parent-child network: Final report, 9/1/79–8/31/82.* Grant No. NIE G 8000042, National Institute of Education, U.S. Department of Education, 1983. (Photocopied)

Levenstein, P., O'Hara, J. M., & Madden, J. The Mother-Child Home Program of the Verbal Interaction Project. In Consortium for Longitudinal Studies, *As the twig is bent.* Hillsdale, N.J.: Lawrence Erlbaum Associates, 1983.

Levenstein, P. & Staff, Verbal Interaction Project. Child's Behavior Traits. In O. Johnson (Ed.), *Tests and measurements in child development, Handbook II.* San Francisco: Jossey-Bass, 1976.

Levenstein, P., & Sunley, R. Stimulation of verbal interaction between disadvantaged mothers and children. *American Journal of Orthopsychiatry,* 1968, *38,* 116–121.

MacGregor, E. *Theodore turtle.* New York: McGraw-Hill Book Co., 1955. (out of print)

Madden, J., Levenstein, P., & Levenstein, S. Longitudinal IQ outcomes of the Mother-Child Home Program. *Child Development,* 1976, *47,* 1015–1025.

Madden, J., O'Hara, J. M., & Levenstein, P. Home again. *Child Development,* 1984, *55,* 636–647.

McKinley, D. G. *Social class and family life.* New York: Free Press of Glencoe, 1964.

Millar, S. *The psychology of play.* Baltimore: Penguin Books, 1968.

Moore, T. Language and intelligence: A longitudinal study of the first eight years. *Human Development,* 1968, *11,* 2–24.

Morrison, G. S. *Parent involvement in the home, school and community.* Columbus, Oh.: C. E. Merrill, 1978.

Moynihan, D. P. *Family and nation.* New York: Harcourt Brace Jovanovich, 1986.

Murray, C. *Losing ground.* New York: Basic Books, 1984.

Myrdal, G. *Challenge to affluence.* New York: Pantheon Books, 1962.

National Research Council. *Risking the future.* Washington, D.C.: National Academy Press, 1987.

Nelson, K. Structure and strategy in learning to talk. *Monographs of the Society for Research in Child Development,* 1973, *38,* (1–2, Serial No. 149).

Norman-Jackson, J. Family interactions, language development, and primary reading achievement of black children in families of low-income. *Child Development,* 1982, *53,* 349–358.

O'Hara, J. M., & Levenstein, P. *Downward extension of the Mother-Child Home Program: Final report to the Rockefeller Brothers Fund.* Freeport, N.Y.: Verbal Interaction Project, 1979. (Photocopied)

Patterson, J. T. *America's struggle against poverty, 1900–1980.* Cambridge: Harvard University Press, 1981.

Phillips, J. R., & Levenstein, P. *Effects of the Mother-Child Home Program on younger siblings of index children: A cognitive profile study.* Progress Report to the Foundation for Child Development. Freeport, N.Y.: Verbal Interaction Project, 1973. (Mimeographed)

Polansky, N. A., Borgman, R. D., & DeSaix, C. *Roots of futility.* San Francisco: Jossey-Bass, Inc., 1972.

Radin, N. Maternal warmth, achievement motivation, and cognitive functioning in lower-class preschool children. *Child Development.* 1971, *42,* 1560–1565.

Rohter, L. Study finds city schools made no progress in reducing dropouts. *New York Times,* May 26, 1985,

Rojankovsy, F. *The tall book of Mother Goose.* New York: Harper & Row Junior Books, 1942.

Rosenthal, R., & Rosnow, R. L. *The volunteer subject.* New York: Wiley-Interscience, 1975.

Rossi, P. H., Freeman, N. E., & Wright, S. R. *Evaluation: A systematic approach.* Beverly Hills: Sage Publications, 1979.

Royce, J. M., Darlington, R. B., & Maurray, H. W. Pooled analyses: findings across studies. In Consortium for Longitudinal Studies, *As the twig is bent.* Hillsdale, N.J.: Lawrence Erlbaum Associates, 1983.

Sameroff, A. J., & Seifer, R. Familial risks and child competence. *Child Development,* 1982, *54,* 1254–1268.

Sameroff, A. J. Caretaking or reproductive casualty? Determinants in developmental deviancy. In F. D. Horowitz (Ed.), *Early developmental hazards: Predictors and precautions.* AAAS Selected Symposia Service. Boulder, Colo.: Westvieco Press, 1978.

Sapir, E. *Culture, language and personality.* Berkeley: University of California Press, 1962. (First published, 1921)

Saretsky, G. The OEO P. C. experiment and the John Henry effect. *Phi Delta Kappan,* 1972, *53,* 579–581

Scarr, S., & McCartney, K. Far from home: An experimental evaluation of the Mother-Child Home Program in Bermuda. Paper presented at the Biennial Meeting of the Society for Research in Child Development, Baltimore, Md., April 23, 1987.

Schacter, F. F. *Everyday mother talk to toddlers.* New York: Academic Press, 1979.

Schaefer, E. S. A home tutoring program. *Children,* 1969, *16,* 59–61.

———. Need for early and continuing education. In V. H. Denenberg (Ed.), *Education of the infant and young child.* New York: Academic Press, 1970.

Schaie, K., & Roberts, J. *School achievement of children 6–11 years as measured by the Reading and Arithmetic subtests of the Wide Range Achievement Test.* Series II, 103, National Health Survey, National Center for Health Statistics, Public Health Service, DHEW Publication, 1970.

Schorr, A. L. *Poor kids.* New York: Basic Books, 1966.

Schwartz, Tony. *Media: The second god.* New York: Random House, 1981.

Seuss, Dr. *The cat in the hat.* New York: Beginner Books, 1957.

Sidel, R. *Women and children last.* New York: Viking, 1986.

Sigel, I. E. The attainment of concepts. In M. L. Hoffman & L. W. Hoffman (Eds.), *Review of child development research* (Vol. 2). New York: Russell Sage, 1964.

———. Language of the disadvantaged: The distancing hypothesis. In C. S. Lavatelli (Ed.), *Language training in early childhood education.* Urbana, Ill.: University of Illinois Press, 1971.

Siller, J. Socioeconomic status and conceptual thinking. *Journal of Abnormal and Social Psychology,* 1957, *55,* 365–371.

Skeels, H. M. Adult status of children with contrasting early life experiences. *Monographs of the Society for Research in Child Development,* 1966, *31,* (3, Serial No. 105).

Skeels, H. M., & Dye, H. B. A study of the effects of differential stimulation on mentally retarded children. *Proceedings of the American Association on Mental Deficiency,* 1939, *44,* 114—136.

Strodtbeck, F. L. The hidden curriculum in the middle class home. In J. D. Krumholtz (Ed.), *Learning and the educational process.* Chicago: Rand McNally, 1965.

Sutton-Smith, B., & Rosenberg, B. G. *The sibling.* New York: Holt, Rinehart and Winston, 1970.

Taylor, D. *Family literacy.* Exeter, N.H.: Heineman Books, 1983.

Thorndike, R. L. Causation of Binet decrements. *Journal of Educational Measurements,* 1977, *14,* 197–202.

Tresselt, A. R. *Rain drop splash.* New York: Lothrop, Lee & Shepard Co., Inc., 1946. (out of print).

———. *Wake up, farm!* New York: Lothrop, Lee & Shepard Co., Inc., 1955. (out of print)

U.S. Bureau of the Census. *Statistical Abstract of the United States: 1985.* (105th ed.) Washington, D.C., 1984.

U.S. Department of Labor, Bureau of Labor Statistics. *Women who head families: A socioeconomic analysis.* Washington, D.C.: Government Printing Office, 1978.

U.S. Department of Health, Education, and Welfare; National Institutes of Health. *Parent-child program series, report no. 1: Mother-Child Home Program, Freeport, New York.* Publication No. 78–659. Washington, D.C.: Government Printing Office, 1972.

U.S. Department of Health, Education, and Welfare; Office of Education. *Model programs, compensatory education: Mother-Child Home Program, Freeport, New York.* OE, 72–84. Washington, D.C.: Government Printing Office, 1972.

U. S. News & World Report. December 24, 1984. 38–43.

Vygotsky, L. S. *Thought and language.* Boston: Massachusetts Institute of Technology, 1962.

Wargo, M. J., Campeau, P. L., & Tallmadge, C. K. *Further examination of exemplary programs for educating disadvantaged children.* Palo Alto: American Institutes for Research in the Behavioral Sciences, 1971.

Wells, G. *Language development in the pre-school years.* Cambridge, England: Cambridge University Press, 1985.

White, B. L., Kaban, B. T., & Attenucci, J. S. *Origins of human competence.* Lexington, Mass.: Lexington Books, 1979.

White, R. W. *Ego and reality in psycholanalytic theory. Psychological*

Issues 3, Monograph 11. New York: International Universities Press, 1963.

Young, K. T., & Zigler, E. Infant and toddler day care: Regulations and policy implications. *American Journal of Orthopsychiatry,* 1986, *56,* 43–55.

Zigler, E., & Valentine, J. (Eds.) *Project Head Start: A legacy of the war on poverty.* New York: Free Press, 1979.

Zion, G. *All falling down.* New York: Harper & Row Junior Books, 1951.

Index

academic achievement: and dropout rate, 35–36, and economic status, 41, 107, 126, 204, 217; of MCHP participants, 12, 114, 117, 120–32, 205–6, 213–14; and parental behavior, 104, 134–36, 147, 159
Adelman, Helen Roth, 71
adoptions, MCHP. *See* replications, MCHP
Ainsworth, Mary, 105
Applebome, Peter, 33, 34
Associates, VIP: conferences of, 175, 181; Workshop for, 198, 199. *See also* Coordinators, MCHP
Auletta, Ken, 30

Baumrind, Diana, 60
Beller, Kuno, 42
Belsky, Jay, 103
Bermuda, MCHP in, 157–58, 174
Bernstein, Basil, 101–2, 105
Bloom, Benjamin, 107–8
bonding, mother-child, 1–2, 43, 105–6, 110, 215. *See also* network, mother-child
books: bilingual, 171–72; and imagination, 215; MCHP criteria for, 65–66, 229. *See also* literacy, print; Verbal Interaction Stimulus Materials, books and toys
Bowlby, John, 105
Brazelton, Berry, 105
Bronfenbrenner, Urie, 105–6, 109
Brown, Roger, 100–101
Bruner, Jerome, 100

Caldwell, Bettye, 108, 110–11, 207
California Achievement Test, 130, 178
Cameron, William J., 126
Campbell, Donald, 139

Cassirer, Ernst, 100, 107
Cattell Infant Intelligence Scale, 13
Cazden, Courtney, 106
Chapter One, Educational Consolidation and Improvement Act, 41, 126, 128, 129, 130, 137, 177, 178
child abuse, 35, 39, 46, 164, 193, 194
child participants, MCHP: autistic, 50; cognitive development of, 41, 99–104, 107, 110–11, 126, 155, 197, 204, 217; creativity of, 62, 65, 135, 207, 214; examples of, 5–26, 52–60, 113–16; individuality of, 73–74; self-confidence of, 135, 155, 207; social-emotional development of, 39, 43, 51, 60–63, 104–5, 109–10, 134–36, 155, 167, 215
Child's Behavior Traits (CBT) measure, 136, 197
Clarke-Stewart, K. A., 107
cognitive development, 197, 205, 207; and environment, 108–9, 110–11; and family relationships, 41, 100, 101–4; and language, 99–101; and mother-love, 104–5; and mother's education, 39; and verbal interaction, 155
Coleman, James, 204
computers, 214–15
confidentiality. *See* Home Sessions, confidentiality of
Consortium for Longitudinal Studies, 42, 122, 125, 137
conversation, mother-child. *See* verbal interaction, mother-child
Coordinators, MCHP, 71–72, 89, 119, 142, 159, 160, 174, 175, 179, 181, 183, 195, 196, 211; conferences of, 175, 181; education of, 71; and MCHP participants, 15, 16–17, 19–20, 21–22, 25, 26, 72, 173, 191; and replications, 172, 174, 176–77, 184–200 passim;

(Coordinators, MCHP, *continued*)
reports on Hesitaters, 159–62; reports on Strivers, 160–62; salaries of, 176–77; as TDs, 72; and TDs, 67, 68, 171–72, 173, 181, 182, 198; training of, 168, 172, 179, 181, 185; work sheet of, 174, 183. *See also* Crawford, Myrtle

Crawford, Myrtle, 6–8, 10–16 passim, 18, 19–21, 22–23, 25, 26, 67

crime, 3, 30, 32–34, 125

cultural/ethnolinguistic differences, 45, 86–88, 95, 96–97, 104, 171–72, 190, 198, 211

curriculum, MCHP, 52–63. *See also* child participants, MCHP, social-emotional development of; verbal interaction techniques; positive parenting behavior

curriculum materials, MCHP. *See* Verbal Interaction Stimulus Materials

Darlington, Richard, 42, 122, 124, 125

Day, M. C., 42

daycare, 38, 39, 129; model programs for, 163–64

depression, of low-income mothers, 37, 40, 41, 44, 90, 97, 116, 119, 160, 161, 162, 208, 209. *See also* mental health

Design I research, 117–37, 213; enrollment in, 118–19, 139, 149, 158; findings of, 120–25, 136–37, 159; flaws in, 137–38; Hesitaters in, 119, 141–46, 158–59; meta-analysis of, 122, 125; methodology of, 117–19, 137–38; questions answered by, 119–20; self-selection of mothers in, 119, 141, 143–44; Strivers in, 119, 141–46, 158–59; summary of, 136–37

Design II research, 137–159, 212–13; control groups in, 145, 146, 148, 149–51; on downward extension of MCHP, 156–57; enrollment in, 137–38, 139, 140, 141–42, 148–49, 156, 157–59; findings of, 147–49, 153–55, 158–59; flaws in, 140–44, 149–51, 158–59, 212; John Henry Effect in, 139–41, 158; lottery condition in, 137–38, 139, 157, 158; and MIB measure, 153–55; methodology of, 137–38, 139–40, 145, 158–59; self-selection of mothers in, 141, 143–44, 149–50, 158–59,

212–13; Strivers in, 149–51, 158–59; summary of, 158–59

Deutsch, Cynthia, 42

Deutsch, Martin, 42

Devito, P. J., 126, 128

distancing hypothesis, 101

dropouts, high school, 2–3, 31, 32, 33, 35–36, 37, 41, 144, 204

drug abuse, 32, 34–35, 194

education: attitudes toward, 104, 204; and employment, 3, 31, 32, 33, 36; and pregnancy, 35, 38; preschool, 41–42, 43; special, 121, 125, 205

educational disadvantage, 41, 110, 120–32, 137, 178, 204–6

ethical standards in home-based programs, 94–97

evaluation research: and federal funding, 128; problems with, 178; and social obligation, 94–95. *See also* Design I; Design II; IQ tests; Mother-Child Home Program, evaluation of; replications, MCHP, evaluation of

families: as educators, 39, 40, 100–4; dysfunctional, 30, 33–34, 36, 41; low-income, 140–41, 145, 201, 204, 216–17; middle-class, 30, 44, 50, 60, 127, 180, 193–94, 200–1, 216, 217; single-parent, 32, 36–37, 39, 40, 97, 119, 140, 207–8

fathers of MCHP participants: absence of, 32, 36, 37; education of, 121, 194; in Home Sessions, 78–79

Family Service Association, Nassau County, 50, 139, 220

Feldheim, Naomi, 186, 187, 188, 196, 199

feminization of poverty, 36–40, 46

fictitious names, use of, 5

Forster, E. M., 214

funding: federal, 108, 128, 177; of mental health centers, 164–65. *See also* Mother-Child Home Program, funding of; Verbal Interaction Project, funding of

Gordon, Brian, 91–94

Gordon, Ira, 42

Gottfried, Allen, 103

Guide Sheets. *See* Verbal Interaction Stimulus Materials, Guide Sheets for

Headstart Project, 42, 170, 212–13
Heath, Shirley, 103–4
Herbers, John, 31
Herzog, Elizabeth, 40
Hesitaters; 44–45, 119, 207–9; children of, 44, 204–5; in Design I and Design II research, 141–51, 155, 158–59; education of, 144–45, 209; in Home Sessions, 75–78; and program enrollment, 44–45, 141–44; become Strivers, 159, 206, 208
Hess, Robert, 102, 105
hidden curriculum, 50, 53, 200, 205
Home Observation for Measurement of the Environment (HOME), 110–11, 207
homelessness, 164–65
Home Sessions: appointments for kept, 116, 134, 191, 206, 211; audio/video recordings of, 67, 151–56, 173, 181, 182–83, 198, 199, 207; bilingual, 86–88, 171; confidentiality of, 95, 96, 173, 211; examples of, 13–21; fathers in, 78–79; and family problems, 88–89, 90; first, 13–14, 18, 51, 64; frequency of, 23, 51, 64, 173, 180, 198; grandmothers in, 77, 83, 85–86, 89; Guide Sheets in, 53–56; and MIB, 141–42; run by mother, 25, 72, 136, 210–11; siblings in, 77, 79–81, 85; twins in, 77; TD descriptions of, 14–15, 16–17, 68–70, 72–94, 173, 183. See also Verbal Interaction Stimulus Materials, books and toys
Hunt, J. McV., 108

intervention programs: center-based, 94–95, 131; funding of, 108; home-based, 94–95, 97, 108–9, 165–67, 213; for infants, 156–57; research on, 107–9
IQ tests: of child participants, 12–13, 27, 113–16, 120–25, 128–29, 131–33, 138, 147–49, 157–58, 167, 178; and PACT, 136; renorming of, 150–51; of siblings, 131–32; usefulness of, 120
Irwin, O. C., 105

Jester, Emile, 42
jobs, entry-level, MCHP. See Toy Demonstrators
John Henry Effect, 139–41, 158

Karnes, Merle, 42
Karon, J. P., 126, 128
Kasarda, John D., 31–32, 36
Keller, Helen, 100
Kerr, Peter, 34–35, 36
Key Elements for Establishing Program (KEEP) instrument, 172–74, 180, 182–83, 190, 191, 195, 199
Kochman, Arlene, 71

language: and cognitive development, 1–2, 99–101; development of, 99–107; mainstream, 95; and socioeconomic status, 101–4; and social-emotional development, 62, 104–5, 155; and symbolization, 99–101, 107
Lazar, Irving, 42, 122, 124, 125
Learning in Joy, 133, 179, 186
Levenstein, Phyllis, 42, 127, 166, 179, 186, 187, 188, 189–90, 191–92, 195–96, 198, 199, 200
linguistics, developmental, 99–107. See also language
literacy: print, 64, 104, 124, 130, 214–15; electronic, 214–15
location-randomized research. See Design I research

Maeroff, G. L., 213–14
mainstream culture. See cultural/ethnolinguistic differences
Maternal Interactive Behavior (MIB) measure, 141–42, 153–56, 198
McCartney, K., 157–58
mental health: of child participants, 60–63, 105, 167, 207; of mother participants, 40, 46, 110, 116, 159–62, 207, 208, 209. See also depression; self-esteem
mental illness, 164, 165
mental retardation, 50, 108–9, 168
Miller, Louise, 42
Mother-Child Home Program (MCHP): acceptability to mothers of, 45, 119, 133–34, 206–8, 211; basic program standards of, 45, 172–74, 175, 180; cost of, 52, 136–37, 176–77, 212; curriculum of, 52–63, 110, 172, 200; curriculum materials of (see Verbal Interaction Stimulus Materials); development of, 1, 42, 49–50, 109, 219;

(MCHP, *continued*)
do-it-yourself version, 200–201, 217;
drop-off program of, 26, 52, 143, 148;
ethical standards of, 52, 94–97, 211;
evaluation of, by mother participants,
16–17, 21–22, 25, 26, 72, 133–34;
evaluation of, by outside experts, 165–
67; evaluation of, by TDs, 67, 173;
evaluation research on (*see* Design I research; Design II research; IQ tests;
Maternal Interactive Behavior measure);
funding of, 1, 49–50, 128, 170, 171,
177, 216–17, 219–21; goals of, 1, 3–4,
12, 17, 42, 46–47, 49, 50, 60–61, 113,
114, 117, 127, 162, 172; hypotheses of,
1, 49, 99, 105, 106–7, 109–10, 127,
136; nonintrusiveness of, 94, 95, 96,
114, 173, 211; replication of (*see* replications, MCHP). *See also* Coordinators;
Home Sessions; Parent-Child Home
Program; Toy Demonstrators; Verbal
Interaction Project, and MCHP
mother-love, 43, 44, 46, 106, 208; and
cognitive development, 104–5
mother participants, MCHP: autonomy
of, 45, 51, 52; demographics of, 119,
192–95, 201; education of, 118, 140,
144–45, 170, 194–95, 201, 209; as
educators, 43–44; employment of, 46,
118, 136, 210–11; examples of, 5–29,
53–60 passim; MCHP benefits to, 25,
26, 46, 116, 132, 159; motivation of,
44, 97, 141–44, 208; as TDs, 14, 25,
52, 66, 72, 116, 136, 142–43, 185, 209,
210–11. *See also* Hesitaters; mental
health; Strivers
Moynihan, Senator Patrick, 31, 36, 37,
38, 39–40
Murray, Charles, 29, 31, 41
Myrdal, Gunnar, 29, 31

National Research Council, 31, 37, 39
network, mother-child, 1–2, 4, 41, 45–
46, 49, 50, 107, 110–11, 136, 137, 156,
159, 206–7

Palmer, Francis, 42
Parent and Child Together (PACT)
measure, 134–36, 189, 191–92, 197
Parent Assist, 175, 186
Parent-Child Home Program, 120, 125–

131, 169, 174, 175, 186, 196, 206, 214;
development of, 126–27; evaluation
of, 128–31, 137, 178
Parker, R. K., 42
Patterson, James T., 29–30, 38–39
Payne, James A., 34
Peabody Picture Vocabulary Tests (PPVT),
128, 129, 191
Polansky, Norman, 40
positive parenting behavior, 51, 56–60,
136, 137, 207
poverty, 29–31, 36–40, 46, 107–8. *See
also* families, low-income; underclass
Proposed Plan, 180, 190–191, 195

remedial programs, 3, 41–42
replications, MCHP, 50, 51, 52, 97, 126–
27, 163–201, 203, 210, 216; documentation of Family Keystone's, 183–99;
evaluation of, 174, 178, 182–83, 199–
200; problems with, 163–65; sponsors
of, 71, 168–71, 174–75, 203, 225–27;
standards for, 172–74, 175; training
for, 172, 181, 185, 186–88, 190; VIP
approval for, 179, 182–83
right to privacy, 45, 94–95, 211
Rosenthal, R., 146, 149, 150
Rosnow, R. L., 146, 149, 150

Sapir, Edward, 99–100
Scarr, S., 157–58
Schaefer, Earl, 105, 109, 110
schools, as sponsors of MCHP, 125–31,
169, 174–75
Schorr, Alvin, 36
self-esteem, of low-income mothers, 2,
16, 20–22, 26, 37, 40, 41, 44, 46, 47,
49, 97, 207, 208, 209; improved by
MCHP, 110, 116, 160, 161–62
Shipman, Virginia, 102, 105
Sigel, Irving, 101
social agencies, 164, 165, 174, 181, 194,
201, 208, 217; referrals to by MCHP,
68, 72, 89, 148, 194; as sponsors of
MCHP, 168–71, 174, 180, 203
Stanford-Binet Intelligence Scale, renorming of, 150–51
Stolzberg, Judy, 175, 186
Strivers, 43–44, 60, 119, 198, 206, 207–9,
213; children of, 44, 146; in Design I
and Design II research, 141–51, 155,

158–59; education of, 144–45, 209; in
Home Sessions, 75–78; motivation of,
44, 141–44, 146
subcultures. *See* cultural/ethnolinguistic
differences
subject-randomized research. *See* Design
II research

Taylor, Denny, 103
technology: and literacy, 214–15; and
employment, 3, 31
television, educational, 21, 42, 151
Title One, 3, 41, 177
Toy Demonstrators, 7, 13–14, 23, 66–71;
conferences of, 64–65, 66–67, 68, 96,
142, 173, 182, 199, 211; and Coordinators, 67, 171–72; education of, 18,
66, 68, 71, 133, 136, 177, 210–11; as
entry-level job, 177, 197; evaluate
MCHP, 67, 173, 211; evaluate mothers,
208; evaluate VISM, 20, 85–86, 173;
evaluation of, by mothers, 67–68, 71,
72, 133; model positive parenting,
56–60, 64, 209; moral obligations of,
95; payment of, 67, 176–77, 212;
reports on Home Sessions, 14–15,
18–19, 20–21, 23, 24, 68–70, 73–94,
142, 211; role of limited, 51, 58, 67,
68, 71, 96, 180–81; training of, 52,
66–67, 68, 72, 96, 172–73, 182, 185;
volunteer, 18, 67, 176–77, 212. *See also*
mother participants, as TDs
toys, MCHP criteria for, 65–66, 229. *See
also* Verbal Interaction Stimulus Materials, books and toys

underclass: and literacy, 214–215; myths
about, 207–8; problems of, 29–40,
207–8; remedies for problems of,
40–47; and use of MCHP, 216–17. *See
also* families, low-income; poverty
unemployment, 30–32
unwed mothers, 32, 35, 36, 37
Ur Education, 105–6, 109, 110

verbal interaction, mother-child, 1–2, 4,
25, 43, 51, 53, 63–64, 65, 102, 105,
106–7, 127, 136, 189, 197; and child
development, 100, 101–4, 155, 159,
192, 206–7; increased by MCHP, 116,
206; nondidactic, 156, 159, 207; and

PACT, 134–36
Verbal Interaction Project (VIP), 3–4, 67,
49–51, 162; Director of (*see* Levenstein, Phyllis); Early Screening Program
of, 139, 140, 141, 145, 146; Field Con-
sultants of, 185, 186, 187, 188, 196,
199; funding of, 49–50, 126, 206; and
MCHP Coordinators, 72, 181, 183; and
MCHP development, 1, 26, 42, 49,
167–68, 220; and MCHP replications,
50–51, 172–75, 178, 179–83, 199–200,
203; technical materials of, 180, 181,
223–24
Verbal Interaction Stimulation Intervention Techniques (VISIT) handbook,
53–56
Verbal Interaction Stimulus Materials
(VISM), 7, 45, 50, 51–52, 63–66, 110,
181, 183, 195, 200, 201, 207, 208–9,
211; books and toys, 13–20, 23, 24,
53–55, 73–94, 161, 173, 192; and child
development, 65; cost of, 176, 189,
212; criteria for, 65–66, 229–30; and
cultural differences, 66, 171–72; evaluation of, by mothers, 65, 161; evaluation of, by TDs, 65, 69–70, 85–86, 173;
as focus of interaction, 1, 2, 51, 53,
63–64, 65, 106, 127; Guide Sheets for,
23–24, 25, 26, 53–54, 67, 116, 143,
161, 173, 183, 195; in Home Sessions,
73–94
verbal interaction techniques, 53–56, 67,
151, 153–55, 173
videotaped maternal interactive behavior, 116, 151–56, 173, 181, 182–83,
199, 207
VIP Update, 195, 196
volunteers, and research bias, 149–51,
158–59
Vygotsky, L. S., 100

Weikart, David, 42, 205
welfare, 29–31, 37–39, 40, 41, 119, 140,
194, 201, 207–8, 209; dependency on,
3, 31, 41; and pregnancy, 37–39
Wells, Gordon, 106
White, Robert, 106, 110

Yeates, Marcia, 198

Zigler, Edward, 42

Phyllis Levenstein, a clinical psychologist, created the Mother-Child Home Program and is director of Verbal Interaction Project, Inc., which guides new replications of the model program. Dr. Levenstein is Adjunct Associate Professor in the Social Sciences Interdisciplinary Program, State University of New York, Stony Brook.

Designed by Jane Forbes.

Composition by Chappel Typography, Athens, Ohio.